Watching China Change

"Between May, 1976, when Mao Zedong was still alive, and February, 1997, when Deng Xiaoping died, was a time of tremendous changes in China—from the 'Great Proletarian Cultural Revolution' and poverty, to the affluent eighties and nineties, from socialism to what looks like unrestrained capitalism, and from a mysterious country wrapped in isolation to one of the key players in modern international affairs. It's a dramatic story, which involves a fifth of the human race and impinges on the rest... I was there, taking it all in."

Thus starts this book, a gripping account by a foreigner living and working in China. What was it like to be there? What was his daily life in that exotic country? What were his insights and understandings as he tried, through the years, to come to grips with the theories and actualities of Chinese life through the great changes?

Cosbey's skill as a writer shows in the details that bring his observations to life: the different dance styles of the two periods, the songs the students sang in the mass demonstrations of 1989, people falling over backward on the escalators of the new Tianjin railway station when they see mural paintings of nude young women, weavers in carpet factories afraid to talk if the boss is present. The details, together with his insights into why China changed as it did, make this book 'a good read' as well as a serious contribution to our knowledge of modern China.

WATCHING CHINA CHANGE

Robert C. Cosbey

For Lloyd Barber, who helped get me to China. Many thanks! And best wishes!

Robert C. Cosbey

(Bob)

between the lines

Published in Canada by
BETWEEN THE LINES
720 Bathurst St., Suite #404
Toronto, Ontario
M5S 2R4
E-mail: btlbooks@web.ca
Website : www.btlbooks.com

Watching China Change
© 2001, Robert C. Cosbey
ISBN 1-896357-43-1
Canadian CIP data have been applied for

Author Photo by Janet Melvin

PRINTED IN INDIA

Published by Sterling Publishers Pvt. Ltd., New Delhi-110 016.
Laserset at Vikas Compographics, New Delhi-110029.
Printed at Prolific Incorporated, New Delhi-110020.

CONTENTS

ACKNOWLEDGEMENTS

There is not space to thank all the people who made this book possible. But I must mention a few, starting with my wonderful graduate students in China. Over the years, many colleagues, friends, and casual acquaintances helped me understand their culture. I learned also from people I interviewed for a series of lectures on China on the Canadian Broadcasting Corporation's "Ideas" program, especially William Hinton, Jan Wong, and Patrick Brown. Saros Cowasjee, of the University of Regina, urged me to get the book published, not just leave it for my grandchildren, and showed me the way. I hope all of these, and many others who helped over the years, will accept my thanks and good wishes. None of them, of course, are responsible for any errors herein, nor for my opinions and conclusions.

Thanks to the President's Office of the University of Regina for a grant in support of this publication.

PREFACE
Who, What, When, Where, And Why

Between May 1976, while Mao Zedong was still alive, and February 1997, when Deng Xioaping died, was a time of tremendous changes in China—from the "Great Proletarian Cultural Revolution" to the affluent eighties and nineties, from socialism to what looks like unrestrained capitalism, and from a mysterious country wrapped in isolation to one of the key players in modern international affairs. It's a dramatic story, which involves a fifth of the human race and impinges on the rest.

I was lucky in my timing: I was there, taking it all in. I want to share it with you—to tell you the history of China and the Chinese during those tumultuous years. But I have to pause before I even begin, to consider what telling my story involves.

The word "history" has two meanings. History is the web, moving through time, of all the millions of lives and events in the world. "Historians" try their best to give an account of that vast web, and the books they write are also called "history."

Nobody can take into account all the millions of lives and events in the great web, not even all those happening at any one pinpoint in time. The historian must select the "period" she or he chooses to block off in that seamless time-web, and must make a selection of the markers which appear to be significant during that arbitrary "period". But the historian can't help seeing the selected subject through the lens of her or his own personality, personal history, and training. No wonder history has to be re-written constantly!

Nevertheless, we find it fascinating, in our own attempts to understand this world and this life, to read historians' attempts to make sense of it, and I think we all feel the urge to be historians ourselves, whether in casual conversation or in the formality of books, or somehow else, to share our own understanding of the piece of the world-web we find ourselves in. At least I know I do.

I don't mean to put down formal historians. They are indispensable sources of information, but maybe there's something to be said, too, for personal observations such as this book aspires to give you.*

What I offer you is simply China since 1976 as seen through the eyes of one fascinated observer.

But who am I to talk about China? My own experiences in China cover the years between my first trip in 1976, three months before Mao Zedong died, and shortly before the death of Deng Xiaoping in 1997—two of the most crucial decades of China's history. And since leaving China I have been busy keeping up with developments through newspapers, magazines and books, through letters and e-mail from my friends in China, and through long discussions and debates with Chinese friends living in Canada and the US.

My first trip to China, in 1976, was an exhausting study tour that lasted one month. In the spring of 1979, I spent a

---

* If you want a solid, 747-page history of China from the late 16th Century to the aftermath of the Tiananmen massacre of June 1989, crammed with details, thoroughly documented, clearly written, with (for the most part) an even-handed treatment of many controversial people and events of those 300 years, look for Jonathan D. Spence's *The Search for Modern China (Norton, 1990.)* But remember that formal historians, too, see the world through their training, their personalities, and their own experience of life. To see this problem, compare Spence's account of the famous Dazhai commune (pages 593-594) with that of William Hinton, in *The Great Reversal (Monthly Review Press, 1990)* beginning on page 124.

month on a similar study tour—one highlight of which was that I was in the first group admitted to the Inner Mongolia Autonomous Region after the Cultural Revolution. Then, in the school year 1979-1980, I took a sabbatical leave from the University of Regina, and taught at Nankai University, in Tianjin. In 1982, I retired from the U of R. From then until the end of 1996 I spent half my time in China and half in Canada. My cumulative time of living in China adds up to just over eight years. While there, I taught Western literature to graduate students of English at Nankai and Xiamen Universities, and I lectured at many other universities and language institutes across China. When I wasn't teaching, I was traveling, and I've been in all the major areas except Xinjiang and Tibet.

So for more than twenty years much of what I've been doing has been living and working in China, seeing as much of it as I could, trying to understand what I saw, and thinking and reading and talking about it.

Over the years, I came to think of China as my second home, and I developed many friendships and other ties there. In 1985, Nankai University made me an Honorary Professor, a rare distinction, of which I am proud. In 1996, the city of Tianjin gave me its Hai He Award "for contributions to the culture and development of the city." In the same year, China's national government gave me its Friendship Award, described in the presentation as the highest honour given to foreigners working in China. Such honours are gratifying, but what has kept me going back to China has been the love of friends and, especially, the friendly and fruitful relationship with my great Chinese students.

Unfortunately, my time for living in China has come to an end. I have chronic bronchitis (which has made me familiar with Chinese hospitals!) and the air pollution in Chinese cities has been getting worse year by year. My bronchitis and their pollution collided while I was teaching at Nankai in the autumn semester of 1996, and I became so ill that it was clear I had to stop going to China—a decision the emotional equivalent of being cut off at the knees.

Now I am moved to get down on paper my memories and observations about that twenty-plus years' experience. Neither a eulogy nor an exposé—just as honest an account as I can make it of the China that I saw and experienced.

Where did my interest in China start? There are three main strands, and who knows how many others. My mother was always fascinated by China, though where that story starts I don't know. Oma never went to China. She never knew any Chinese people, and as far as I know had never even met anybody who had been there. She was especially attracted to Tibetan Buddhism, and I remember a big book with large wonderful black and white photos of temples and people. (Was it hers? Had she borrowed it? If hers, where is it now?) But she was also interested in the customs of ordinary Chinese life.

To raise money for the church, she used to give Chinese dinners (teaching herself Chinese cooking out of a cookbook). There were Chinese characters on butcher paper hanging on the walls (the characters drawn by a local Chinese shopkeeper— and who knows what they said?) Oma presided over the festivities wearing a traditional *qipao* with tight neck and slit sides. The people who paid to eat had to wrestle with chopsticks; if anyone demanded knife and fork, that cost extra. I have often surprised Chinese people by telling them that it was my mother who taught me how to use chopsticks, back in the 1920s.

Then there was the pull of exotic places, of which China always seemed the most exotic. There was Marco Polo, and *The Good Earth*, and *Oil for the Lamps of China*, *Man's Fate*, and *Moment in Peking*, and Fu Manchu, and Charlie Chan. The pull of the exotic became even greater after World War II, when China was isolated from the world and very few foreigners could get there.

But by the time I was thinking seriously of how to get to China, the big pull was the possibility of seeing socialism in action. I suppose my thinking about society has always been in some sense socialistic. The idea that the purpose of a society is to ensure a good life for all its members has always seemed to me the merest common sense. And the aspect of Christianity which I accepted wholeheartedly is represented by Matthew 25, 34-46: "Insomuch as ye have done it unto the least of these my brethren ye have done it unto me." And the message on the wall of the parish house: "It starts with me. If not me, who? If not now, when?"

When I came of voting age, my first vote was for Norman Thomas. When I lived in southern Illinois, I was the only white person on the executive committee of the regional NAACP. Well, this is not an autobiography, except as it describes my years in China, but that's the background. So when an opportunity to see China came along, yes, there was a strong pull to the exotic, but the strongest pull was the idea of seeing socialism in action.

I learned a lot, fast, in China, and some of it was disillusioning. It seems naive, now, to have assumed that the customs of a country could be changed in a few years to some universal thing called socialism. Actually, the history of modern China has been its attempt to create socialism in a country whose folkways were as different from socialism as could be imagined—a country with a three-thousand-year history of ingrained feudalism and imperialism—a brave attempt, which some Chinese say has greatly succeeded, though others will tell you that socialism failed and has disappeared.

To give you a feeling for the ancient folkways socialism hoped to overcome, but which still persist: If socialism means respecting the dignity of all human beings, I don't know where to find socialism in this world, but China ranks even lower than Western capitalist nations in this respect. The Chinese, though they deny it, have a ferocious sense of class. Intellectuals (which in China means anyone who works with brain rather than with hands) despise the workers. Not everybody, of course. You must accept from the start that when I enunciate a generalization like that, I could give many exceptions. Isn't that true everywhere? But look at some examples:

In May, 1979, I was on my second study tour of China. I had a contract to teach for a year at Nankai University starting in September so I took a day off from our tour and went from Beijing to Tianjin with an interpreter to visit my new colleagues. We were met in the Tianjin railway station by a minor official of the city, all affability and smiles. To leave a train in China, you must show your ticket to prove you have paid, and the line at the gate is always long, crowded, and impatient. But our host took us to the head of the line, and with a strong gesture simply swept some peasants out of the way and ushered us through with a big smile. What hit me at once was that nobody—not the peasants, not the other people in line, not the ticket inspector—nobody seemed to see anything unusual about that. That was my introduction to "socialist" Tianjin.

Some time later, as I was going alone through a similar line-up, the young peasant woman ahead of me, I think not familiar with railways and not anticipating that she must show her ticket, held up the line, fumbling through her cloth bundle. This time, the ticket inspector, a woman of about the same age, simply shoved her aside, so rudely that she fell down. The people behind shoved me, and I popped through the gate—the inspector didn't even glance at my ticket. Again, nobody, including the peasant woman, seemed to find anything unusual. Nobody registered any objection—not even by frowning.

There was the time my class was having a party in my room in the foreign teachers building, and some construction workers stood outside watching. One of my students slammed down the window shade, her eyes blazing, saying, "Who do they think they are?"

I could give a lot of examples, including the time one of my brightest students said to me, "They tell me 'Learn from the peasants.' 'Learn from the peasants.' I'm an educated man. What can I learn from stinking peasants?"

These few examples (I could cite many others) will, I hope, give you some feeling of the immense job of trying to convert China to socialism.

On the other hand: Yes, there certainly is the other hand, which encouraged me to write home, in 1979, saying "It feels great to be living under socialism." I wasn't lying.

First, the structure of society: Under socialism, working people in China were guaranteed jobs, and the factories or other units they worked for provided them with housing, medical insurance, schools for their children, and old age pensions. When I visited the Tianjin Household Products Company (where they make those wonderful silk-and-bamboo kites as well as more mundane things such as lampshades), the first thing I noticed when I entered the grounds was the pleasant appearance—the entrance court was bright with flowers and shaded by trees—and the first thing I heard was the happy noise of a daycare playground. After touring the factory I had lunch in the cafeteria. The place was clean and bright; the food was tasty; the workers told me they elected the committee which administered the food service. The dining hall was forbidden to make a profit: any money left over at the end of the year was used for a banquet for managers and workers. Similarly, they said, the factory's net profits at the end of each year were discussed by a joint meeting of managers and workers, to decide what to do with the money—how much to put into research and development, how much to improve workers' housing, or to build a workers' cultural centre.

Don't misunderstand me—I present this as an exceptionally good factory, not as a representative one. I have also visited horrible factories, which I'll get around to. But here was a solid example of a factory that existed not only to produce high-quality goods at a profit, but also to make a good life for the people who worked there. That's one of the signs of what I call socialism, though really I think it should be just plain common sense.

As for the relationship of workers and management: I could tell horror stories about that, too, and probably will, but here's an example of the other side: In the wonderful botanical gardens outside of Xiamen City, where they have over 200 species of bamboo alone, a research institute but also a lovely public park, the director himself took time to show me around. I gave him a book, a manual of Western trees which I had brought with me as a gift. He stood on the path, looking through it with pleasure. Three workers who were weeding and raking nearby downed tools, and came and looked over his shoulder. He explained to them what it was. They passed the book around, admired it, gave it back to him, gave me thumbs-up, and went back to work.

As for the spirit of the young people, especially my students, they had grown up under socialism, and most of them had imbibed socialist idealism from the start. Many of their personal names showed it, to begin with, for Chinese parents don't take names from a common stock of proper names, but make up names for their children. So in my early years there I had students with names like Wei Hua ("For China") and Hong ("Red", meaning socialism) or Hong Hong or Dan Hong , both of which mean "Double Red". The girls, especially, had names very unlike what girls had been supposed to be in their grandparents' times, names such as Lan Yan ("Stormy Petrel"—the bird that flies right through storms over the ocean) or Zheng Bo ("Big Wave").

I want to give you examples of the socialist idealism which that generation grew up with, and which many of them retain. If some examples look like just decency and thoughtfulness and cooperation, that seems to me no incongruity—that's one of the signs of socialism, as far as I'm concerned.

Item: I was in Beijing for the weekend, staying at the Friendship Hotel in the north-western part of the city. I had spent the day in the downtown area near Wangfujing Street, and when it was time to go back to the hotel I took the trolley-bus as far as the zoo, and there I was to change to the 322 bus to the hotel. There was, as usual, a mass of people waiting (Chinese buses are always incredibly crowded), and it looked as if I might not get on the next bus. I was just beginning to learn Chinese, but it's my custom to learn by doing, so I asked a young man and his mother "*Youyi Binguan ma?*" ("Is this the right bus for the Friendship Hotel?"). They shook their heads emphatically, and explained in a rapid Chinese I couldn't understand. Then they laughed, and gestured to me to come, and left that line and went with me to another "322" line, and crowded onto that bus with me, and told me when it was my stop for the hotel. Only later, I learned that the first line was for the express bus to the Summer Palace, far beyond the hotel, and realized they had taken the tedious local bus in order to be sure the old foreigner got to his hotel. I could give dozens of examples of things like this.

Item: In 1976, our local guide in Beijing was Li Susu, a petite young woman with beautiful clear English, a very thorough-going socialist youngster. I knew that she must have spent two years in the countryside or in a factory, as was the custom then, before applying for training to be a guide-interpreter. I asked her where she had worked. "I had hoped to go to the countryside; I thought that would be healthy. But I was sent to a bicycle factory in the north-east." "Were you disappointed?" She looked really puzzled. "What do you mean?" "I mean you wanted to go to the country but they sent you to a factory. Didn't that disappoint you?" "But you don't understand. I was needed in the factory." As if explaining the obvious to a slow learner. Li Susu was not being ideological or waving the flag—she had quite internalized the concept that in the struggle for socialism young people should be happy to do whatever was needed.

Hey! Wait a minute! Here you've been mixing up 'socialism' with being nice to people, and with religion and with idealism! What exactly do you mean when you say 'socialism'?

Fair enough. I'll be using words like *socialism*, but I want to dig deeper and link up with broader concerns. Rousseau was not the first to point out that human beings live with a tension between two basic impulses: the impulse we call individualism and the impulse we call altruism, or community. As with most tensions, taking either of these to extremes gets you into trouble: extreme individualism becomes selfishness, greed, unconcern for others. Extreme altruism may lead to a phony selflessness, or to obedience to leaders (waiving your right to think for yourself). You may already have thought that my example of Li Susu raises this question: is she an idealistic youngster who sees what needs to be done and is happy to do it, or is she a brain-washed automaton happy to obey orders? That's a very large question in China — you'll see me wrestling with it throughout this book — but it's not just a Chinese question, is it? In our schools in the West, why is it so hard to get students to think for themselves? Isn't it because the big lesson we teach in schools, from kindergarten through the Ph.D., is obedience to the teacher, who is also the judge, who puts on record how well each student has lived up to the demands of the teacher? We don't teach democracy in our schools; we teach (or at least try to teach) obedience. I could carry this idea over into our politics, too, but let it go.

Okay, when I say "socialism" I mean two things: one is idealism, community, working together—what the Chinese mean when they say that in the 1950s "we were brothers and sisters." The other is economic and political systems which assume and encourage all that. In these terms, I don't expect to see a socialist country in my lifetime. I call the China I get excited about "socialist" because they almost had it once, and they still have aspects of it. The basic idealism of the Chinese is still socialist, and those aspects of its economy and government that are true to its Revolution are socialist. At the same time, as I'm always pointing out, when idealism becomes obedience, or, on the other hand, when individualism becomes selfishness and greed, China (or any other country, for that matter) is in big trouble.

Now, let me get back to those "items" about what I saw as socialist in China.

Item: One of my Xiamen students told me how, during the Cultural Revolution, his school had been closed and the students sent to work in the countryside. Later, he came back to his city, and had various odd jobs there. He had started studying English in high school, and wanted to keep it up, so he got together with ten others to study English in the evenings. All eleven of them had had their education disrupted by the Cultural Revolution, and saw no chance of ever getting to university. "We felt frustrated because we couldn't be part of building socialism. We asked each other how we could help our country, and decided all we had was our English, so we should find a useful book in English and translate it into Chinese and get it published." Which they did. I remembered the year I graduated from high school into the Great Depression, unable to find any kind of work, with no hope of getting to university—a bitter time, during which it would never have occurred to me or my mates to ask what we could do for our country—all we could think of was what the country was doing to us.

Item: Having supper with friends at Nankai University, the wife, a teacher of English, the husband, an administrator in a university office. The ten-year-old daughter: "Ma, I'm going out to play now." "Have you studied your homework?" "I don't need to study. I'm the best student in the class." The mother proceeded to ream her out. "Does China need a silly, stuck-up girl like that? If you are smart, the country needs you more than others, not less. Get in there and study!"

Item: In February 1985, I was in a small dingy room in a Guangzhou city hostel, all by myself on Spring Festival Day. I'd had a harrowing long trip by bus from Hainan, which I'll tell you about later, and had missed my flight to Chengdu to spend Spring Festival with friends. I was exhausted and frustrated. But I looked out of the window and saw the tall, sparkly-white mass of the new White Swan Hotel, and thought: 'In that international hotel there's a bar, and in that bar there's Scotch whiskey.' So I went there, and sure enough found the bar, almost empty, and a young woman on duty as bartender. I got my Glenlivet, and started to talk with her, my Chinese by this time being good enough for that. "Too bad you have to work on Spring Festival Day," I said, just to make conversation. She straightened up and answered sternly. "*Weishenma bu hao?*" ("Why is it too bad?") "If I don't work, how can people be served?" Hey, here it was the post-socialist period of China, when the in thing was simply to get as rich as you could, and here, in the belly of the beast, socialist idealism surfaced.

Item: During my first years there, my Chinese colleagues in the universities where I taught, especially the younger ones, worked very hard indeed, and were full of team spirit, getting together often to compare notes on the best way to do this or that and improve their teaching, so devoted to their students that they would spend much out-of-class time coaching them, in small groups or as individuals. In China at that time there were no grades and no degrees and no exams, so there was no question of playing favourites—teachers and students worked together to raise the whole class to the optimal level.

Item: The struggle between old feudalism and new idealism took place not only between individuals but often inside one's head. The same bright student who had asked what he could learn from stinking peasants became a teacher in the department in which I was teaching. In 1989, when the students occupied Tiananmen Square, he heard that some of the hunger strikers were refusing even water. He came to me in agitation. "Those are my students up there in Tiananmen! They don't know anything about fasting, or how soon they can kill themselves if they don't get fluids! I've got to get up there and help them understand." So off he went, this shy introverted old-fashioned scholar, up to the tumult of the demonstrations, and stayed there for a week doing what he could to help his students.

You'll understand by now that my time in China coincided with big changes in society. In May 1976, when I first went there, Mao Zedong was still alive. The "Great Proletarian Cultural Revolution" was still on. All factories and other units were run by "Revolutionary Committees" made up of young and old, men and women. We were not, of course, shown any of the brutal excesses of the Cultural Revolution—I learned about them later as my Chinese colleagues learned to trust me; but I was lucky in 1976 to find many people who were working hard to make the Cultural Revolution work—I saw the positive side of it, which has since been officially denied. Once Deng Xiaoping had ruled that the Cultural Revolution was a ten-year disaster, it became unsafe to suggest that good things, too, had been happening.

By the time I finally left China, Deng Xiaoping had moved the country into the very different period of capitalism (well, officially it is "socialism with Chinese characteristics," but it has the marks of 19th-century unregulated capitalism), and Deng himself was dying—he died early in 1997.

I'll have a lot to say about Deng's decade, but here's one example of how the mood changed: An American teacher of English at Nankai, starting a unit on the structure of English sentences, said "Give me a sentence. Any sentence." No response. She called on one student, who looked embarrassed, then blurted out, "In agriculture learn from Dazhai." That had been one of the most popular slogans of the socialist period. But the whole class burst into laughter and it took the teacher five minutes to get them under control and back to work. So much for socialism! So much for working together to make a better world! So much for Li Susu! The slogan Deng Xiaoping gave the country was "To get rich is glorious!" and the mood of the new period was look out for yourself, or at most your family. Forget about society. And yet, you know, I found something significant about the hysteria of that laughter, and the fact that it lasted so long and was hard to control. My reading of the mood in China today is that when there is no longer hope for idealism, the only thing left is self-interest, but the deeper feeling is that there *ought* to be hope. Events have convinced me that as soon as people, especially young people, find a door opening on such hope, they will forget about self-interest and go for it. That's the basic message of Tiananmen—I'll get into that in detail.

And I have learned to look for the same thing in other countries, especially the US, where so many people have a cynical attitude towards society (including the majority of eligible voters who don't bother to vote). When they see a chance of change——well, this is a book about China, not the world, but think of the student movements of the 1960s in the US and you'll be better able to understand what the student demonstrations in Tiananmen Square were all about.

Enough by way of preface, eh? Now let me tell you how it all was, in the eyes of this one old foreigner.

1

To China!

It was far from easy to get to China back in 1976. I managed it only because I was a member of the Canada-China Friendship Association, and because the Chinese, who had invited a small group of Canadians to come and see China on a study tour, insisted that the members of the group should represent the major areas of Canada, and because a friend phoned me and asked if I'd like to be the prairie person on that trip.

Going to China then had an excitement not far short of going into space, and people I hardly knew stopped me in the halls of my university, saying with awe, "You're going to CHINA!" Today, when you just drop in on the nearest travel agent and buy a ticket, it's hard to remember what an inaccessible country it was then, and how much that inaccessibility heightened the excitement.

At the same time, it was a chance to see what the "Cultural Revolution" was all about. We had heard vague and conflicting reports, but on the whole it seemed the Chinese, having won their revolutionary war, and having set up their socialist government and economy, were now taking the big step of making their whole culture socialist. To make society more just and more humane — that was in the air in the 1960s and early 1970s, if you remember. In the US and in France, students and others were demanding big changes not only in universities but in society. This Cultural Revolution thing must be part of all that, and perhaps the most promising part of all. You must

remember that the dark and brutal side of the Cultural
Revolution had not yet been exposed, so our hopes for a more
just and humane society in China were still unsullied.

It's not easy to describe the complex emotions that kept me
awake and excited on that first trip, in May 1976. The excitement
kept me sleepless through the ten-hour plane trip from
Vancouver to Tokyo, the four-hour trip the next day from Tokyo
to Shanghai, the two-hour trip, after clearing customs, from
Shanghai to Beijing, and in China kept me pressed against the
window of the plane looking down, and against the window of
the bus from the airport, staring at everything and everybody,
delighted just to be there.

Our bus from the airport brought us to the Beijing Hotel
in mid-afternoon. Three of us immediately set out from the
hotel to walk around and see for ourselves this China. (I have to
comment here, ironically, that we were much freer to do that in
1976 than members of commercial tours are now.) We turned
off the big main avenue, looking for residential areas. In the
narrow side street, the buildings on either side presented only
blank walls right on the edges of the street, with no sidewalks—
and in the walls, at intervals, gateways with mysterious glimpses
of courtyards. We passed a tiny restaurant, with low stools and
tables outside, and many people eating.

There were a lot of people in the narrow streets, as there
had been alongside the roads from the airport. All of them,
men and women alike, wore what Westerners call "Mao jackets"
and pants—those plain baggy standardized blue clothes that
led some Western reporters to call the Chinese "Mao's blue ants".

The lanes we wandered through, the walls of the one-storey
buildings, the glimpses we had of courtyards, all seemed plain
and stark, and even drab, but clean and quiet. After turning
from one lane to another, we got lost. But our guide had given
us a card with the name of the hotel in Chinese characters, and

the first young man we showed it to smiled and beckoned, and went with us all the way back, trying in vain to talk to us and making us ashamed that we had not had time to learn a smidgen of Chinese before we came.

But I for one was more interested in our visits to a "barefoot doctor" clinic, and a local neighbourhood headquarters (where I suddenly realized that the reason they were showing us their rather drab lanes was that they were, in contrast to the old days, spotlessly clean), and the Institute for the Minorities. I found out later that dreadful things were happening in minority areas, with Red Guards destroying temples and forbidding people their local customs and languages. But here at the Institute we saw youngsters from many minorities, in their traditional dress, eating their traditional food, and—what impressed me more— seeming free to talk frankly to these foreigners. One Tibetan young man told us that in his home area there was a saying, "Don't use a rock for a pillow or a Han for a friend." ("Han" means the majority ethnic group—what we usually think of as "the Chinese").

Also, in the Institute for the Minorities, I remember the art teacher—a small, old woman with a beautiful face, full of wrinkles and energy. She told me her students were not there because they had been asked to paint a mural in a new railway station, so they were off working on the railroads for three weeks, some on the trains, some in maintenance. They worked all morning, made sketches in the afternoons, and had noisy meetings in the evening planning their mural, in all this following Chairman Mao's advice to "take society for your big classroom."

From Beijing, we went by plane to Xi'an, stopping halfway to have lunch in an airport, since China didn't yet have food service on the planes. We saw the sights in Xi'an, as everywhere (not the Qin Emperor's tomb, though—it was not yet open to the public). We went to the Wild Goose Pagoda, where one member of our group asked the director, "Why does socialist China not embrace Buddhism? It is, after all, a religion for the common people." To which she replied, "We believe that a religion which teaches submission to bad things rather than the will to change them, is not acceptable."

It became obvious to us that big struggles were taking place. We were asked not to photograph the big-character posters that were being put up everywhere. We were told that there was still a deep suspicion of foreigners, so we should not initiate conversation with local people for fear of getting them in trouble. But I remember that one evening, after we had seen a movie, three of us walked back to the hotel rather than take our bus, and passed through an area of apartment houses. We came to a place where we heard lively Chinese music coming from an apartment window. As we stood there listening, a door opened, and people came out with stools for us to sit on as we listened. That little episode is eloquent: they did not dare invite the foreigners into their apartment, but they found a way to show their friendship anyhow. And we felt that this mixture of caution and friendliness summed up a lot of what we saw around us.

One day we asked our guide, Fu Feiying, to let us talk with a group of women about the position of women in China. She was able to assemble for us at a few hours notice the woman in charge of the city's birthcontrol program, the principal of a highschool, the head of a factory's management committee— about a dozen women in such positions, who assured us that one of the big goals of the Cultural Revolution was to bring women closer to equality with men in their new society. One of them told us: "Marx says you can tell the precise level of development of a country by the position of its women."

From Xi'an we took the train to Luoyang, and visited the famous East is Red Tractor factory. I used to be a factory worker, and I went quickly to the precision grinding workshop, where I found a young woman working at a machine that looked familiar to me. I asked her what those objects were that she was working on, and she told me just how they fit into the tractor. (I, by contrast, in a Western factory, had been told not to ask what the things I worked on were for—just take them from this box, grind them to this tolerance, and put them in this other box).

She told me that there were eight workers in her group, who rotated from one machine to another, and also rotated in the position of foreman—and that whoever was foreman spent part of his or her time working at a machine, and another part in the factory's Workers' College studying mechanics and engineering. She said they decided as a team how to meet the quotas given them by the management committee. The feeling of newness was everywhere in this factory, which I still remember as one of the happiest factories I've seen anywhere. We felt the mood so strongly that when we reached the end of the production line and saw a tractor roll off the line and out to the proving ground, we applauded. As I've said before, I have seen dreadful factories in China, but also exemplary ones—this was one of the best.

In the East is Red Number Four Primary School of the factory, we watched little kids in one of their two weekly "production classes", taking the wires that go from distributor head to sparkplugs, crimping a metal connecting unit on each end of a wire, then running to test it at a device that lit up if they had done it right, dropping it in a box, and running back for another wire — as if playing a game. Later, when we visited the workers' homes, two sets of parents told me their children were proud of working for the tractors, "like Mom and Dad". That evening, the schoolchildren put on a performance for us, including a dance by the little ones, called "Working for the Tractors". A funny little dance, with the dancers waving the wires they had finished. In the middle of it, one boy came down front and shouted, "Let's break the production record! That's the important thing!" But another boy shouted, "No! Let's be sure all the wires are fixed right, so the farmers can have good tractors. *That's* the important thing!" And they all shouted and went on with the dance.

In Changsha, we spent a day in the Hunan Provincial Hospital. As in every unit we visited, we were welcomed at the gate by the managers—and in this case by about a dozen doctors—then sat behind what we would call coffee tables and drank tea while they told us about the work they did there, and their problems, and invited us to ask questions.

The high point of that day was when we all donned white clothes and caps and masks, and were admitted into an operating room where they were using acupuncture anesthesia. They put five flexible needles, with fine wires attached, in the small of the patient's back, then turned her over, and sent very light electrical pulses through these wires. They covered her except for the area they would operate on, and put a shield so she could not see what they were doing, and then, as she talked with one of the nurses (the anesthetist, it turned out), the surgeons cut her open and took out an ovarian cyst the size of a hen's egg. I turned to the Canadian next to me and said, "Okay, I believe. But who will believe me?"

For me the most interesting part of the whole tour was our visit to the Hunan Number One Normal College in Changsha—the school where the young Mao Zedong started his own teaching. There was a beautiful large red screen in the entrance lobby, with raised golden characters in his handwriting: "*Xiang shi renmin de xiansheng/ Xian shi renmin de xuesheng.*" That is, "If you want to be the people's teacher, first be the people's student."

In this college, we spent hours talking to the teachers about how they were trying to change the system of education, to make it less elitist and more relevant to the needs of society. In the process, they brought up questions that had been bothering me, as teacher, for decades.

There were no entrance exams here, because that system keeps out people who come from poor backgrounds but might be talented. They gave aptitude tests, and depended also on recommendations from fellow workers and previous teachers, and even neighbours. In the classes, there were no grades and no exams and no degrees. That excited me, because I have long held that grades corrupt the learning process, forcing students to work for grades instead of for learning, and since the teachers who give the grades are not only teachers but judges, the students at all levels of schooling are encouraged to please the teacher rather than learn to think critically. They agreed with me strongly when I told them this. They said their system made it possible for teachers and students all to work together to raise the competence of the whole class. They also pointed out that when students graduated they were still considered students of the college, and often came back for advice on how to handle problems, or to ask someone to come and criticize their teaching. In short, these teachers were trying hard to break down artificial walls, and bring the system closer to its basic objectives.

I must add that when I started teaching graduate students at Nankai, in September 1979, there were no grades, no exams, no degrees. It was heaven for a teacher! These students had been carefully screened, and certainly didn't need the discipline of grades. They worked together, and spent time in the library finding out more about the subject, and sometimes came to class waving a book, saying, "Look at this. Why haven't you told us about this?" Later in the school year, the rules were changed by order from Beijing, and I had to give them exams and grades—the result was that they were soon asking, "Is this going to be on the exam?" And they didn't dare spend time in individual research in the library. It was a lesson to all of us, as I made sure they were aware.

I've always been glad I was in China in 1976, to see and hear about positive aspects of the Cultural Revolution, because these aspects have since been denied or repudiated. The fashion now, in China as in the West, is to consider the Cultural Revolution as, in Deng Xiaoping's phrase, "a ten-year disaster".

One of the things that impressed me most about China was the sense of its antiquity. I knew it was ancient, of course, but that's not the same thing as being there and seeing the evidence all around me.

I had read Marco Polo's accounts of life in China in the 13th century. At a time when no city in Europe had a population of more than 100,000 people, he describes cities ten times that large. I knew that during the Ming dynasty (A.D. 1368 to 1644) China was the most advanced country in the world, technologically and culturally, and that the Chinese had invented paper-making, had invented printing, had invented the compass, gunpowder, the seismograph, and many other important things, and that Ming ceramics and painting are still considered among the world's artistic treasures. But when I got to China, in 1976, I actually saw some of these ceramics and paintings, and saw how modern artists still work in these traditions. I saw ancient temples, and statues, and began to realize how much of old China is still alive, how much their long past is part of the Chinese people's present.

In Qu Fu, I was shown a cemetery with the graves of seventy-two generations of the Kong family, stretching back more than two thousand years. One grave was that of Kong Fu Zi (whom we call Confucius). That same Kong family still flourishes in China.

For many centuries the Chinese believed that their country was the centre of the world, even of the universe. (They don't call their country "China". They call it *Zhong Guo*, or the country at the centre.) The emperor connected heaven with earth right there at the centre, making contact with the Emperor of Heaven.

Around that central country were barbarian tribes who were sometimes troublesome. Beyond these were unknown areas with which the Chinese sometimes condescended to trade, sending out fine silk and tea and porcelain and bringing back condiments, handicrafts, strange foods.

(The language of China preserves the memory of where some of these foods came from, as the word *huluobo*, or carrot, means "the root crop of the north-western barbarians", *yangcong*, or what we call the common onion, means "the kind of onion which came from across the ocean", and *xihongshi*, or tomato, means "the red persimmon that came from the countries to the west of us". All of them, you see, coming to China, the centre, from strange places out there on the world's margins.)

To stand in a temple, as I have often done, with red pillars going up to the shadowy ceiling, with the Buddha and his attendants looming over me, and the thick smell of incense in the air—to stand there and watch the yellow-robed monks at their service, with small drums, hand bells, and monotonous chants, and to realize that with the exception of short periods of disruption this scene has been enacted on this same spot daily for many centuries, sends shivers down my back.

In 1980, when I first climbed Mount Tai, the Daoist holy mountain, I was told that in olden days poets had carved poems on the rocks. When we came to one, I asked, "Is this an old one?" My Chinese companions studied it, then said, "No, that's not old. It's only four hundred years old." A little later, they said, "Here's an old one. This one is one thousand five hundred years old." You climb Mount Tai up stone steps all the way, in the company of hundreds of other climbers—and in the ghostly company of many thousands of others, whose soft cloth shoes have over the centuries worn deep depressions in the granite.

Chinese culture and Western culture developed in isolation from each other, so of course they developed ways of doing things which are different from ours. The Chinese eat with what I once heard a tourist describe with disdain as "two little sticks". In the south, especially, they eat things which Westerners do not consider food, things such as sea slugs, "ancient" eggs, dogs and cats, snakes. (For their part, most Chinese are disgusted by our eating cheese, and by our carving at the table great hunks of rare meat. And the waitresses at the Nankai Foreign Teachers Guest House once asked me to explain something they thought simply insane: Why on earth do foreigners drink ice-cold orange juice and hot coffee in the same meal?)

The Chinese use a gesture meaning "Come here" which looks like our gesture for "Goodby". According to our thinking, they give their last names first and first names last. On crowded local streets, until just a few years ago, the drivers of cars were forbidden to keep their car lights on at night, as I learned when the police stopped our car and scolded the driver.

The Chinese street scene in 1976 was very different indeed from ours (and from the Chinese streets of the 1990s). The streets for centuries had belonged to pedestrians, so there were no sidewalks. People on foot gave way only grudgingly for bicycles or for the rare auto. Traffic on main streets was heavy, but almost silent because it was almost entirely bicycles.

People of all ages rode bicycles. It was nerve-wracking to cross a city street if the light changed and you saw masses of bike-riders charging at you—though on the other hand I have more than once seen an old grandmother calmly walk across the street in the middle of the block through all the traffic, looking neither right nor left as the bicycles flowed around her like schools of fish.

China has changed tremendously since my early days there. But the old ways of China still have a charm for me. I remember the time I first saw water buffalo up close, a line of them beside the road, with a small boy astride each one, as they could have been seen for thousands of years. I remember the day I first saw a herd of wild camels running across the loess plateau. I'm glad I was able to work in old Xiamen, before it became a modern New Economic Zone, and in Ningxia, on the edge of the Gobi Desert, when "undeveloped" Ningxia was not yet open to foreigners except those with work permits. I'm glad I was able to talk with shepherd boys herding lean sheep on Ningxia's wild plateau as they have done for centuries, and with *muma ren* (horse-herding nomads) in the far north of Inner Mongolia in their yurt homes. I'm glad to have been invited into several of the Dai people's traditional stilt houses in the southern Yunnan jungle, and on one wild long afternoon got rather drunk playing drinking games with old Dai men. I'm glad one of my Xiamen students comes from an isolated mountain village (only a mix-up in plans prevented me from visiting her family there) where the villagers still go in procession to bring gifts and prayers to the oldest tree and ask its blessings. I'm glad I know where the old bird and flower market is in Kunming, and the old teahouse with traditional storytellers. I'm glad I know where to find the parks, in Kunming, Jinan, Tianjin, where old people still gather on Sunday mornings to sing traditional opera tunes to the music of the two-string *jing hu*.

In short, I love the old ways of China—I love them so much that it took me years to realize that the gift of the past in China is twofold, and that some of its ancient traditions have been hostile to socialism, and a drag on its realization.

2

Socialism In China

Socialism, like most things in this world, is created not in a vacuum but in pre-existing circumstances. I have to admit that I first went to China naively, looking for something called "socialism", some universal thing, without stopping to think that it would have to be different in different cultures. I soon learned that in order to understand Chinese socialism I'd have to consider what forces or elements in Chinese culture favoured the development of socialism there, and what worked against it, and how the mix produced *Chinese* socialism.

Where should I begin? Perhaps with Liberation.

On October 1, 1949, Chairman Mao announced to a huge enthusiastic crowd in Tiananmen Square, "China has stood up!" Although during the previous civil wars the areas won by the Communist armies had been called "Liberated Areas", and although in these areas much of the structure and spirit of socialism had been established, still in the minds of most Chinese people "Liberation" means October 1, 1949, when the nation officially became a socialist country.

But if you aren't familiar with the history of pre-Liberation China, you might be puzzled. Liberation? From what? What was so bad about the previous conditions that throwing them off was an act of liberation? I wasn't there, of course. By the time of my first visit to China in 1976, the Chinese had been living with socialism for 27 years. But I think the Chinese have more awareness of their history than most Westerners: I heard many accounts of "the bad old pre-Liberation days".

My colleague, the late Hsieh Peichih, Professor of Asian History at the University of Regina, started life in old China. He told me about it, beginning with the famine of 1943 when he was a small child. There in his village he saw a man lying on the ground dying of starvation. Nobody offered to help him— so many were dying that it was hopeless. The child went often just to look at him, until he died and someone carried off the corpse.

To realize the awfulness of those days, Professor Hsieh said, think first of some of the things happening in the world today. Think of the thousands who are starving, and the millions of children severely malnourished. Think of the warlords of Somalia, and the slayings in Rwanda and Algeria, and the genocide in Bosnia, and the incredible inflation in many countries. Put them all together, he said, and you'll have some idea of what China was like before socialism. When the Communists offered a new kind of world, some people agreed, he says, simply because they thought nothing could be worse than what they already had.

Bill Hinton, the author and agricultural expert who has been working in China since before Liberation, told me that China then was "a basket case".

But how had China got into such chaos? My Chinese friends start that story with the year 1840, when the British, who had built up a massive illegal trade smuggling opium from India into China, were told by a high official that the trade must stop. The official took the intolerable step of seizing a shipment of opium and burning it, to which the British responded by bringing up the Royal Navy and Army and storming ashore. They not only imposed their opium on China, but forced the country to cede "concessions"—that is, areas belonging to the British, where British law, not Chinese, ruled—the bases from which they controlled more and more of China's economy. This was a time when the Qing Dynasty was slowly dying, collapsing into impotence, corruption, and chaos, so the Chinese were in no position to resist. And in the wake of the British, many other countries demanded equal treatment, and "expropriation" became the golden door to exploitation of China's resources.

After seven decades of war, uprisings, turmoil, and corruption—and fruitless attempts at reform—the moribund Qing Dynasty was overthrown by the followers of Sun Yat Sen, and my Chinese friends date the beginning of modern China from that 1911 event, the end of the last imperial dynasty.

Sun united in his "National People's Party", or "Guomindang", both the new Communists and the Nationalists, but in 1927, two years after Sun's death, Chiang Kaishek (Jiang Jieshi) turned violently against the Communists and thus began the long bitter warfare between Communists and Nationalists that ended in 1949 in Liberation. Meanwhile, beginning in 1927, and intensifying massively in 1937, the Japanese invaded China, at first to grab territories in the north-east as an industrial base, and later trying to subdue China by terror in order to free their armies for action further south. For years there was no effective national government, and local areas came under the control of warlords and were raided by bandits and slid into chaos and misery.

That's a painfully simplified account of very complex events, but my purpose is only to remind you of those times in order to indicate something of the conditions the new socialist government inherited.

The first great problem of socialist China at Liberation was how to bring food, housing, medical care, and education to a desperate country of 500,000,000 people (a number that would double in thirty years.) You can judge the results either way: old people in China, looking back at the old days, tell me with great pride how far the country has come. Young people, before the boom of consumer goods in the 1980s, saw how much poorer their lives were in material ways than those of the Americans and Europeans and Japanese, and were ashamed.

In 1979, while I was at Nankai, it was announced that for the first time an American program would be broadcast on Chinese television. At that time, no people I knew had their own TV sets. To watch television, you went to the TV room in your hotel, or dormitory, or workplace. So the TV room of the foreign students dorm in which I was living was jammed tight with people, and many heads in the doorway. The program was one episode of a silly series called "The Man From Atlantis", in which a web-fingered hero comes up out of the ocean and saves the situation, then goes back into the ocean—an old Tom Mix plot. Later, I asked my students how they could be interested in such a stupid story, but they said, "Story? What story? Didn't you notice how any time those people went anywhere, they got into their own autos? And every time we saw the inside of a house, there were carpets on the floor, and big rooms with fine furniture, and only one family living in a whole house?"

Fair enough. In that context, they were right. As many people said to me back then, "You shouldn't have to be poor to be socialist!" And what they had was, by Western standards, poverty, no matter how superior it was to pre-Liberation China. After providing a minimum lifestyle for the people, the socialist government concentrated its resources on crucially needed infrastructure and heavy industry, at the expense of advances in consumer goods. When I visited my Chinese friends, I sometimes found them living in housing that people on welfare in Canada would have refused.

One family I often visited were living in two tiny rooms, not even close to each other. They shared a dark little toilet room with three other families. They bathed in the communal showerhouse three blocks away. Their "kitchen" was nothing but a small coal stove out in the common hallway. In these conditions lived the father, the mother, two daughters, and a grandmother. And these parents had relatively good incomes— she was a university teacher; he was an official in the university administration.

(But this was the same family I've mentioned before, where the mother scolded her ten-year-old daughter for not doing enough for her country.)

To give Chinese socialism its due, we must look at the other side, the side that many young people in the 1980s and 1990s have forgotten. Yes, the people had lifestyles far less comfortable than those of most Westerners, as the country's resources went predominantly to building up infrastructure and social programs. But to be fair, we must consider what they got from that division of scarce resources.

If you had been born in 1949, in the world the socialists inherited, you could expect, on average, to live only to your mid-thirties—thirty years later, average life expectancy had doubled. In old China, so many babies died in infancy that the custom was to wait and see if your baby survived for a hundred days—if so, you could assume it might live, so formal "hundred days pictures" were taken to show family and friends. Under socialism, so many more infants survived that although people still take "hundred days pictures", young people have forgotten the reason for the custom.

The most pressing job was to provide food for five hundred million hungry people. Socialist China succeeded in this, except for the three dreadful years 1959 to 1961. Food production increased so steadily that as their huge population doubled to a billion people, production kept up, although the amount of arable land actually decreased. They have fed their burgeoning population—20 per cent of the world's people—on 7 per cent of the world's arable land. How could they do this? Mostly through the great development of water conservancy and irrigation. Everywhere I went in 1976 and thereafter, I saw new aqueducts, some as large as the old Roman ones, soaring across valleys with large arches, carrying not only precious water, but sizable canalboats; some so small that they were waist-high and carried tiny streams from hillside springs to lower-lying fields. And everywhere new dams, irrigation canals, reservoirs and holding ponds—and all of these built without the heavy machinery available to Western countries. Everywhere we went on our study tours, one of the things people were most proud to show us was their water conservancy accomplishments. I have photos of our study group standing with local officials in front of dams, or aqueducts, or water gushing out of pumps into irrigation ditches.

Between 1949 and 1979, socialist China also developed a well-rounded industrial base, including a steel industry, a chemical industry, a greatly expanded railway system. They were soon making and exporting railway locomotives. (I remember reading in the 1950s or 60s an essay by the Chinese-become-American writer, Lin Yutang, expressing his astonishment that the Chinese had been able to manufacture a locomotive.) By 1979, China was leading the world in the development of small hydropower technology, enabling villages with small streams to develop their own power, and in biomass energy—people still come from around the world to learn from the Chinese how to use vegetable and animal waste to produce and use methane gas. It developed solar cookers which have relieved people in semi-desert areas where the trees have long since been cut down and people were burning wheat and rice stalks for cooking instead of plowing them back into the ground. It developed small wind-power machines, enabling nomads in north China, following their herds, to set up their yurts, then their windpower machines, then go indoors and turn on the light or the television.

(Notice, please, the emphasis on making technology serve ordinary people, which I see in sharp contrast to the mega-projects of the 1990s, such as the Three Gorges Dam and the nuclear power plants.)

In medicine, socialist China pioneered in the treatment of burns and of severed parts of the body, sent teams of doctors as teachers to other Third World countries, and set up a system of first response, the "barefoot doctors" I'll describe later. Socialist China developed a space program which put dozens of satellites into orbit. And (whatever we may think of this) it built atom bombs, hydrogen bombs, and nuclear submarines.

It's crucial to remember that, whatever its shortcomings in housing and so on, the socialist period developed the infrastructure—the water conservancy, the railroads, the ports, the energy systems, the industry—in short, the economic base which made possible the spectacular development of consumer goods in Deng Xiaoping's decade of the 1980s. And what credit have the socialists been given for that, either at home or abroad?

I hasten to add that these technological advances, important as they are, are not what impress me most about socialism. Neither is the system of central planning by which they got their economic system started (which I'll talk about in detail when I describe a factory in Tianjin).

To me the evidence of the success of socialism in China is the spirit it inspired in the people. Not all the people; remember that one theme of this book is that the struggle to convert the Chinese from age-old folkways was only partially successful. More than one of my own students said to me, "Not everybody in a socialist country is a socialist." But I'm impressed by how many people had, and indeed still have, that spirit of socialist idealism. I see it most clearly in the older people whose memories go back to pre-Liberation days. But I see it also in the assumptions and attitudes of most of my Chinese students, in the idealism that endears them to me, and expresses itself not only in their tremendous enthusiasm for hard work but their taking it for granted that their work must do good in the world. Many slogans of the socialist years were only slogans, but "Serve the people!" is still taken for granted as what one ought to do. That spirit has been under great stress from the materialism of the 1980s and thereafter, but it was the strongest incentive of the students who demonstrated in 1989 and of the millions of people who came out to support them.

One of the old-timers I met is a woman who started life at the same time I did—in November, 1914—but her life started in poverty and in constant hunger. She was a child in a world I find it hard even to imagine. When she was little, her mother bound her feet, which means she forced them back under so the girl was walking on the top of her inverted toes, and then bound them tightly with strips of cloth. When the daughter grew up, her adult foot was less than four inches long. The mother thought this would help her find a husband. But times got worse and worse, and the daughter, now an old woman, remembers with great bitterness how, while still a child, she was sold in the marketplace. "Like a cow or a pig!" she says. Some of the first laws the socialist government passed outlawed foot-binding and the buying and selling of people. And when I met this woman, she was looking back at those days from the security of a socialist old-age home.

Another old-timer, a friend of mine, was in the 1940s a grubby, barefoot peasant girl in a mountain village who never got enough to eat. Her whole family was illiterate. After Liberation, when she was eleven years old, the new government opened a school in her village and encouraged not only the boys but the girls to go to it. With the backing of the Party, she went through primary school, high school, and university. The teachers, she says, always encouraged her to show the world what girls can do. Now she's an administrator in a big research institute. She still sprinkles her talk with the slogans of Mao Zedong Thought. "After all," she says, "I work for everybody, and everybody works for me." "I tell my girls, `Dare to think! Dare to speak! Dare to do!'" She has no patience with young people who think only of having American jeans and lots of money, and going abroad.

When China was "a basket case", how did it happen to turn to socialism, rather than (as had happened many times before in history) to another imperial dynasty, or to a charismatic leader taking them down the road to a more modern dictatorship and fascism? Where did the mass enthusiasm come from that enabled the Chinese under socialism to build dams and aqueducts and other massive things without heavy machinery? A lot of books have been written to give detailed answers to these questions; a complete answer would have to record the contributions of many thousands of people. But the one person who must be considered is of course Mao Zedong, who focused in himself many of the strengths of the revolution. He was a great tactician in warfare, a wise planner of a society, a great socialist theoretician and teacher, and an extremely charismatic leader.

It was Mao who based the revolution on the masses—which meant, in China, the peasants who were (and are) the overwhelming majority. It was Mao who realized that the first thing the peasants needed and hungered for was land. Without the peasants, and without land reform, no revolution. It was under Mao's leadership that the Red Armies developed the guerrilla tactics that enabled them to survive and then outfight the invading Japanese army and the armies of Chiang Kaishek. And he, more than any other person, taught the Chinese people what socialism meant and enlisted their energies, enthusiasms, and idealism to build and cherish it. Without that enthusiasm, no socialist China.

Was Mao Zedong a saint? No indeed. Along with all the strengths that made him one of the great leaders of the 20th Century, he carried inside himself elements of the old imperialist China which were to cause great problems. I'll get to them. For now, let's concentrate on the socialist spirit which he, more than any other individual, inspired.

I remember a funny but moving example of that spirit, from our 1976 study trip: In the city of Zhengzhou, the capital of Henan Province, we were invited to a performance by high school students, a variety of acts before a large audience of which we were the only foreigners. One act was a dance which a group of girls had developed from the elastic-skipping game—the most popular game of Chinese girls everywhere, in which an elastic string goes around the ankles of two girls, forming a long loop, and others skip in and out of the loop to a set chant, performing various twists and turns and ways of catching up the string with their feet, after which the string is raised, and the game starts over, ending (I'm told, though I never saw it go this far) with the string around the necks of the two girls holding it, from which height the players have to bring it down with their feet.

In the performance which they had developed from this game, one girl stood in the center of the stage while elastic strings went out like the spokes of a wheel from her ankles to the ankles of eight other girls standing around her in a circle, and another around the rim of the circle. A group of girls ran out and did a graceful dance in and out of the strings, to the chant of the skipping game. Then they ran off and the rim string was raised neck high.

A single, rather short girl ran in. She was supposed to bring that string down with her foot, but there was no way she could possibly reach it. She came downstage and mimed the action of crying. But another girl came in, and urged her to try again, which she did—but it was obviously impossible, so she cried again.

Then the second girl did something the meaning of which was obvious to all the Chinese. She took the ends of a red neckerchief which the short girl was wearing and held the ends up in front of the girl's face. The gesture, our guide whispered, meant "This is the neckerchief of a Young Pioneer. What does Chairman Mao say to the Young Pioneers? He says, 'Think! Experiment! Never give up!'" At that the short girl drew a deep breath and marched over and tried again—but, of course, it was still no use.

All of a sudden, she thought of the answer, and ran and did a cartwheel at the top of which her foot caught the string and brought it down, and she danced triumphantly while the whole audience rose and clapped and laughed and stamped on the floor.

I've often thought about this dance while trying to understand what "Mao Zedong Thought" meant. When a brain surgeon told me his team owed the success of an operation to Mao Zedong Thought, I'm afraid I snorted. But the point is that socialism at its best was "grassroots socialism", in which Mao gave them general principles ("Think! Experiment! Never give up!") but not, of course, specific solutions to all problems.

Pat and Roger Howard, of Simon Fraser University, who have been studying and working in China since 1971, told me about an example of this grassroots socialism, in the resolution of a heated debate in one commune, on the issue of men's work and women's work.

In the commune, workpoints were assigned to each member for the work he or she did each day. At the end of the year, the profits were divided according to each person's total workpoints. The problem was that men earned ten workpoints for a day in the fields, but women only seven or eight.

There were actually two problems. One was that the men considered work which women traditionally do, such as transplanting rice seedlings, easier than men's work. Therefore women should get fewer points. The women challenged them to a rice-transplanting contest. The men not only lost the contest, but had sore backs and swollen ankles. They agreed that the women deserved full points for each hour worked.

But the men had another argument: the women didn't spend as much time in the fields as the men, because the women went home early at noon. The women were indignant. Why did they go home? Not to rest or play! They went home to gather firewood, make the fires for cooking, and prepare lunch for everybody.

After much debate, they came to an agreement. The women were given the same workpoints as men for equal hours at field work. And they all built a solar water heater, so the women didn't have to spend time gathering firewood and could stay in the fields longer. (Give some credit, incidentally, to the men, who in a very sexist society agreed to settle the problem by Mao Zedong Thought rather than by macho tradition.)

A striking example of grassroots socialism was told to me by our guide on the 1976 study tour, Fu Feiying. Fu was always ready to talk to us while we traveled by train from one place to another. One day we talked about one of Chairman Mao's mottoes: "Overcome the divorce between theory and practice." She understood the basic idea: Theory without practice is ignorant. Practice without theory is chaotic. Since I'm a teacher of English, I asked her how she thought this might apply to the teaching of English. She told me about a debate in the Beijing Foreign Languages Institute in Beijing, where she had studied, precisely on this subject.

We found a way. At my institute there were big debates. Some said you can't unite theory and practice in the teaching of English, therefore English should not be taught. That was leftist extremism. Some said the teaching of English is an exception, so it must not be asked to unite theory and practice. That was rightist extremism.

But our group won: we found a way. We all spent a month on a commune farm. In the mornings, we worked with the peasants. In the afternoons we studied English. In the evenings we wrote up our notes. Then we spent a month in a factory the same way. We wrote two books in English, one about farm work and the other about factories, which are now being used as textbooks in high school English classes.

Can't you hear them? Hours of meetings, arguments, proposals and counter-proposals about how they should be learning English, in order to make the process socialist! And they did not look to leaders for answers, but worked them out themselves.

One day in June 1980, it was the turn of the Nankai University Foreign Languages Department to harvest the wheat on an allotted section of the university wheat farm. So at four o'clock in the morning there assembled on the wheat field all the students, teachers, administrators, secretaries, janitors of the Department, to spend that day all together in manual labour. My son Aaron, who was visiting me from Canada, was there, and although the foreign teachers had been told they were not obliged to help, almost all of us were there, too. (For myself, though, I have to admit that I didn't make the 4 a.m. deadline.)

We harvested the wheat in a way that might have been familiar to farmers of the Old Testament, but seemed quite strange to Aaron and to me, coming from Saskatchewan. The instrument was a stick about two feet long, at the end of which a sharp blade about eight inches long was attached at right angles.

You seized a handful of wheat stalks with one hand, and pulled the knife towards you to cut that bunch, which you laid down behind you. Other workers gathered this up into sheaves, and still others carried the sheaves to a truck which would take them to the threshing floor.

The atmosphere was more like a holiday than hard labour. We got an amazing amount done, but without working up much sweat, and with a lot of joking, and singing, and conversation. And on my part, at least, a lot of thinking. I was reminded that in 1976, at the end of our study tour, I had asked Fu Feiying what she would do next, after seeing us off. "Oh, I'll be back in the office in Beijing for a week, writing up my report. Then it's time to go down to the countryside and spend a month getting in the wheat. I'm good at that!" She spoke as if it was a holiday she was looking forward to, and for sure it would be a break from the pressures of being our guide, and from working in an office—the change, the fresh air, the spirit of camaraderie and of helping the country, helping feed the people.

(Please remember the schoolgirls' dance, the debates in the commune and at Fu Feiying's institute, the spirit of our wheat harvest, and Fu's anticipation of going to the countryside to help get in the wheat. They are "grassroots socialism" in action, based on local thinking and planning and enthusiasm—within the framework of socialist ideology. When China turned more and more to decisions being made at high levels and then *imposed on* local people—as, for example, when people were *sent*, or *sentenced* to the countryside, enthusiasm like Fu's died out, and China's socialism was in trouble.)

During that 1979-1980 school year at Nankai (a ten-month school year, with only July and August off) there were many times when my students and I did things together. At six o'clock every morning, exercise music came over the ubiquitous loudspeakers, and everyone ran out to do a set series of exercises.

Classes started at 7:30. At 10:20, music rang out again, and students and teachers ran out to exercise together for a quarter of an hour. The students of each undergraduate class spent two weeks each semester working on the campus, clipping hedges, weeding flowerbeds, cleaning junk out of the little canal that crossed the campus. As for my graduate class, on our time off (which mostly meant Sundays, since the Chinese work-week was six days) all my students and I went to the parks together—rowing in the water park, strolling through the zoo, having picnics. Every now and then the whole class came to my apartment and cooked up a huge pile of *jiaozi* together—those "dumplings" which they say are the ancestors of ravioli and perogies—everyone joining in the making and cooking and eating, with lots of jokes and songs and laughing. It's a lovely thing to do, especially with a new class, to break the ice and make us a social unit.

I was lucky in my timing, getting to China in time to be part of those days. If I went there now for the first time, I'd find a very different Nankai. There's no university farm anymore—that whole area is taken up with new buildings. There's no more exercising together; in fact, there is nothing that teachers and their whole classes do together outside of the classroom, unless they organize a birthday party or some such special festivity. Students don't have to get out for morning exercises now, though some choose to do that, and students don't work on the campus grounds (and so don't feel responsible for them, so tend to litter, and break through hedges, and things like that.) Students are no longer classmates in the old sense. In 1979-80, students stayed together as classes: each class took the same courses, lived in the same dormitories, ate in the same dining halls, and met in the evenings for study sessions to be sure everyone understood the subject. Today, I can no longer tell one student that I forgot to ask the class to bring a certain book to our next session, knowing that the whole class would get the message. They don't all take the same courses anymore, or live as a close-knit group for their university years (and no longer have that bond which makes students stay in touch with each other for years after graduation—I can ask any of my old students from those days what the rest of the class are doing now, and get a detailed answer, and once, on a trip through the south with Chinese friends, we went fifty kilometres out of our way so one of them could say hello to a classmate she hadn't seen for ten years).

In fact, the whole feeling of Chinese society has become much less communal than it was then. Dams are not built by masses of people working together, but by professional construction workers and heavy machines. In the socialist days it was taken for granted that everyone would pitch in to change things—my favourite example (it happened before I got there, but I heard a lot about it) was the campaign to eliminate flies, during which everybody, including Chairman Mao and all his ministers, and the millions of Chinese people, each had a quota of how many flies to kill each day. The flies are making a comeback, but are still very much fewer than in other Third World countries I've visited—that's especially noticeable in open-air butcher stalls in the markets.

There are many such reminders that under socialism society was more communal. I was in China for a short time, relative to the great sweep of changes over several decades, but even I saw enough of that spirit to miss it in these very different times.

That reminds me of another memory—one which illustrates the fact that I'm not alone in my feelings. In 1987, I went back to Xiamen to visit some of the friends I had made while teaching there previously. I found an older student, who had been herself a teacher while studying for her MA with me. She and her husband and little girl were living in a new development, a group of five seven-storey apartment buildings near the ocean—a wonderful improvement over the cramped quarters they had lived in before. I had a long leisurely supper with them, and we got talking about the changes they had seen.

After boasting about their apartment, showing me through the rooms and pointing out the television set and the washing machine, their talk took a different turn.

"Did you notice," said the husband "there are bars on the windows of this apartment? We refused to have them installed at first, but our neighbours convinced us they're necessary because we're on the ground floor. And you know everybody has more things now—like our big-screen TV, and our cameras. There are more thieves now that we have things worth stealing."

"It's not only that," the wife said. "Not just because there are things to steal. You know, before, if anyone noticed a man in the market grab a woman's purse, they'd shout, and everyone would run and catch that man, and take him to the police station. But now, nobody wants to get involved."

Then they pointed out to me that the bars on their ground-floor apartment were only the beginning. Now, if you go outside and look, you'll see that there are bars on the second and third floor windows, because thieves can carry ladders. And there are new steel doors outside the regular front doors of all the apartments in all these buildings.

"And that wasn't enough," they say. "So the people who live in these apartment buildings had a meeting, and now at any hour of the day or night we have a citizen's group—we all take turns—patrolling the area."

My student looked embarrassed, and changed the subject, and made more tea—but they couldn't stay away from the subject very long.

"You know, in the early days there were food shortages, and shortages of just about everything else. But there were no locks on people's doors. We may not have had very much, but we had each other. We were brothers and sisters then."

Romantic nostalgia? In part, I guess. The same could be said of some of the banners that the demonstrating students carried in 1989, that read "Mao Zedong's ministers had clean hands. Deng Xiaoping's ministers are all millionaires." I mentioned these banners to Peter Gzowski once, on his "Morningside" radio show, and he said in a shocked voice, "You don't mean to tell me they're nostalgic for the Maoist days?" Well, yes, I do mean to tell you that. My student's husband said it: there were many hardships and problems back then, but "we had each other."

Socialism is both a feeling, an emotion, a relationship of people to people—and, at the same time, a political and economic structure. These are not separate: the structure, at least in theory, is designed to bring about the basics of a good life for the people, and to engender feelings of community. As to the structure, I'll go into details later. Here, I'll just note what seems to me the most basic difference between Western capitalist systems and Chinese socialism. Mao Zedong once said, "When you are seeking the answer to any broad social problem, ask yourself *for whom* you are seeking a solution. If your answer is anything less than the mass of the people, you are wrong. Start over again." Which reminds me of a passage by Henry David Thoreau. He was writing it at about the time that Engels was making his study of the condition of the "operatives" (that is, the workers) of England, which would be incorporated into the Communist Manifesto. (Thoreau, of course, was not a communist, nor a socialist, but an aggressively independent observer of American society.)

> I cannot believe that our factory system is the best mode by which men may get clothing. The condition of the operatives is becoming every day more like that of the English; and it cannot be wondered at, since, as far as I have heard or observed, the principal object is, not that mankind may be well and

honestly clad, but, unquestionably, that the corporation may
be enriched. In the long run men hit only what they aim at.

(Walden, Chapter 1)

That points up rather neatly the difference between the
socialist doctrine of production for use and the capitalist
production for profit. It's true, of course, that the distinction is
not 100 per cent: capitalist theory includes the premise that it
will ultimately benefit the consumer, and socialist theory does
not rule out the hope of profits—but the distinction is clear.

A truly socialist structure is designed to produce a good life
for the people, and to engender feelings of community. The
feelings, are, in turn, the generators of the enthusiasms which
make the people accept and support and defend the political
and economic structure.

New China needed dams, aqueducts, roads, new farm fields,
housing, in order to feed and house the people of devastated
China (half a billion people at Liberation, remember, and
doubling in just thirty years.) It needed educational and medical
systems. It needed factories, and transportation, and the
distribution of goods. There was a whole new system to be
planned, as well as a mass enthusiasm to carry out the plans.
Both were needed. If the people ever lost their trust that the
government was working for the fine new socialist world, or if
the leaders of the government ever lost contact with the people
and their feelings, the whole thing was in danger—and in fact,
that might be taken as a brief statement of the crucial problem
of socialist China.

(To jump ahead, when the soldiers not only smashed the
student demonstrations in Tiananmen Square on June 4, 1989,
but for three days kept on shooting at the people
indiscriminately, what they killed was not so importantly
individual people, awful as that was—what they killed was the
faith of the people in their leaders, and their government—

which, for many of them meant their faith in socialism—which left a void in people's minds and hearts. After Tiananmen, many students said to me, "I just feel empty inside.")

But come back to the socialist beginnings. When the city of Beijing was liberated, one of the first jobs was to clean up the filth which had accumulated in all the lanes. The people enmasse tackled the job with enthusiasm, and long lines of handcarts carried the refuse off to dumps outside the city, with a general feeling that they were cleaning out the filth of the old society. The great irrigation projects I've described were built by mass labour—think of masses of people building large earth dams with no machinery but hand tools and handcarts! Think of the great campaign to eliminate flies by everyone in that populous country joining to kill their quota of flies each day! And think of the effect on the people's morale when they proved what could be accomplished by working together.

What happened to the enthusiasms of those days? I remember saying to a student in 1991, "I'm beginning to understand. You don't love socialism. You don't hate socialism. You just never think about it." She said, "Yes. That's all ancient history!" (Actually what she said was *gudai de gushi*, which literally means "an ancient story"). These days in China the popular mood is "Get what you can; forget the other guy." Many people today would agree with Margaret Thatcher's slogan, "There's no such thing as society." How did they get from there to here?

Socialism had to struggle against a number of forces, from the start—both internal forces and external enemies. Of the internal forces, I want to concentrate on three: hold-overs from Old China; bureaucracy; and a war mentality.

Many aspects of Old China were precisely what socialism intended to change—but changing folkways of about three thousand years is not to be accomplished in one generation. The theoretical bedrock of Old China was Confucianism, a theory built on the concept of hierarchy and obedience. Only when children are obedient to parents, wives to husbands, widows to sons, women to men generally, servants to masters, all citizens to the emperor, and the emperor himself to the mandate of heaven, could there be a peaceful and proper society. The concept has always reminded me of the "great chain of being" described by Alexander Pope in the 18th Century, to break any link of which would cause disaster to the whole. Such a system, obviously, justifies a society in which some are wealthy and powerful while others are poor and miserable. Give Confucius his due—what he preached was virtue and benevolence, from the emperor down through the social ranks. Only when the masters are virtuous, he said, will there be justice and peace. Nevertheless, the basis of his thinking was hierarchy and obedience, and that concept of how society must be run was very deeply imbedded in Chinese culture, and has by no means been eradicated.

Many social ranks had, of course, vested interest in the old system, and would have to give up power if the system was to be changed—but it is asking more of most people than they are capable of giving, to ask them to give up power. For example, the question of women's rights. The Constitution of socialist China says, "Women enjoy equal rights with men in all spheres of life." But the facts of Chinese life, even today, after decades of socialism, are somewhat different. In almost all families, although both husband and wife have jobs outside the home, at the end of the working day the husband's job is finished but the wife's is not—she has two jobs, one at her outside work and the other in taking care of the house, the cooking, and the children. And although both may be ambitious in their work, the man's work is "obviously" the more important; so he must be free to study, perhaps, while she washes the dishes. Men do not easily give up the prerogatives of a macho culture, or the concept that the role of women is to support the men. It follows, in the Confucian tradition, that women should not be educated except in those things which will make them better wives. As an example of how persistent that tradition is, these days it's common knowledge that the smartest young women students have problems finding husbands. In 1996, on three separate occasions, young men said to me (expressing opinions they would not have felt free to express a few years before) "Confucius was right: Intelligence in a woman is not a virtue."

Another point: although socialist China officially has no such thing as social class, in fact, the class system is still so strong that I sometimes think of it as a caste system. You remember my student—an intelligent, upright person—who asked what he, an educated man, could learn from "stinking peasants".

The power of officials has been, traditionally, a personal power. The old Chinese system was run not by law but by authority. There has been a socialist campaign to change to a system of law, binding on everybody, but it has been an uphill battle which is still far from won. In Old China, the law was whatever people in power said it was. For officials to accept that they, too, are bound by law, will take a long time to work its way through the system.

It has fascinated me and saddened me to see how the top leaders of socialist China carried over the old idea that society is run by leaders deciding and people obeying. One incident has seemed symbolic to me: when the Communists won the civil war and took control of the country, in 1949, they decided that Beijing would be the capital. One question was where the government headquarters should be. It was suggested that it should be in the Forbidden City, the old imperial palace complex. That was a shocking idea to the more radical members of the leadership, some of whom said it would be more appropriate to burn the old thing down. Mao Zedong decided that the new government's headquarters, and the living quarters of the leaders, should indeed be in Zhongnanhai, part of the old palace complex. Some of the revolutionary leaders refused to live there, but to this day that is the resplendent headquarters of the socialist government, guarded by sentries in splendid uniforms, and barred to anyone without very high official business.

Chairman Mao had his share of contradictions. Although he was a great Communist leader, he also carried inside himself the old assumptions of hierarchical leadership. He changed the collegial system of leaders, which had won the revolution, to a single top leader—himself—and gradually assumed the role, though without the title, of emperor. He let himself be worshipped, as the emperors had been.

One of my colleagues at Xiamen University told me that when she was a girl there was a picture of Chairman Mao on the wall beside her bed. Every morning, she had to bow to the Chairman three times and promise to be a good girl that day. Before every meal she bowed to him, and before going to bed she confessed to him everything she had done wrong that day and promised him to be a better girl.

Mao's pictures were in every home and every office; his statues in every city and town. His face was on Chinese stamps, depicted as the sun, with rays shooting out around it, beaming on the earth beneath. You were expected to wear a Mao badge at all times, and Lord help you if you pinned it on at a slant. Any time your photo was taken, you'd better be holding the Little Red Book (*Quotations From Chairman Mao Tse-Tung*) next to your heart. To criticize Mao would be blasphemy.

For me, Mao Zedong towards the end of his life is the prime example of how Old China persisted into New China and distorted its socialism.

The more I think about it, the more I realize that this is a very basic and widespread problem, not just a matter of Mao and his shortcomings. The idea that leaders decide and the people obey, that holdover from Confucianism, saturates the society. You see it in the classrooms, where the teacher is the expert and the students are privileged to listen and take notes without questioning anything. You see it in families, and in factories, and everywhere—the commonest pattern is leaders deciding and those under them obeying.

Students in classes and all people in daily life are expected to take their ideas and attitudes from the leaders. So they never get much chance to develop the habit of thinking, and analyzing, and developing their own slant on things. That's why when Deng came to power and opened China to the world, and Western ideas and customs came flooding in, most Chinese people had no scepticism, no habit of examining and questioning—so they welcomed the new ideas, and customs, and consumer goods with uncritical delight. It was easy for them to forget about socialism, that old story, and just be delighted by the new story.

Another of the internal forces acting as a drag on the development of socialism has been a bureaucracy which is the despair of anyone who wants to get things done. In part, this bureaucracy grew out of the circumstances of Liberation. The Communists came to power in 1949 abruptly, much sooner than they expected. So they were suddenly faced with the complex problem of building a new society. Since there was already a bureaucracy in place, running local government, running a police department, a post office, and so on, the easiest thing was to take it over and keep it going, while energies were concentrated on those things it was most crucial to change and

make new. Unfortunately, that meant taking over a bureaucracy
that was notorious for delays and corruption, a bureaucracy that
had given currency to the term *mandarin* meaning devious,
inefficient, and corrupt.

At the same time, there was urgent need of a whole new
bureaucracy in Beijing, to run the new socialist system. The
new school system was planned in detail in the Ministry of
Education, to set the rules for schools everywhere. When
students graduated from high school or from university, they
were assigned to jobs where their skills were needed. (Remember
Li Susu? "I was needed in the factory.")

One ministry was in charge of factories everywhere, to be
sure they all ran on socialist principles, and that each factory
was doing its part as one element of the whole economic plan.
Experienced managers were few, so they were brought to Beijing
to be in charge of the nationwide system in which they were
experts. Under this system, a factory making generators, for
example, would be told by the ministry in Beijing what kind of
generators to make, and how many. The raw materials would
be ordered and sent to the factory by the ministry. The working
conditions, etc., were decided by the ministry. The ministry
took the finished products and distributed them where they
were needed.

As the start-up mechanism for a system of socialist schools,
factories, and so on, it made sense. But as you will be suspecting,
it developed into a huge, ungainly bureaucracy, in which the
danger was ever-present that the deciders in Beijing would be
out of touch with the problems at the grassroots. Theoretically,
central control should have loosened to overall supervision,
rather than running everything everywhere—but that would
involve the bureaucracy giving up its power, and as I've often
said, to ask people to give up power is to ask more of them than
most people can give. The system became a heavy bureaucratic

blanket on the ability of specific local schools, factories, etc., to solve their problems and do their work.

The third factor from the past which hampered socialism was militarism. For twenty years before Liberation the revolutionaries had been engaged in bitter war against the Chinese Nationalists and against the Japanese invaders. During most of that time, they were the underdogs, opposed by overwhelmingly larger and better-equipped armies. Part of their strategy was to wait for times when they had an advantage, then strike hard, without mercy. One of their slogans was "Beat the dog in the water", that is, if you have the enemy at a disadvantage, smash him. That attitude of being engaged in a life-and-death battle against dangerous enemies was carried over into peacetime. It was easy to decide that anyone who disagreed with official opinion was an enemy. Dissenters were enemies. Enemies had no rights.

Add to the internal traditions of obedience, bureaucracy, and militaristic attitudes, the fact of external pressures. The United States had, throughout the long civil wars, backed Chiang Kaishek and his Nationalists against the Communists, giving Chiang millions of dollars, armaments, military advisors—even transporting Nationalist army units in US planes, and after Chiang was forced to retreat to Taiwan, sending the US Seventh Fleet into Chinese waters to keep the Communist armies from following Chiang and finishing the war. After the Communists set up their socialist government, the United States organized a boycott of China like the boycott they have for decades enforced against Cuba. For many years, the Chinese took it for granted that the US was going to invade them, so they wasted millions of dollars and untold energy and resources preparing for invasion (moving factories away from the coast, digging air-raid shelters, building up the army, scrambling frantically to develop the atom bomb).

More recently, socialism in China has been challenged by materialism, calling people away from a sense of community and into self-centred goals. I'll hold that story for my chapter on Deng Xiaoping.

Can you see why I started by saying that socialism in China is not so much a state as a struggle? Or why I had to get over my naive idea that there's some abstract thing called "socialism", with the implication that socialism will be the same in all countries calling themselves socialist? Chinese socialism has always been, and still is, a struggle. Let me put off to the end of the book my take on how the struggle is going, and only say here that it is far from over.

Now, enough for this overview—let me get to some of the specific things I saw and lived with, during my years in China. First, some examples of how quickly and strikingly the country changed while I was there, followed by some of my own experiences.

3
Changes: Two Dances

The two key words about China are certainly *struggle* and *change*. During my years of going back and forth between Canada and China, every time I returned to China, even if I'd been away only a month or two, all I had to do was look at the people and the traffic in the streets to notice the changes—in clothes and in vehicles especially. Bicycles and pedestrians and men pulling heavy loads on two-wheeled carts, and horse-drawn carts with huge loads, giving way to trucks, autos and taxis. "Mao jackets" and home-made sweaters giving way to an increasing variety of factory-made clothes in increasingly varied colourful styles. Even the way women wore their hair changed from year to year, from one long braid or two short ones, to page-boy cuts, to many varieties of perms.

The changes went a lot deeper than these outward signs, of course. You remember the dance of the high school girls in Zhengzhou, based on the ubiquitous elastic skipping game? Ten years later, I saw another group of high school girls perform a dance based on the same game, this time in Tianjin. It was a charming dance, and the audience was tickled at the girls' ingenuity and grace. But what struck me was that its message was only the (admittedly important) one that the things of daily life can be the material of art. It certainly did not bring people to their feet.

There was an ideological shift during those ten years, which those two dances correspond to. But perhaps it would be fairer to show that contrast in two full programs of dances I saw, both put on by professional dance companies, one in 1976, the other in 1985. Both of them were impressive, entertaining, memorable experiences. But when I put them side by side in my mind, it's almost as if they had been designed to show how China had changed in those brief years.

The first was a performance of the Xi'an Municipal Dance Troupe. The very existence of such a troupe is significant. Everywhere I went in China then, I was struck by the fact that although China was a poor country the socialist government had found the means of supporting municipal, provincial, and national opera companies, acrobatic troupes, children's theatres, puppet theatres, and dance troupes. (I found that true of Cuba, too, by the way, when I went there in 1987.)

That evening a small group of us went to the municipal auditorium, making our way among crowds of workers. I noticed, here and elsewhere, that in China at that time audiences for theatre, opera, and dance were mostly working people, who did not dress up for the occasion.

The dances we saw that night were an odd mixture: some beautifully done, some amateurish; some broad comedy, some very serious. What they all had in common was that one way or another they all celebrated socialism. The unspoken theme was a triumphant cry: "We are building a good new socialist world!" To show you what I mean by that, here's the whole program:

The opening act was a scene from the modern ballet "Red Detachment of Women". This ballet is a blockbuster, a strong, stylized dance of revolution, the story of oppressed women serfs who escape and join a women's combat regiment of the People's Liberation Army. In the 1960s and 1970s it was performed too often, and young people of the 1980s didn't want to see "that old stuff", but I'm glad to see that in the 1990s it's being brought back.

"Going to the Fields" was a farce, with a great deal of slapstick humour, showing three Korean-minority men with shoulder-poles taking lunch to the workers in the fields.

"The Coming of Electricity" opens on a scene in Yunnan Province, among the Yi people. We are high up a mountainside. A small cottage is at one side of the stage. An elaborate backdrop gives us a view of a broad valley stretching away to another mountain. An excited young Yi couple, in traditional dress, dance the situation for us: at six o'clock the electricity from the new power dam will be turned on and the light bulb outside their cottage will light up. They hardly know whether to believe it or not. All of a sudden, sure enough, their light goes on—but then we see blocks of lights going on all across the valley and up the side of the other mountain. A very dramatic effect: I surprised myself by being quite moved by the coming of electric power to the Yi's valley.

In "Under the Apple Tree", a young woman in a remote mountain village is tending her family's one apple tree when a soldier appears. She is terrified, and runs to hide; soldiers in the past have always brought disaster. But this soldier is different. This is the People's Liberation Army, the friend of the people. He would never harm her or steal her apples. All he wants is to fill a bunch of canteens at her well. He wins her confidence in a beautiful dance, and finally she comes out and helps him fill the canteens, and stands with her arms around her precious tree watching him go off to his company. (I have to interject here that unlike other armies the PLA really was regarded as the people's friends—right up to the 1989 "incident" in Tiananmen.)

"I Love My Job" was a funny little solo dance-mime, with deliberately grotesque movements, about an overworked waitress in a restaurant who takes comfort in the fact that her work is needed. Serving the people!

"Golden Seeds" was a schmaltzy melodrama, with a slinky villain who hides his face in his cloak and scowls at the audience when they hiss him. The boy and girl high school students guard the grain and foil the evil ex-landlord's attempt to poison it.

"Women Militia of the Grasslands" was a lovely dance, very simple and unlike the others, expressing its meaning solely through dance, with no scenery and no story, and no props except short rifles over the shoulders of the dancers. The Mongolian Women's Militia is seen first at drills, riding their imaginary horses swiftly through complex maneuvers, then on guard in the grasslands, conveying a sense of space with sweeping movements and incredible graceful leaps.

Nine years later, the national Oriental Song and Dance troupe, called the leading dance troupe of China, came to Tianjin, and of course I went to see them

The titles of their dances were "Old China", "Pakistan", "India", "Kites", "Japan", "Brazil". It was obvious immediately that the underlying message had completely changed.

"Old China" was the dance of the emperor's chief concubine and her maids, in quite lovely costumes. Their bound feet were represented by tiny clogs, which were out of sight most of the time behind long gowns. They glided as they walked. Beautiful—but with no suggestion that life in old imperial China might have been less than perfect, or that bound feet were anything but attractive.

"India" acted out the dream of a flute-player in a Hindu temple. A row of dancers representing the temple statues, some with raised arms or legs, held their positions amazingly while the flute-player played and supplicants came to pray and offer flowers to the statues. Then the supplicants left, the flute-player went to sleep, and the statues slowly came to life and danced. A wonderful performance, beautifully choreographed.

"Japan" was not so successful. It was a duet of two young Japanese women with colourful parasols—not expertly done. Some Japanese men sitting behind me were rude enough to laugh at it.

"Pakistan" was a water dance. A line of Pakistani women dance in unison, with water jugs balanced on their heads. They are joined by a line of men, and as they go through faster and faster motions we have to wonder: Are the jugs somehow fastened to their heads? Can there really be water in the jugs? At the end of the dance, the men lift the jugs from the women's heads and pour water from them to show us.

"Brazil" was a dance that would have been unthinkable in 1976. They would all have been in jail. A large group of women doing a samba. They wore very scanty Brazilian costumes, just scant bras and frilly little panties that my sons might have called "butt twitchers". They did the samba steps correctly, and they shook their fannies at us—but they did not look in the least Brazilian. Han Chinese women do not live in their bodies the way Brazilian women do. They looked, indeed, like ten-year-olds trying to be sexy. But they were obviously having great fun, and the audience loved it.

The Latin American finale involved colourful swirling skirts, revealing lace pantaloons. The men were in gaucho costume and had Charlie Chaplin mustaches. Very colourful and active; I enjoyed it very much, as indeed I did the whole program. But it certainly was different from the dances of 1976.

Here, there was no socialist message at all. Of course, there was a message, since all art expresses meaning. The theme was "Aren't we living in a big, varied, exciting world!" It was a dance equivalent of China's economic opening to the world.

That theme was probably quite deliberate, but there were other messages which I think were not deliberately put there. One was the assumption that there's no longer anything to say about socialism, which can disappear without comment. Another has to do with the status of women. In the 1976 performance, the women portrayed were varied. The farm girl in "Under the Apple Tree" was shy and winsome. The women soldiers of "Red Detachment of Women" were battle-hardened fighters. The waitress of "I Love My Work" was small and funny. All of them, however, had a kind of strength. Their dancing included many strong, straight-arm, confident gestures.

In the 1985 performance there were no straight-arm gestures by women. Their gestures were all curved and soft. Don't misunderstand me: I have nothing against gracefulness. But in 1976 there could be graceful gestures too, but there could also be strong, confident ones. In 1985, *all* the women's gestures were soft and graceful.

In 1976 there were strong women characters, but in 1985 the women were all subservient and flirtatious. The emperor's concubine and her maids were gentle and nice; I'm sure the emperor had much pleasure in them. The dance called "Kites" was an imaginative piece of choreography in which the women were all kites, their imaginary strings controlled by men. All this is perhaps more important than it may at first seem. At the same time that the dances celebrated China's opening to the world, they also reflected the concurrent fact that the position of women was slipping in China. I saw that in my classes, where the women were then much more likely to let the men answer questions than in my earlier classes, and were obviously more interested in cosmetics and looking attractive.

By the way, here are some contrasts between 1976 and today: In 1976, you remember, people did not dress up to see a stage performance. Now, they do. And they arrive by taxi, not by the old crowded buses. And whereas the workers in 1976 paid a few *fen* (the Chinese penny) to get in, the theatre-goers of today pay several *yuan* (the Chinese dollar).

Times have changed even since 1985, of course. The present scene in Chinese dance is as complex as everything else these days. Now, dance companies from Europe, Africa, the Americas, and Asia give performances in China's cities. China's minorities bring their own dances to Beijing. Researchers and choreographers are reviving ancient Chinese dance styles. So dance troupes in China these days have a vast variety of forms and styles (and implied messages) to witness, to be excited by, to draw on or reject.

At the same time, television, with its shallow song and dance routines imitating American commercial programs, draws audiences away from live companies. Also, these days governments at all levels are shifting their attention to what helps business make profits, so they reduce or eliminate their support for the arts. As the then Minister of Culture told a *New York Times* reporter, China has millionaires now—let them support the arts.

Today, arts organizations must make profits. We see the results of that most starkly in the movies, where studios are pouring out junk full of violence and superstition, which seems to be good box-office. A leading woman director told reporters that for every serious movie she makes (several of which have won prizes) she must also make three of these money-making films to keep the studio solvent.

Such pressures will be hard on dance troupes. But if we are lucky, dance in China will survive and will draw strength from the proliferation of forms and styles. If we are *very* lucky, Chinese dance will then find its own base, and come to be an expression of what it really means these days to be Chinese. It'll be exciting to watch what develops.

4

Changes: One Factory Twice

When I've had the chance, I've gone to look at factories in China. Partly, this is because I know something about factories from the inside, having worked my way through university and graduate school by working in them. I know what to look for, and what questions to ask.

Also, I think factories pose an interesting problem for socialism. The whole idea of what a factory is and what it should look like was developed during the Industrial Revolution by the owners and managers for their own benefit, without any thought of the well-being of the workers. But a socialist regime is supposed to benefit all the people. So a big question for socialists is, what's the difference between a capitalist factory and a socialist factory?

This is basically, of course, the question of the relationship between the worker and the boss. In the factories I worked in, in the United States during the 1930s, that relationship could be described simply: it was warfare. The boss tried to get as much work for as little money as he could; the workers tried to get as much money for as little work as they could. The whole thing struck me as not only dismal but enormously inefficient. In any of the factories I worked in, the workers could have told the boss how to do the work more efficiently, but there was no incentive for them to do that and they probably would not have been listened to anyway. In none of the factories I worked in was there incentive for the workers to do their best work, or to think about the quality or the usefulness to society of what they were producing. When I was a precision grinder I never knew what those pieces of metal I worked on were for. (Remember my surprise, in the East is Red Tractor Factory, to find that the young woman at the precision grinder knew exactly what she was working on, and how it fit into the tractor?) I was not much more than a piece of the machinery. It was excruciatingly boring.

You can see why I was curious to find out what socialist factories were like.

Some of the things I saw were impressive. In the standard model of a Chinese factory at that time, the workers didn't have to worry about getting fired—their jobs were for life. The factory provided housing for the workers, and schools for their children, and if it was a fairly large factory it also had a workers' "cultural palace", where there would be a library, a theatre for movies or performances, and rooms for playing cards or for group meetings. The factory paid the medical expenses of workers and their families, and paid pensions to retired workers (who also continued to live in the factory's housing).

In many instances, this was a humane and efficient way to run a factory. But there were unsolved problems. One of the biggest was that the workers had no say in what would be produced, or how it would be produced—that was decided by a bureau in Beijing. (Even the managers of the factory could not make local decisions, but had to take their orders from Beijing.) So the worker was as alienated from his or her work as the Western worker. I saw this in other units besides factories— notably in department stores, where there were more workers than needed, and they had no say about how the work might be carried out. One saleswoman talked to me at length about this—they could not say that there was big demand for a product so it should be kept in stock and prominently displayed. Nothing like that. So they were as bored I had been in the factories where

I worked—and bored sales clerks do not give good service. In short, the system had been only partially socialized.

Another problem was that as soon as China began opening up to the West and foreign companies were permitted to open factories, those factories, which had no burden of housing, medicare, or pensions, could undercut the socialist factories in the marketplace.

An even larger problem was that many factories were set up without any thought of socialism at all, factories in which the workers were exploited as badly as anywhere in the West — worse, in fact, because there were none of the Western laws about worker safety, etc. In a weaving mill in Huerhot, Inner Mongolia, I found people working in such appalling noise and such a cloud of lint, that I scolded the manager, much to his annoyance. He told me workers are not interested in such things as ventilation or noise reduction. He himself was interested only in production, and in persuading the government to let him export "his" products.

Another depressing place was the famous Hero Fountainpen Factory in Shanghai. There, I saw a young woman putting the nibs on fountainpens with a crimping machine which she worked by a foot pedal. She took a pen out of one box, set a nib on it, pushed it into a slot, stepped on the pedal, and put it in another box. She worked in a dark, stuffy, noisy area facing a plain brick wall, with nobody else close enough to talk to. In answer to my questions, the director told me that she worked only on that one machine, eight hours a day, six days a week, fifty-one weeks a year. She had been doing it for two years, since graduating from high school. When I asked how long she might be doing it, the director shrugged impatiently. "Perhaps twenty years," he said. He was annoyed that I would ask such questions when he wanted to talk about sales and new models.

I've seen textile mills with no safety devices, where unguarded moving belts come up out of holes in the walkways. I've seen so-called factories in the countryside which were nothing but noisy, dark, dirty sheds with no amenities, not even toilets, where teenage girls sat at horribly screeching machines stamping out fittings for suitcases from sheets of metal. I have wished for their sake that they were back on the old commune farms where at least they had sun and air and a variety of tasks and companionship. I've been in carpet factories where the women workers were afraid to talk to me if the boss was with me, even to answer innocuous questions such as how long they'd been working there. They looked at him in panic for some clue as to how to answer. Two of the bosses in such carpet factories told me that women have "nimble fingers", so they weave the carpets, but men are good at reasoning and planning and meeting people, so they are the bosses.

On the other hand, you remember, I've seen exemplary factories. (Who ever said China was simple?) Remember the Households Products Factory in Tianjin, and the East is Red Tractor Factory in Luoyang? I remember with pleasure the docks in Shanghai, where I saw them unloading wheat from Saskatchewan. There, I was greeted by a Workers Committee, not a manager; there the workers had a great sense of being in control, and a strong memory of the fact that it was Shanghai dock workers who began the uprisings that eventuated in the socialist revolution.

In November 1979, I was returning by train to Tianjin from a weekend in Beijing, traveling with two young Canadian women, foreign students at Nankai University. At that time I could not yet speak Chinese fluently, but they could, so we were able to get into conversations with two factory workers,

Comrades Song and Che, big, hearty men in a jovial mood, coming back from a conference in Beijing.

Obviously they'd had a good time—among other things, they were bringing presents home to their kids, and they whipped out jointed wooden snakes and tried to frighten the young women with them.

Like most of the men on the train, they were chain-smoking, inserting the butt of one cigarette into the end of the next one so as to get the whole thing. They were drinking tea from jars they had brought along, which the attendants replenished with hot water.

Before the train reached the Tianjin station, Che pointed to their factory as we passed it, and asked us to come and visit it, and wrote down the name and address. Of course, we were eager to do that, so when I got back to the university I asked the Foreign Affairs Office to arrange a visit. The official looked at the address and frowned. "Nobody has ever asked to go there before!" I told her that was exactly why we wanted to see it; we wanted to get beyond the model factories which are shown to tourists.

On the appointed day, the university provided a car and driver, and we went. We were reassured by the fact that the driver lost the way and had to ask directions. Finally we stopped at a compound where a sign arching over the gateway proclaimed the Tianjin Generator Factory (*Tianjin Dongliji Chang.*) Within the gates an elaborate welcome was waiting for us: on a blackboard were English words in large letters surrounded by pink flowers: "Warmly Welcome Canadian Friends!" Standing beside the sign was the management committee, with Song and Che. They all clapped as we got out of the car, and we clapped back, Chinese style.

They took us to a meeting room where we sat and were given tea, cigarettes and cookies while the leaders told us about the factory and its history. Then they gave us a tour of the plant, followed by more tea and an opportunity to ask questions, taking the whole morning and most of the afternoon to be with us. I wasn't at all sure why they would do all that for strangers, though perhaps I understood before we left.

Coming out of the meeting room to tour the factory, we passed a large bulletin board with photographs of various groups, and red ribbons next to each photo. We asked what the groups had done. "This group has the top production record. This group has the best safety record. This group is recently-married couples who have pledged to have only one child."

In 1979, you see, the population policy had not yet been made law. In the best Chinese style it was first a three-year educational campaign, with voluntary restraint. These volunteers were honoured here along with other high achievers.

We toured all the workshops of the factory, in big buildings with overhead cranes. We were escorted down wide aisles between the rows of machines: metal-working lathes, precision grinders, compound drilling machines, planers. I noticed that many of the workers on these machines, and the operators of the overhead cranes, were women, and I stopped to watch one of them work a precision grinder. She gave me a friendly smile and explained what she was working on, and I told her that in my youth I had worked on a similar machine, and showed her that the tip of one of my fingers is missing, and urged her to be careful.

We were struck by the order and cleanliness of the workshops: the floors were all clean; there was no litter anywhere. When I mentioned that, Che and Song were quite tickled—it turned out this was their responsibility; they had been pulled off machines six months ago and put in charge of bringing cleanliness to the factory after the chaos of the Cultural Revolution.

After the tour, we left the Management Committee and visited the home of Song's family: just one small room, the whole living space for the parents and two small children—their own segment of a block-long one-storey building which was one of many such buildings, in rows exactly alike. The lane between two rows was so narrow I could stretch my arms and touch the buildings on both sides.

Then on to Che's three-room home in the same kind of row housing, and there we had a splendid lunch. We discovered that not only Che's wife and oldest daughter, but some of the neighbours and even the driver of our car had been busy preparing the meal. Che's wife and daughter didn't eat with us; they were too busy cooking each course while we were eating the previous one; but they did stop now and then to talk to us. They both worked in the factory, they said. The second daughter was still in high school, and the little kids, who had disappeared after being introduced to us, were in primary school.

It was quite a lunch: Two kinds of wine, rice, liver with coriander leaves, scrambled eggs with some kind of chopped greens, a dish of spicy beef, a vegetable dish with black mushrooms and another with tiny salt shrimp, a soup, and several side dishes, including shrimp-chips and "ancient" eggs. All the time we were eating, small astonished faces rose and fell at the window close beside us as people outside lifted their little kids to see the foreigners.

After lunch we had a lengthy meeting with the Management Committee. There were five of them, headed by a grizzled man named Zhou. One of them, a woman, was the head of the design department. All these managers had started as workers in the factory and worked their way up, and they were very familiar with the problems at all levels, and with the plant's history.

The factory had been set up by the Japanese in 1939, during the Japanese occupation of Tianjin, and run by conscript labour. At that time it produced only simple engines. Working conditions were terrible; there were frequent attempts at sabotage by the workers, who were brutally punished. Production was low, the quality of the engines poor. In 1941, production was changed to making guns for the Japanese occupation army.

In 1945, after the Japanese surrender, the factory was taken over by Chiang Kaishek's Guomindang. This was a period of great confusion. The new bosses were hated by the workers, who believed the Guomindang had left them at the mercy of the Japanese, spending all their energy fighting the Communists instead of the invaders. The Guomindang, for its part, was on edge with apprehension about communism and saw any labour unrest as collaboration with the Red Armies. There was corruption and misuse of funds by managers, and sabotage and strikes by the workers. Many times management said they could not meet the payroll for the 400 workers.

In 1949, after the triumph of the Red Armies and the setting up of socialist China, the factory began to recover. The State invested funds for rebuilding and expansion, and the plant was gradually built up to its present 4,800 workers. In 1951, it started producing the diesel-powered generators on wheels which were still its product.

During the Cultural Revolution, they told us, things became chaotic again. "Things were in a mess!" Production, as the main goal, was replaced by class struggle, and anyone who worried about production was suspect. Looking back on it, they told us that the politics that had taken up most of their time was "empty"; it consisted of many posters, the shouting of slogans, mass meetings ending with raised fist salutes and shouting of quotations, but no study, no discussion, no understanding of the issues, only mass demonstrations and rigid conformity.

At that time management of the factory had been by a Revolutionary Committee, consisting (as was then the custom) of young, middle-aged, and old workers. In 1976, at the East is Red Tractor Factory, the Revolutionary Committee had been doing a splendid job, but here, they said, the committee was ignorant both of technology and of how to run an enterprise. The theory was that anybody could run a factory if his political ideas were correct. The result was bumbling, factionalism, and endless arguments and discussions, while very little work got done.

Zhou told us his understanding of the relationship between ideology and production: "The business of a factory is production. In a socialist factory, there must be common-sense attitudes. `Being a worker in a socialist state, how can I make my best contribution to production, to help build socialism?' Without socialist consciousness a worker cannot do his part for production."

His statement fascinates me. It's a basic question, isn't it? What *does* motivate a person—any person—to do his best work? My experience as a factory worker in the West had taught me very clearly that where workers are given minimal pay, bad working conditions, and no respect, they are never motivated to do even moderately good work, let alone their best.

In this factory, the workers seemed busy, but at the same time relaxed and unafraid. (And it's only common sense that when people work at dangerous and expensive machines they should not be driven frantic if you want steady, efficient production.)

It was during discussions with the managers that I suddenly thought I realized why they were spending so much time with us, feeding us so well, and discussing things at such length. My enlightenment came during a description of their problems.

The system they were working under, with absolute control from Beijing, had been necessary for the re-establishment of the factory after the Japanese and Guomindang periods, they thought. The State allocated funds for running expenses, including worker salaries. It told them what products to make, and how many. It assigned new workers to the factory, who could not be rejected by the managers and were there for life. It supplied the raw materials and took all the products. It took all the income and paid all the expenses.

In theory all this was necessary to be sure the factory fitted into the planned economy, using only its share of raw materials, supplying just the right kind and number of products, providing jobs for the right number of people. It's true, too, that when socialist China had to set up a whole new system in a hurry, knowledgeable managers were in short supply, so were brought to Beijing where each could be in charge of large numbers of factories.

But this was thirty years later. One of the problems of revolutions, as I've said before, is that although strict central planning and a large bureaucracy may be necessary to get things started, socialist theory says that such a power structure must give way to more democratic decision making and "grassroots" socialism. But people in power have a devil of a time agreeing that the time is right for giving up power—that's the big problem. So here, thirty years after the start-up, all the affairs of this factory (and of thousands of others, remember) were at the mercy of an enormous, cumbersome, sleepy bureaucracy up in Beijing which made decisions in ignorance of local needs. These managers were desperately frustrated by not being able to make any decisions for their factory.

Specifically, they had two immediate problems. Wu, the head of the design department, told us about one of them. She said they had been trying for years to get permission to change the design of the generators: they had designed one that would be both much lighter and more powerful, use less steel, take less energy to produce, and be cheaper. But their proposals to switch to the new design were simply ignored. No permission ever came, and when they objected they were told, over the years, that the matter was "still being considered".

Second, they were frustrated by the quota set for them. Not that it was hard to meet—just the contrary. Here it was early November, they said, and they had almost met their quota for the year. Soon they would have to stop working for nearly two months because they couldn't get materials to make more generators and couldn't get permission to use that time making something else.

They were obviously distressed. How could a poor country like China afford to have them drawing pay and overhead for almost two months of the year while doing nothing?

Zhou, especially, was eloquent and emotional, and it was while he was speaking that I had a flash of insight. These people had no idea who we were or why we were there. They were taking the long chance that this old man might be somebody important, somebody who could help them, could put in a word for them in the right place in Beijing.

My reaction was deep embarrassment. I felt like a fraud. But, of course, in Chinese style they never came right out and asked me to help them, so in Chinese style I didn't have to reveal my powerlessness, and we parted as friends.

Six years later, in June 1985, I went to see the Tianjin Generator Factory again. At that time the government was trying out a new policy for State-owned enterprises. (Part of a long campaign to do something about the inefficiency of those enterprises and the huge amounts of money the government was paying to cover their losses.)

The stated goals of the new policy were to overcome low productivity, slack management, and the drain on State resources, and to modernize Chinese technology. The two most drastic changes concerned management. Each factory was to be responsible for its own debts and liabilities, and was to buy its raw materials on the open market. It was also entitled to keep its own profits after taxes, and the managers of the factory were free to make most of their own decisions. After fulfilling the state quota, they could use their time and resources to buy raw materials, make whatever goods they thought would sell, and sell them in the open market. When I heard all this, I thought my old friends in the management committee would be happy.

But then I heard the rest: each such factory was to be run by one manager, with broad powers to make decisions. He could hire only those workers he chose. He could fire workers for cause. He could give or withhold bonuses.

Theoretically, the manager was to be controlled by a Workers Committee, an elected body which in many factories must approve the manager's appointment. But the manager's great powers make it very unlikely that workers would oppose him. Actually, I'm told, Workers Committees tend to be rubber stamps.

(I remember an exhibit of newspaper cartoons that was held in one of Tianjin's Workers Palaces, about this time. One cartoon showed a worker standing in the huge hand of his boss, the fingers of which were closing in on him. The fingers were labeled "Job assignment", "bonus", "promotion", "housing assignment", "marriage permit". The caption said, "Why workers do not criticize their leaders".)

I decided I must go and see the reformed generator factory for myself.

The changes were obvious from the start. Waiting for me, without any "Welcome Canadian Friend" sign and without any clapping, were just two people: my old friend Che, and the new director. The director was a man of about forty-five, with a hatchet face and a brusque manner. Clearly he was under no illusions that I could be of any help to him.

That was fair enough.

But there was another change which I find more significant the more I think about it. My friend Che, though he greeted me with a smile and a handshake, was a different person. He smiled only that once. He was obviously nervous. He was at the manager's side throughout my visit, and kept his eyes on him nervously. When the manager addressed a question to him, which he did without looking at him, Che gave a little start and blurted out a brief answer. There was no opportunity for me to talk to Che alone, but I think I know what was the matter.

We walked along the main street of the plant. The director pointed out new buildings, but we didn't go into any of them. "Here", he said, "is the biggest change. In this building is the new assembly line, which we have completely re-designed. The generators being turned out here today are only half the weight but have twice the power of the old model, and the assembly line is state-of-the-art."

Then he pointed to a new building, a handsome brick one, with sunny-looking windows, which was the new clinic, with a staff of nurses and a doctor always on call.

We passed three of the old workshops, which he told me had been modernized.

We went to the meeting room for the obligatory cup of tea, and the director answered my questions. I noticed that whereas the former managers had relaxed in deep armchairs, he sat bolt upright on a straight-backed chair.

In answer to my questions, he told me that the factory's output had almost doubled, and its income had more than doubled. As for the workers, they now got not only higher wages, but bonuses.

It's true that the bonus could be withheld by him, if either the individual or the workshop did not meet production quotas. And certainly "the iron rice-bowl has been broken," meaning the workers no longer have job security, and they don't "eat out of one big pot," or all get equal wages.

"What about women workers?" I asked. The director seemed to expand while he answered this; it was obviously of interest to him. "You must understand," he said, "that in the past we had to take any workers the State sent us, and therefore one-third of our workers are women. Now we have the right to choose, so we don't hire women, and we are gradually moving the women we do have, out of the workshops."

"But why is that?" I asked. He looked at me in surprise, as if I didn't understand the obvious. "This", he said, "is a machine factory."

I pushed the point. I always do, in China, because the tension between old macho ideas and new socialist ideas about women is always there. Would it not be better, I suggested, to say simply that each individual should do the work that he or she is good at?

He jumped at that idea. "Exactly!" he said. "That's exactly my point. I agree with you about this. And what women are good at is running the lunchroom and the nursery and keeping the books. Men are better at running machines and being administrators."

The director went on, relaxing and expanding as he talked. He was really excited about the new generator—Number 6310 as he kept referring to it fondly. "It's lighter, it has twice the horsepower, it's sturdier and needs less maintenance. It's in great demand. And we subject it to rigid testing. We're always improving it. One of the largest buildings I showed you is our research and development laboratory. We have adopted the motto, 'Modernize and Improve.' You may have noticed it over the doors of the workshops. And we have laid out a three-step policy: First: overhaul the plant. You saw the new assembly line [Not quite true, unfortunately.] You saw the new buildings. We've also built a more efficient steam-generator, generating power for the plant.

"Second: Develop the product. This I have already told you about.

"Third: Train the workers and the supervisors. Our assistant directors are now younger, between the ages of 38 and 49. All five of them are university graduates. One is now abroad studying Western technology.

"Our intermediate cadres we send to night school at the universities or to the factory's own technical school. As for the workers themselves, the old ones are gradually being brought up to the equivalent of a high school education, and any new ones we hire must be high school graduates. They must also pass an entrance examination, and they are on probation for the first five years. We assign workers to our Workers College and give them time off with full pay to attend classes. All our supervisors now pay strict attention to the quality of work of our workers.

"Under the new bonus system we lay out the work expected from each worker and each workshop in a yearly contract. Those who fulfil the contract get the bonus. We are determined to keep this system honest and clear of favouritism.

"We try hard to give our workers a new spirit, to make them be proud of mastering new techniques and be aware of the factory's contribution to modern China."

Could I see the new assembly line? Could I talk to some of the workers? Could I visit workers' housing? He looked at his watch. No, he was very sorry. There would be no time for any of those things. He stood up, to indicate that the visit was at an end, and walked out with me to my waiting car, where he shook hands with a firm grip. For my part, I thanked him sincerely for giving me such a clear understanding of the changes.

That 1979 factory had been, I think, one of the best possible under the old system. As far as the restraints it was under would permit, it was efficient. (It completed its annual quota two months early, remember.) The management committee would have changed it for the better if they had the authority; they were certainly not slacking off.

It was a clean and orderly workplace, where people had time to be friendly, where workers could invite me to the factory and to their homes, where a young worker busy on a machine gave me a smile without any idea who I was, and took a couple of minutes to explain what she was doing. It was a pleasant working atmosphere for the workers.

The 1985 factory was surely one of the best under the new system. Now that the manager did not have to send all the profits to Beijing, he was using them for upgrading the plant, re-designing the assembly line, the product, the workshops, building a research lab and a clinic, training the workers at all levels.

I had to admire these changes. Society had more and better generators; the factory had better physical plant; the workers had more money and better training. The new director, whose drive and imagination and managerial skills had accomplished this, was a model of what the new economic policy expected.

But everything has its price. All this was accomplished at what cost? The most obvious answer was that although the factory was more efficient it was no longer such a pleasant place for people to work. True, the workers had higher wages now—but now they had always the fear of being fired, and if unemployed they would lose their medical coverage and their pensions, which at that time came entirely from one's work unit.

And now they were at the discretion of one man, who had a great deal of power. His own prejudices inevitably influenced his policies. That young woman I saw doing a good job on the precision grinder—was she now sweeping floors, or washing dishes in the cafeteria, or out of work altogether? And where was designer Wu? A great many problems were reflected in the nervous face which Che kept turned towards the boss.

The big question in my mind is why was it thought necessary, in order to make the good changes I saw, to put everything under the control of one all-powerful manager? The management committee of 1976 had wanted to make many of the same changes. Was the new director's proud boast, his generator Number 6310—was that by any chance the one the old committee couldn't get permission to make?

The Chinese, like other people, have a tendency to throw the baby out with the bathwater.

But it's important to remember that in terms of the new policy's objective, the 1985 director was without any question one of the best. If all the new managers had been like him, perhaps the question of what to do about the State-owned enterprises would not still be on the table. We heard about many others who were not at all in his class. Many stories reached the newspapers about the managers of other factories. In one case, the new manager, having been approved by vote of the workers, immediately fired all the other candidates and the workers who had supported them. Other news stories reported rampant nepotism, corruption, even reigns of terror, and managers using company funds for big banquets, or expensive vacation trips, or to build themselves expensive houses.

Certainly the history of China does not inspire confidence that unsupervised power will be used humanely.

It's significant that within a couple of years the new economic policy was quietly forgotten, and "experts" still continue to give their varied opinions about what should be done with the State-owned enterprises.

This book comes to you as a free gift from me. It puts you under no obligations whatsoever.

However, if after looking the book over you agree that it is worthy of having a lot of readers, please consider the fact that the publisher is not one of the giants which have large budgets for advertising, etc. (In fact, the big publishers, I'm told, now spend a lot more money on various forms of advertising than they do on producing the book.)   If this book is to get readers, that will happen only because people who see the book take steps to help. So if you should feel the urge to help spread the word, please consider one or more of the following:

1. Talk it up. Mention the book frequently, to a lot of people.

2. Encourage people to buy copies of the book, and tell them where and how they can do that. (Any bookseller can order it, or anyone can order a copy from the publisher by phoning 1-800-718-7201.)

3. Show your copy to local bookstore managers and urge them to order at least a few copies and display them prominently.

4. Ask your local public library and your school or university library to buy copies., and ask your local newspaper or magazine to review the book

5 Anything else? Use your imagination, okay?

All this, please remember, is dependent on your judgment that the book should be supported. You are under no obligation to do any of these things.

5
Places: Nankai

On my study tour of China in 1976, I told everybody, "I can't take in your Chinese world in just a few weeks. I've got to come back." "Well," they said, "we need teachers." So back in Canada I pestered the Chinese Embassy in Ottawa, telling them I wanted to teach in China for a year. That wasn't as easy in the 1970s as it is now: it took me two and a half years. Finally, I got word that I was assigned to Nankai University, in Tianjin, for the 1979-1980 school year.

I was so ignorant that I had to look up Tianjin to find out where and what it was—an industrial city of six million people, the chief port of north China. When I arrived at Nankai, full of zeal and ignorance, I found myself in a university in some ways like the ones I had left behind in Canada but, as often happens in China, it was partly familiar but in many ways a different and fascinating world.

I had never realized how isolated our Western universities are, how restricted to certain age groups, how much of ordinary life they exclude. Nankai, by contrast, was a teeming village, for not only did all the students live there but so did almost all the teachers, administrators, secretaries, janitors and other workers. And so did their families. On campus you could see all ages, from new babies to very old people. There were nursery schools, kindergartens, primary schools, a high school. Besides the classrooms, dormitories, sport grounds I had expected there were groups of apartment buildings, called "North Village", "Southwest Village", and so on, also shopping centres, a bank, barber shops, a post office, general stores, restaurants, bicycle repair places, all within the high walls of the university campus, to say nothing of peddlers with pushcarts and peasants with fresh vegetables spread out on cloths beside the roads.

At Nankai in 1979, loudspeakers pulled everyone out to do exercises together at six a.m. Then for half an hour before breakfast you could see people running, or practicing badminton or *wu shu* martial arts. Students sat on stone benches under the willows beside the lotus pond, hunched over textbooks or loudly practicing their English lessons. Groups of retired people did graceful *tai ji quan* exercises in unison ("Like a slow ballet", a visiting dancer commented.) Grannies pushed babies in prams made of bamboo, which could be adjusted to let the babies lie flat or sit up.

After breakfast, I heard the bird-like voices of little kids drifting to school in groups of two or three, neat and clean, their hair nicely brushed. In winter they wore thick home-made cotton-padded pants and jackets. In spring the boys went into short pants and the girls into simple home-made dresses, the height of the hemline depending on how leggy the girl had grown in the years since the dress was made. They all wore knapsack bookbags and carried plastic canteens with boiled drinking water. The youngest ones had clean handkerchiefs pinned over their hearts. They chattered along with plenty of time to stand and look for fish in the pond or stare with speechless wonder at a foreigner, or squat and show each other things in their schoolbags.

The campus roads became crowded with bicycle traffic as students came from dining halls or "small eat" places and cycled off to class. In front of the classroom buildings students and teachers coasted to a stop and parked their bicycles, and the irregular rows of parked bikes grew until it was hard to pick your way among them to get to the building.

A bit off the main road of the campus was an open space, bordered at one end by an outdoor stage at the rear of the Administration Building, and at the other end by a large movie screen. Here there were sometimes formal gatherings, when the space was filled by hundreds of people on chairs, facing the stage listening to speeches. Here, on Saturday evenings, hundreds of students faced the other direction, sitting on little stools they brought with them, watching outdoor movies. Here, in 1989, great rallies took place, from which hundreds of students and their supporters marched out into the streets of Tianjin to join other hundreds in demonstrations.

The Nankai campus, in short, was a lively place. Some people might prefer the isolation of our Western campuses. There's something to be said for ivory towers. For my part, I can lose myself for hours at a desk in quiet, slightly musty library stacks. But when I come out it's a pleasure to be part of the bustle of life again.

When I first observed the Nankai campus I had no idea how much of what I was seeing was loaded with history, and no idea how soon what I was seeing would change or disappear as China moved through the 1980s.

I came to Nankai, in August 1979, through noisy Tianjin streets teeming with people, some on foot, some on bicycles, some straining to pull heavy-loaded two-wheel carts. Then, crossing a malodorous little canal and passing through the main gate, I found myself on the main street of the quiet Nankai campus. To my left and right were five- or six-storey apartment buildings, their balconies cluttered by potted plants, mysterious objects wrapped in plastic cloth, and clothes hung out to dry on horizontal bamboo poles. The ground alongside the road and between the buildings was plain dirt, which (I would soon discover) was mud in wet weather and volatile dust when dry.

There were no flowers, no grass. I soon passed, on my left, an ugly dump with all kinds of rubbish.

What surprised me most was the dozens and dozens of little brick houses about the size of our house-trailers. They were everywhere—alongside the road, all over the athletic fields, in every available spot. Some had been built around trees, which stuck out through the roofs. All of them had stovepipes sticking out, at various angles.

Soon I came to what I was told was the main classroom building, which didn't look at all Chinese. As I found out later, it's a replica of a building at the University of Kiev, and a memento of the time when the USSR was China's "Big Brother". Inside, I also found out, the tower had been sealed off as unsafe. The elevators, people said, would be back in service any day now.

Past the classroom building and other academic buildings, I looked across a canal at the western half of the campus, most of which was a large wheat field. That's where, in June 1980, Aaron and I would (as I've told about) join the entire Foreign Languages Department (students, teachers, administrators, support staff) in harvesting our allotted section of the field.

It was only gradually that I found out how much of what I saw in that first view was what you might call normal, and how much reflected historical changes, or was itself about to become history. Those little brick buildings everywhere, and the damage to the classroom building, were the result of a massive earthquake in the summer of 1976 (shortly after I left China that year.) The epicentre had been at Tangshan, a hundred miles north, where over 250,000 people died and the city was wiped out. In Tianjin there was also massive damage to buildings, though the loss of life, I was told, was remarkably small.

After the quake, the Tianjin city government quickly set up soup kitchens. The army came in with trainloads of bricks and mortar, soldiers taught people how to lay brick, and the people built themselves these little houses everywhere: all over university campuses, in all the city parks, right on the sidewalks in many parts of the city, some of them even jutting out into the streets.

I saw them everywhere, and marveled at how the Chinese are able to cope—I think that's what they're best at, actually: dealing with whatever comes along and getting on with their lives.

I visited several of these "earthquake houses". They had no running water, no electricity, no sewers—everyone used the facilities of the nearest public building. Cooking was done over tiny coal-burning stoves. What struck me was how clean and neat the interiors were, with their brick floors and compact arrangements for cooking, storing things, and sleeping—like our house-trailers. Young women came out of these houses in bright, clean clothes, with white gloves and wide-brimmed white hats, and cycled off to work. Little kids came out all spruced up for school.

People expressed their personalities in the way they built these houses. Some found windows and doors from damaged buildings and worked them into the new homes, including one couple that had somewhere found two large round stained-glass windows.

My favourite was one built at a busy intersection in the centre of town, jutting out from the sidewalk right onto the street under a bright streetlight. In the evening the family brought out a table and set it right in the street, and the father read the paper, the mother knitted, and two little girls bent over their homework, while the traffic (bicycles, of course) flowed around them

These little houses were there for over three years, partly because no one wanted to rebuild until they were sure the earth had really settled down. (I felt two mild tremors that first semester at Nankai.) But in the early 1980s Mayor Li Ruihuan announced that within two years the "earthquake houses" would all be gone, and there would be new apartment buildings for the people to move into—and Mayor Li, unlike a great many politicians and bureaucrats, was a man of his word. A row of hopelessly damaged buildings which I occasionally passed on my way downtown disappeared so quickly that when I bicycled through that street I thought I had lost my way. In an area on the south edge of the city, farm fields were turned into an area of apartment buildings, thoughtfully laid out, with every sixth street a broad through street and the others narrower, with short dead-end streets branching out from them, with trees, and grass and the new buildings, none of them more than three storeys high. I've been in some, and can testify that they are nicely designed.

The handling of this emergency was impressive. There was no moving of masses of the homeless into refugee camps. None of the problems that come from ignorant decisions made at high levels and imposed on the people—only programs to help people help themselves, and then gradually the provision of new buildings.

However, a very Chinese problem arose. When some families were told they had been assigned new apartments, they said, "Fine. Half of us will move there, and half stay here. That way we'll have more space." It was a lesson to me. One of the assumptions I'd had about China was that when the leaders said "Jump!" everybody jumped. But there was no way, apparently, that the government would force these people to move. The university had to appeal to them: Please let us have our playing fields back! The government appealed to patriotism and publicity, and gradually the little houses disappeared, and peasants came from the countryside, carefully cleaned the bricks, and hauled them away on two-wheel horse-drawn carts to be re-used somewhere else.

Another aspect of the campus which gave me a history lesson was the dusty grounds everywhere, also that rubbish dump beside the main road. Nankai, my friends told me, had once been a beautiful campus. But during the Cultural Revolution there had been a massive attack on beautiful things, as being frivolous and distracting people from studying Mao Zedong Thought or working to develop socialism. I have a lot of trouble getting my head around this one, I must admit. The idea that beauty, especially natural beauty, is counter-revolutionary is hard for me to comprehend, especially since Mao himself celebrated his love for flowers in famous poems.

In any case, that dump had once been a famous rock garden, with beds of roses, a wisteria arbor, and flowering trees. Alongside the main campus street, too, there had been flowering trees— plum, peach, crabapple—and shrubs such as forsythia and flowering almond, and many beds of flowers. The little canal that empties into the lotus pond, which in 1979 was choked with refuse and black with pollution, had once been clear and pretty. All of these had been systematically trashed during the Cultural Revolution.

How things change! If you went to Nankai any time after about 1990, you wouldn't find the dump. That is again a pretty little park, with tall picturesque rocks, flowering trees, wonderful displays of roses. It's a fine place to sit and rest awhile, and in the evenings a favourite place for couples (known informally among the students as "Lovers' Park").

The little brook is clear again, and bordered by flowering shrubs. The dusty earth, which in 1979 the wind used to whip up into dust storms so that there were times when you couldn't see six feet in front of you, and many people wore surgical masks, while young women covered their heads completely with sheer silk scarves they could see through—that earth is now covered by grass, on which little kids play. The "earthquake houses" are all gone, replaced by grass and by a great many new trees, the result of tree-planting campaigns.

Some of the changes are not as welcome to me, personally, as all those. The open area in front of the classroom building where we used to do exercises together is now filled by covered sheds for parking bicycles. (No matter: there are no more exercises at 10:20, and no more group exercises at all. In fact, there's nothing outside of classrooms that students and teachers regularly do together.)

The western half of the campus, where we once harvested wheat together, is crowded with new buildings now, including the new Foreign Languages Building and a fine large new library. (Again, no matter: universities don't have wheat fields any more, and academics no longer do physical labour.)

Is it just me? Am I never satisfied? I stand at the main gate of the Nankai campus these days and look along the main street at the trees and grass and flowers, and see the fine new buildings in the distance, and I think it's all very good, and exciting. I admire it. Is it only because I'm stubborn, or (as one of my students says) incurably romantic, that I miss some of the things that are gone, especially those things we did all together? It's a fine university, and I'm always glad to get back to it—but sometimes I wonder if it was necessary, in order to have such progress, to lose the feeling that here we were building a new kind of university in a new kind of world.

Come back to 1979, before I started having such feelings. I arrived in Beijing with my son Tim, who was to study Chinese for a year at the Beijing Language Institute. We were met by Mr. Dong, a very polite, quiet, proper young teacher, assigned to shepherd me to Nankai. But there were problems in getting

Tim into the Language Institute, although he had been notified that a place was being held for him. We went there, were warmly welcomed by administrators, saw his room, met his roommate, bought his books and his meal tickets—but he could not move in because an official letter admitting him had not been received from the National Bureau of Education, across town. We went there, and were assured that the letter had been written and signed and would be forwarded very soon. Please be patient. It was hard for me to be patient. After a few days I asked Dong why we didn't pick up the letter and take it to the Language Institute. He was horrified. That would make several people lose face, he said.

To distract me, he took us to plays, movies, an opera, and to parks. At one point we went to the Friendship Store and bought a bicycle for a mysterious "Miss Margaret", a teacher at Nankai, and put it on a Nankai University mini-bus and watched it roll away to Tianjin while I fretted in Beijing.

Finally, the letter achieved the trip across town, and Tim was installed. He and I parted, each feeling more alone now in a strange country, and Dong and I took the train to Tianjin.

On the way, I asked him where I would be living. He said, "You will live with Miss Margaret." He was in an anguish of embarrassment when I explained the implications of that. It turned out that I would be staying in the Tianjin Number Two Municipal Guest House, where Miss Margaret also lived. (Poor Dong! Miss Margaret and I are still laughing at the embarrassment he hasn't even yet overcome.)

The Guest House was exactly what I did *not* want. It was a fancy expensive hotel, originally the mansion of a French big shot in the days of foreign occupation. My room alone cost the university each month more than the average annual salary of a factory worker. The meals were too rich and elaborate for a daily diet; there was even a pastry chef.

Worst of all, the Guest House was in another part of the city from the university. It had a high wall around it, and dragon-like gatekeepers whose main job, apparently, was keeping out anyone who wanted to see me. I was to phone the university for a car and driver any time I wanted to go anywhere, including getting to class every morning.

When people asked me how I was, I complained that this was not at all what I wanted. But we developed a cross-cultural misunderstanding that it took weeks to sort out. According to Chinese manners, it was polite of me to say that the Guest House was too expensive and ornate. The more I complained about the pastry chef and the chauffeur, the more my hosts thought what a polite person I was; they took it as a way of expressing my satisfaction with these privileges.

Finally I told the driver he was a good young man but I didn't need him, and I bought myself a bicycle and crossed the city every day. My hosts were horrified. It was a crisis. An old man must not think of riding a bicycle in Tianjin traffic! Well, I said, in the first place I'd been riding bicycles for several decades and felt competent. In the second place, I had no option. To call for a driver wasted time, and since there was no place for me on campus, what else was to be done? "*Mei ban fa*," I said, using one of the first Chinese expressions I'd learned. "Nothing can be done about it."

That was how I met Yan Tiezheng, an official in the university's Foreign Affairs Office, who has since become a good friend. She came to see me, bringing an interpreter (since I then knew only a few words of Chinese and she has never learned English). "There is a place you could live on campus, in the Foreign Students Dormitory. But I know you wouldn't like it."

"How do you know that?"

"Because last year there was a foreign teacher who asked to be moved on campus and we put him there, but after a month he asked to go back to the hotel."

I said, "Miss Yan, I'm very glad you let him make his own decisions."

She gave me a shrewd, startled look, then burst out laughing and said, "Come and see," and took me to exactly what I wanted: a spacious room on the first floor of the foreign students building, three steps from an unpretentious but good dining hall, where I could get my lunch and take my bowl and chopsticks and go sit on the front steps and talk to people while I ate. My students' dorms were close by, and they came often to see me. It was just what I wanted—but cultural misunderstanding kept me from it for almost two months.

It was my fault as much as theirs. My frustration grew out of my culture; their providing the best accommodations for a guest grew out of theirs. I learned. And I started a lasting friendship.

It took me much longer to realize that another misunderstanding was based on cultural differences—this one involving the books I had brought with me to give the Foreign Language Department.

In May of 1979, when I was on my second study tour of China, I had taken a few days off to come to Tianjin and case the place where I would start work in September. I looked at the library and was dismayed to see that there were very few books—almost none—in modern Western literature. There were good holdings in 19th Century and the first half of the 20th, but the axe must have fallen about 1960; anything published after that was not there. A twenty-year gap—and I found out later that there was that same gap in the other departments.

It was much later that I realized what political movements were responsible for this (including the US boycott of China.) But it was clear that something had to be done. So in the summer of 1979, I appealed to colleagues and friends in Canada to donate books for Nankai, and raided my own collection, since I was about to retire anyhow, and came to Nankai in August bringing over a thousand books.

They were welcomed enthusiastically. When the crates were delivered to my room in the Foreign Students Building, teachers and students of my department came with a big hand-cart and we took them to the Foreign Languages Reading room in a joyful procession. There, the administrators decided to put them in a special room, called the Friendship Reading Room.

So far, so good. The misunderstandings started soon after. I had already seen that what few foreign books the library owned were kept by teachers for their own use. My mission was to get the books to the students, so I insisted as a condition of the gift that the books must be available to students and must not be taken out on loan. (Teachers everywhere tend to take books out on loan and do not return them.)

The authorities agreed, and there was a ceremony. I have a formal photo of the occasion.

My zeal was admirable, right? Unfortunately it was also ignorant. It's a mistake to go into a different culture and set about putting things right. My zeal was based on reason, enlightenment, concern for the students. What humanitarianism! What energy expended to do good in the world! Yes, and what ignorance of what I was intruding myself into!

As soon as I was gone from Nankai after that first year, the Friendship Reading Room was closed down and the collection merged with the regular departmental reading room, open only to teachers and some graduate students. What was worse, the books began to disappear. I estimate that a third of them are no longer there. I was told on the sly that one teacher had mailed ten of them to a friend at another university.

All this was outrageous. When I came back to Nankai I told the dean I was not going to get any more books for the department. I was very angry at the teachers for acting in childish, unproductive, not to say unsocialist ways. From now on, I would bring only the books my students needed in my classes, and give them directly to the students.

But you know, getting angry ignored some important facts. One was that such books really were in extremely short supply, and it really was important for teachers to get first crack at them. In China a teacher has, traditionally, a dignity to uphold. To give students books which the teachers themselves have not studied puts the teachers in a very embarrassing position—that's a deep part of the culture, not to be brushed aside.

I've noticed, sheepishly, that as the department has been able to buy more books, the rules have loosened and more and more students have access to them.

Now, I try to be just a bit more aware of what I'm getting into, to be a little less like a militant missionary. These days I take copies of the contemporary novels we use in my classes, and give them to my students, but I also bring a few copies of the same novels for the departmental reading room. Outside of that, I let the Chinese decide what the Chinese ought to do.

Gradually, as I lived and worked there, I learned about the history of Nankai—strikingly different from the histories of my Western universities. It was established in 1919. That's not old compared to the universities of Europe and England and New England, but there's a lot of history packed into its lifetime. In the year of its founding, the May Fourth Movement broke out, a popular movement for reform and for opposing the continued occupation of China by foreign armies and "concessions". A Nankai student, young Zhou Enlai, who was to become China's best-loved Premier, was one of the organizers of the May Fourth Movement in Tianjin. On the Nankai campus, at the end of a peninsula jutting out into the lotus pond, is a memorial to Zhou which is visited by people daily and is banked with flowers on *Qing Ming*, the day of honouring the dead.

Zhou is celebrated as one of Nankai's greatest students. There's irony in this, since he was there for less than a year and even then must have spent little time in the classroom. In 1919, he was busy with the movement. The next year, he sailed to France where he spent many years as a student and, incidentally, joined the Communist Party. When he came back, it wasn't to Nankai but to the revolutionary struggles in the south of China.

In 1931 and again in 1936, Nankai students were among the leaders of the demonstrations against the Japanese invasion of China's north-east. In 1937, when the Japanese war machine smashed into China's coastal cities, it started the invasion of Tianjin by suddenly bombing Nankai from the air, leveling almost all the buildings and killing many people. The surviving faculty and students gathered up books from the library and fled on barges down the Grand Canal. They set up a university in exile, first in Nanjing and later in Kunming, where Nankai joined two other universities in exile to form the wartime Southwest University.

During the Cultural Revolution (1966-1976), Nankai, now back in Tianjin, was a focus of the Red Guard campaign to radicalize education and root out old-fashioned ideas and old-fashioned thinkers. No classes were taught, I'm told, for four years, and at one time the campus was in a civil war in which two factions of revolutionaries were shooting each other with rifles and taking captives in raids. Finally, a group of workers and peasants, whose prestige during the Cultural Revolution was high, took over the campus and restored order.

In 1976 came the great earthquake, and the quake victims taking over much of the campus to build their little brick houses.

In 1989, Nankai was the rallying point for the great student marches of the city of Tianjin, and some of my own Nankai students were in Beijing's Tiananmen Square when the army smashed the student movement.

It's a history that doesn't make you think of ivory towers. It helps me understand the mood of today's China, when people want to forget big social struggles and just live in peace.

My 1979 students had lived through a lot of history themselves. They were very different indeed from the tamer students of the mid-1980s, who came to university straight from high school. These students were older—in their late twenties or early thirties. They had all lost a lot of years during the Cultural Revolution, when their schools were shut down and they were sent to the countryside. Now they were back, eager to get at the books and make up for lost time. How they worked! How they pushed me! It was an exciting year.

It was the students themselves, from the start, that made teaching at Nankai such a pleasure for me. The classrooms did not inspire joy. In the main building, where we held our classes, the elevators seldom worked. The halls and stairways were dark and drab. In our classroom there was chalk dust everywhere— my students brought dust-cloths to wipe off their desks and seats before they sat down. (Chinese chalk is more crumbly than ours.) About once a week, the students, prodded and led by me, brought pails and cloths and washed the blackboard and the desks. In winter, a modicum of heat was provided, but that heat was not turned on until the first of December, the room was on the north side of the building and the cold wind came in around the edges of the windows. Towards the end of November I found myself teaching class while wearing long underwear, heavy pants and shirt, a sweater, a sheepskin overcoat, and a fur hat. But I didn't complain. Those students made teaching a delight, and I often thought of the phrase "plain living and high thinking".

When I started teaching at Nankai, in September 1979, there were no grades, no exams, no degrees. The theory was that since only a few of the best students became graduate students, and since they would all be in demand after graduation, there was no need for grades. It was enough to say they had completed the program at Nankai University. So they did not see themselves as competing with each other. They helped each other. They studied together, and supported each other. They saw the purpose of the class as bringing all of them to the required high level of achievement.

Can you imagine what it meant to me as a teacher to find I had eager, smart, hardworking students, to whom I was not a judge but a guide and a friend? I have always tried to be what I call a demanding friend to my students, but we always knew that at the end of the semester I was going to be the judge and hit them with grades. Those Nankai students and I really could be friends, at the same time that we were all working very hard indeed. (I've never had a school year that left me more exhausted.) As friends, they dropped in on me for tea. They came shopping with me, to show me where the stores were. We went rowing together in the Water Park. As students, they would come to me and say, "That's an interesting writer you talked about. What else did he write?" —and they'd go to the library and find those other books and read them. They ranged over the subject.

In the eighth month of our ten-month school year, the dean came to me and said, "I'm sorry, but Beijing has changed the policy. There will be final examinations, and you must give them grades. And next year they must write theses and get MA degrees." Our relationship changed abruptly. We were still friendly, but there was an anxiety in the air, and they started asking that dreadful question, "Is this going to be on the exam?" The system forced it on them. The change was a lesson to all of us, as I made sure they understood.

What has not changed, in spite of the grades I must give them, is that my Chinese students have been both very hardworking and very friendly, and our relationship has stayed cordial. We work hard together, and then cook meals together, go to movies together, bicycle to interesting places together, and we stay in touch with each other through later years.

Students in Chinese universities have the old Chinese respect for teachers and elders. They also have the strengths and weaknesses of traditional Chinese schooling. One strength is respect for learning, for the subject. Another is the development of amazing memories. In the lower schools, students learn languages by reciting model sentences together in loud voices. They memorize enormous amounts of material. In first grade the kids have several new characters to learn every day. In all grades they memorize. My students could all recite Chairman Mao's essay on Dr. Norman Bethune ("The Great Internationalist") from beginning to end. That first year, we had a ten-month survey of English literature, meeting eight hours a week. We covered an amazing amount of material, but at the end of the year my students had it all at their fingertips.

The emphasis on memorizing, however, goes along with a weakness of the system. The student, traditionally, is there to receive knowledge, not to develop his or her ideas or opinions or power of reasoning and analyzing. The teacher is the expert. The student is privileged to sit and listen, and memorize. You can see how easily this would fit in with the tendency of Chinese socialism to slide towards obedience.

What did it mean, then, to say I was teaching in a socialist country? Westerners frequently ask me, "What did they let you teach?" I have to chuckle about that. As far as my classes went, I saw no restraints. No one asked me what books I was giving the students to read, or what positions I was taking. One administrator told me, "You are the expert on Western literature. It is not for us to tell you what to say, but to learn from you."

Other foreign teachers have had different experiences, as they've told me. Chinese socialism, as I've said before, has two faces. One is the socialist base of idealism and feelings of social responsibility, the idealism which young people in China cherish. But the other face, which is also called socialism, is that leaders are experts, and the people are there to listen and obey. I can't tell you how much I hate that!

In general, life in China was much less noticeably socialist than I had expected. My students were interested in ideas in general. They were ready to look at the world through any author's eyes. They were quick to apply to their own lives what they saw in the novels we read. They loved *Catcher in the Rye*, partly because they could easily point out to me aspects of hypocrisy and pretentiousness in Chinese life similar to those that were driving Holden crazy in America.

But what they rejoiced in was new ideas, new approaches. They did not want to read *The Grapes of Wrath*. They groaned. Not one more epic about heroic peasants, please! When my Xiamen University class read Marge Piercy's *Woman on the Edge of Time*, with her fantasy about what the United States might become if all the progressive movements got together, I expected a hot debate about how her vision of the future differed from that of socialist China, but except for two students (out of sixteen) they were emphatically not interested. "The only boring thing you've given us to read!"

I'm sure I used the word *socialism* more often than they did. They had been crammed with agitprop novels, stories, movies, and operas, in a kind of orthodoxy that permitted no deviance, and they were eager for new ideas, new approaches. Unfortunately, having never been given a chance to exercise analysis or criticism, they jumped at the new ideas (and, later, the new clothes, music, food, and so on) uncritically. I think that sums up a lot of what has happened in China as it came in contact with the West.

On the other hand, it is still true that at a deep level they took two things for granted. One was the basic rightness of socialism, for all the glaring faults of what passed for socialism in their lives. Another was that the social function of literature is to help people understand and deal with the problems of society. I was not surprised that they didn't like Vonnegut's *Slaughterhouse Five*, but I was dead wrong about their reasons. The fantasy did not, as I had expected, repel them. They were indignant about what they saw as his basic ideas: Sure he went through hell in Dresden, but he had twenty years to come to grips with that before he wrote the book. China went through a lot more hell than that during the Japanese invasion, but our literature is not like that. Why is he bogged down in helplessness? What good is a book that says nothing can be done? Their own basic idea was that expressed by the well-known woman writer Ding Ling: "We should write about the socialist upheaval and the scars caused by it, about privilege-seeking and corruption, and the dark side of life. . . [But] no matter how much we shock or anger the readers, in the end we must give them strength." (Quoted in *Beijing Review, April 13, 1981*)

After that great first year (1979-1980) I taught in China until the end of 1996, spending half my time in China and half back in Canada. Most of that time, obviously, was in the 1980s, Deng Xiaoping's decade, a crucial period marked by great changes. The buzzwords were "open up to the world", and "modernize". (Though a lot of the time it has seemed to me that "modernize" really means "Westernize", and comes close to being synonymous with "Americanize".)

I'll get into those changes in detail when I give a chapter to Deng Xiaoping. Here I'll note the change that was most obvious in my classroom. Year by year through the decade, students had more freedom from the rigid control of their lives. For example, in 1979 dancing was strictly forbidden at Nankai, but by the mid-eighties on Saturday nights there was a dance in each of the seven dining halls on campus. In 1979 such frivolities as hobbies were considered outrageous distractions from the serious business of life. By 1989, almost all people had hobbies— collecting stamps, taking photos, building miniature gardens in pots, keeping pets—you name it.

In my classroom the important difference was that year by year my students felt freer to express their thoughts. When we read *One Flew over the Cuckoo's Nest*, one of the students started our discussion by saying loudly, "China needs McMurphy!"

In 1979, a stranger might have thought that the Chinese were sexless, and in fact some Westerners wondered how the population could have increased so much. There was almost no possibility for social relationships between the sexes. Young women might hold hands with each other, or walk with their arms around each other. So could young men, whom I often saw holding hands while riding bicycles side by side—without the overtones such things would have in the West.

But you never saw boy-girl couples together, much less holding hands. That has changed year by year and is now drastically different. Now it's common to see girls riding on the carriers of their boyfriends' bikes and snuggling up to them, and it's common to see couples walking with arms around each other. On Saturday nights during the late 1980s if you walked or rode through the street that joined the Nankai campus with the Tianjin University campus, you made your way through surging crowds of young people all spruced up and looking for excitement. The sense of healthy young sexuality was almost palpable. And in "Lovers' Park" in the late evening two people, as the saying goes, cast one shadow in the moonlight.

(However, the excitement on that inter-campus street offended the conservative Party leaders of the two universities, so a high wall was erected right across that street, and the young people have gone elsewhere.)

What I've written so far might give the impression that life at Nankai has been tumultuous. But day by day life has felt placid—the changes seem rapid looking back, but were not so important day by day. My deepest feeling has been a sense of peace there, a gentler rhythm of life than in the West. I've always felt glad to be living there. The friendships, with students mostly, but with colleagues too, and with people I've met casually, the sense I have of the Chinese people's genius for making the best of things and enjoying life, coupled, I must certainly add, with a feeling that my work was appreciated—all this added up to a way of life which for me has been pleasant indeed.

Shortly after my first year in China, after coming back to Canada, I wrote down something which I can still quote as a valid expression of my feelings as I look back:

> I was restless one night, unable to sleep, so a bit after midnight I got up and dressed and went for a walk. I left the campus, exchanging greetings with the watchman, and crossed the canal to the busy street. It was, indeed, still busy. No bicycles at this time of night, no trucks, no buses. Now the street was full of the quieter sounds of horses' hooves as peasants brought in fresh vegetables for the next morning's markets, bricks for construction projects, and many other things, on large two-wheeled carts pulled by three-horse teams. They are not permitted on the city streets by day since those streets are so crowded, so here they came, working through the night. On top of most of the loads, drivers and their helpers were

stretched out, many sleeping, until time for unloading. There were no reins; the horses just plodded ahead waiting for a voice command to turn or stop.

In the dim light, the pleasant patter of these horse teams as they came into sight and melted again into the darkness seemed to me the sound I would remember best from this city that never sleeps. Always something is stirring, and life goes on. It was comforting, somehow, and I walked back to my room ready for my sleep, realizing that for me living and working in China was not just an interesting job, not just an adventure, but a deeply peaceful experience as well.

6

Places: Tianjin

When I go out through Nankai's main gate onto the streets of Tianjin, I realize that although the university is like a small village complete in itself, it is surrounded by a different world. On the street which runs in front of the campus, life is noisier and more turbulent, and in many ways more fascinating. Up until 1996 (by which time the streets had been taken over by cars, trucks, buses, and taxis), I made it a habit to get out of the university every day, usually on my bicycle, to explore this different world.

On campus it's a common sight to see eight- or nine-year-old girls in pretty clothes, with big hair-ribbons, riding the new child-size bicycles. Outside the campus, although you may see equally well-dressed people you will also see people who scramble for a living, and children in patched or torn clothes wandering around with runny noses and dirty faces and dirty hair, and no bicycles. Officially, China is a classless society, and when I once asked students in a conversation class to discuss the classes of Chinese society, they were puzzled and said there's no such thing. Don't believe it! A peasant, a factory worker, a university teacher, a government official, a movie star, all live in very different worlds indeed, and so do their children. But on the streets of Tianjin many of them jostle each other in the crowd.

On the street, just as on campus, I see history all around me. When I first saw this area, in 1979, it was drab and quiet. Everything was sold in State-owned stores, in which the service was bad and the supplies dismal. The street traffic then made little noise; it was thousands of bicycles, and carters straining to pull heavy loads, people carrying loads on bamboo carrying-poles, and crowds of people just walking.

The government was beginning to relax the system of State monopoly and let people bring their own crops or those of their communes and sell them in "free markets" in specified areas, one of which was a couple of blocks from the university gate. The idea was so new that everyone was nervous about it, not sure the government really meant it. The sellers would not let me photograph them: nobody wanted to be on record, in case the policy changed again. One ingenious young man built a sort of cabinet on the carrier of his bicycle, which opened up into a repair shop so he could repair pots and pans and other household things, but could close shop and be off at a moment's notice.

Today, that's all changed. Now the whole city sometimes seems to be one big market, clumped in formal areas but also spread out alongside the streets here and there, with many kinds of goods sold from wagons or pushcarts in the street or just laid out on the sidewalk: fresh vegetables, fresh fruits, peanuts, grains, soft drinks, clothes, magazines, knick-knacks. In their seasons you can see spread out on cloths on the sidewalk piles of lovely fresh field-ripened tomatoes, green peppers, sweet corn, eggplants, many kinds of squash, garlic, ginger, coriander leaves. In June and July there are regular hills of small, round watermelons, ripe, sweet, and delicious.

Young men sell "seconds" from their pushcarts—things rejected for export: toys, clothing, kitchenware, plates and bowls, plastic sheets—whatever the factories have available—and shout their wares with loudhailers.

Sitting on the curb beside the road is a line of young peasants, men and women, who have come to the city looking for work, have bought hand-operated sewing machines, and will repair your shoes or handbags while you wait. Beyond them, a young man has spread his tools on the ground and is busy repairing bicycles. Beyond him is a barber, with a plain wooden chair for his customers, and a mirror hanging on the trunk of a tree. An old woman walks by, selling copies of the daily newspaper from a stack on the carrier of her bicycle.

The government tries to control this dispersed selling. It has rules about licensing, about honest weights, about overcharging. But these are hard to enforce in the shifting scene. In newspapers you frequently see scenes of policemen nabbing cheating vendors, but the frequency of such pictures shows that the problem is far from solved.

One day as I came out through the gate of the university, I was almost run into by a young peasant woman, carrying her sewing machine and running towards me but looking back over her shoulder. She had spotted police vans coming and was running to hide, which means that she was in the city illegally and had no business license.

The police swooped, in three vans, and swarmed around a few of the vendors, while the other vendors quickly pushed their carts down the lanes. They caught an acquaintance of mine, a young man from one of the Tianjin counties. He had started business by sitting on the curb selling peanuts from a basket, and had worked his way up to a handsome pushcart with colourful awning where he specialized in the latest fruit from the south—the first peaches, or grapes, or watermelons. As I came up to them, the police were shouting at him and shaking their fingers at him. They imposed a heavy fine, which they collected on the spot.

He explained to me later that doing business in the street is illegal because it interferes with traffic. Vendors are supposed to use lanes and side-streets. But he says the ones who work in the street get all the business and he can't afford to do differently.

A few minutes after the police left, all the vendors came out of hiding and it was business as usual.

Across the street from the Nankai gate, behind the line of vendors' pushcarts, is a row of small stores where you can buy soy sauce, spices, matches, soap, candy, cooking oil. There's a bookstore, and a post office, and a stall with newspapers and magazines and paperback books. People line up in front of a small window behind which some one is selling fresh noodles. (You must bring a container, for they just hold out the damp noodles to you.) Right alongside that is a store selling computer software. All in all, it's much livelier than it was in 1979.

If I go on my bicycle for ten minutes, I reach the Lhasa Street market, where I park my bike (for ten Chinese pennies) and walk around looking at everything for half an hour before buying what I came for. There are several streets in this market: on one, aquarium fish are for sale, some displayed in large aquariums, some in mason jars—lots of different kinds of tiny lively fish of amazing colours. On another street are *penjing*, the miniature landscapes the Chinese love, and the materials for making your own: grotesque stones to represent mountains, live dwarf trees, tiny ceramic temples, boats, bridges, storks, and people; in another street it's flowers and plants and accessories; in another ladles, knives, chopping boards and such, sold by the people who make them; in another many kinds of clothes. The longest street is for foods: meat, vegetables, fruits, grains of many kinds, live chickens, live fish in tubs—all sorts of things. Often I see vegetables that are new to me, and once or twice when I've asked what they are and how to prepare them the peasants have given me free samples. "Come back and tell us how you like them."

There are modern stores in downtown Tianjin now, including new international department stores like fancy expensive ones anywhere in the West, but I stick to the local places. I like to deal with people who make the things or raise the food that I buy.

The markets prospered year by year during the 1980s, and the supply of goods for ordinary people has increased amazingly. In 1979 there was almost no meat, or fish, or eggs. All these and many other foods were rationed. If a shipment of meat came to a store, the news was shouted from person to person and everyone ran to line up, and bought whatever there was on sale. Today, there is so much meat available, all unrationed, that shoppers are fussy and won't take any that's too fat—so the farmers are starting to breed leaner pigs.

In the 1979-80 school year, from November to April the only green vegetable we could get was *bai cai*, Chinese cabbage. In the fall, long lines of trucks brought *bai cai* from the farms. Vendors piled them up in hills and covered them with thick quilts. Many people bought a whole winter supply at once, and stacked them up outside their doors. The mounds were quarried all through the winter, for one thing you can say for *bai cai* is that it can keep for months and still be edible. But I can tell you that after three months or more of nothing but *bai cai* it takes real hunger to eat it without making faces. These days, however, there are many kinds of vegetables to choose from, coming by train from the south.

But come back to that busy scene outside the campus gate. As I stand by the gate, at my right is a large elevated clover-leaf traffic interchange, the off-ramp of which empties its traffic right into the bustle of this street. What a new thing! In 1979 there wasn't nearly enough traffic to justify it, and nobody had even heard of such a thing. It's part of the new ring road that circles the city and links up with the speedway which has cut the time it takes to get to Beijing by more than half.

This clover-leaf was inaugurated in a ceremony up on the road itself, with red flags and official speeches. The people who had lived in a run-down area that was cleared to make room for the new road had been invited, and stood in a line with big red paper roses on their chests as officials formally thanked them for giving up their old homes for the good of society.

For weeks after that ceremony, people flocked up the down-ramp by the hundreds to see this new thing, and it was hard for trucks and cars to get through, but now it's just part of the busy scene.

The trucks which crowd noisily down into our street have almost entirely replaced the old way of moving things. You see very few men pulling hand-carts or using bamboo carrying poles, and horsecarts only at night. So quickly does China change! There are still lots of bicycles, of course, but the work of carrying goods, which used to require human muscle and sweat, is now done by machine. That's a fine change, of course—but we have the constant noise of the traffic now, and it's increasingly dangerous to cross the street—and the air, which used to be fairly clean, with interesting smells, is now heavily polluted with exhaust fumes. Such trade-offs are part of the changes taking place all over China.

In 1979 there were absolutely no advertising billboards. (When the first was put up, in the centre of town, crowds gathered to watch the painters at work.) But there were slogans everywhere, some of them golden characters on a deep red background, others paper posters with bright pictures: quotations from Chairman Mao, or exhortations to observe safety rules, to follow good hygiene, to give children a balanced diet, to support the policy of one child per family.

Now the slogans are entirely gone, but on busy downtown streets billboards are everywhere, advertising a jumble of things in a joyous outburst of commercialism: rubber boots, bus tires, shampoo, ball-bearings, quick-cooking noodles, Scotch whiskey, trench coats, tractors, skin cream, medical scalpels, Chinese medicines, textile machinery. (I took this list from one row of billboards in downtown Tianjin.) It's characteristic of the changes in China that at one time there were no commercials, only slogans, and a short time later no slogans, only commercials. Such dizzy swings from one extreme to the other!

Traditionally in China selling things was considered a demeaning profession. When I went to a movie with a friend in 1980, a young man came in late and joined a group behind us, who whispered to each other. My companion whispered in my ear, "He's explaining why he was late. He stopped outside to talk to some of his old high-school classmates who don't have jobs. They're selling peanuts outside the theatre but were too ashamed to talk to him."

That attitude towards buying and selling has been swept away, though I still hear echoes of it—I think that's what's behind the anger of university teachers when they tell me that street vendors make more money than professors these days. But on the streets you won't see any sense of shame—it is now eminently respectable to make money. As Deng Xiaoping said, "To get rich is glorious!"

The new commercial prosperity is the key to Tianjin these days. The city is booming. It's a steel-making city, a city of factories turning out bicycles, elevators, trucks and buses, taxis, coal-mining machinery. It's a textile city specializing in high-fashion clothes; a city of fine handicrafts (carpets, jade carvings, cloisonné); an oil-refining city; a fisheries city; a railway and waterways transportation hub; one of China's largest seaports; a New Economic Zone; a hustling, noisy, smelly sprawl of six million people with another two million in its suburban counties. If you want the feeling of it, read Carl Sandburg's description of his city in the poem "Chicago".

In Tianjin the *Ding He*, or "Placid River" flows in from the north-west, and the *Ziya He*, or "Child's Tooth River" from the south-west. They meet the North Canal flowing in from Beijing, and the famous Grand Canal which for more than five hundred years has been bringing barges 1600 kilometres north from the Yangtze River. They all converge to form the *Hai He*, or "Ocean River" which flows through the city and on to the sea. This whole area is low-lying and flat, so the rivers drop their silt here, and the *Hai He* has silted up so badly that large ships which used to come up to the centre of the city must now berth fifty kilometres downstream at Tianjin's seaport.

Water has been important in Tianjin's history. It's the lowest coastal city in China, so low, in the old days, that there were canals everywhere, serving both for transportation and for drainage. One of them, the *Wei Ci*, ran diagonally right across the city. But as the population increased and industry developed, the demand for water increased and many wells were dug. The groundwater was used up, the watertable dropped, and the drainage canals weren't needed. The *Wei Ci* was filled in and paved, becoming a busy street (called, under socialism, *Shengli Lu*, or Victory Street, though now, when reminders of socialism are disappearing, it's just plain Nanjing Road).

A new problem developed as the groundwater was used up: the city began to subside. According to *China Daily* (March 5, 1992) between 1959 and 1985 some parts of the city sank by more than two metres, with disastrous effects on roads and buildings. Since then the city has spent millions of dollars buying and sealing the wells, over 700 of them in one three-year campaign.

But that left the city short of water for homes and factories. The *Hai He*, ironically, was too polluted for use. So the Chinese government, in a huge engineering feat, turned around a river in the north-east and brought it through tunnels and canals to

Tianjin. (The Chinese, like the Americans, love the whole idea of huge projects. For myself, I had to wonder if it wouldn't have been cheaper and easier to clean up the *Hai He*.)

Besides being a waterways hub, Tianjin is the great railway hub of northern China. Trains from Beijing turn north from here to the rich industrial north-east and on all the way to the former Soviet Union. Or they turn south and go all the way to Shanghai, connecting there with all of south China. Rail lines converge here from all over inland north China, so Tianjin is a gateway to the ocean and to international trade for many inland provinces and autonomous regions, including Tibet, Ningxia, Inner Mongolia, and Xinjiang. In 1992, Tianjin held a big trade fair at which representatives of those inland places showed 10,000 kinds of agricultural, industrial, and crafts goods to businessmen from many countries.

With all this commerce it's no wonder that Tianjin's new railway station has been, until just recently, the largest in China. (An aside I can't resist: In that new railway station the ceiling of the main lobby is a large dome on which is painted in heroic dimensions the goddess Jingwei with her attendants. Jingwei, in ancient myth, was a beautiful woman who was cruelly drowned by the sea. Turning into a bird, she vowed revenge, and ever since then she has been carrying pebbles and twigs and throwing them into the ocean to fill it up. She will, too, some day, the legend says. Like the Foolish Old Man who moved mountains, she stands for what can be done by perseverance. In the dome, Jingwei hovers above us on broad wings in a circle of light. She and her attendants are shown not as birds, though, but as young women, painted realistically as if the artist worked from living models. But they are startling in puritanical China because they wear no clothes, only their midsections being fortuitously covered. If you watch the people crowding the escalators directly under the dome, every now and then you'll see somebody catch sight of naked Jingwei and the others overhead, and be so startled as to almost, and sometimes quite, fall over, creating such a jumble that the attendant must stop the escalator until it gets straightened out. Jingwei comes out of the mist of legend, bypassing the art of socialist realism which would have put revolutionary heroes in that dome, and presides over the new openness and internationalism. Not a bad symbol for Tianjin, that ancient city, the booming centre of prosperous newness.)

The modern period in China is usually dated from the Opium Wars of 1840-1842, in which the British invaded Guangdong and forced on China the opium trade and the system of "concessions", or areas under foreign control. For the next hundred years China was wracked by wars and uprisings and other disruptions as the old empire slowly died and various political movements, local warlords, peasant uprisings, and foreign armies contended for control. Tianjin was often the centre of these troubles, partly because of its industry and its importance as a communications centre, partly because any invaders coming from the sea and striking at Beijing had to go through Tianjin.

In 1858, the French and British together shelled and occupied the city and forced on the Chinese government the Treaty of Tianjin, opening more areas to foreign control. In 1860, British and French warships again shelled the city and forced the Chinese to concede more "rights" and more areas. In 1900, the Boxer uprising was suppressed by the combined armies of Europeans, largely in Tianjin. At this time the invaders forced the Chinese to destroy Tianjin's city walls, which Dutch travelers had described, 475 years earlier, as 7.6 metres high and very imposing. All that's left now is the east gate.

From then on Tianjin was carved up by foreigners, as were Shanghai and other coastal cities, into concession areas in which the foreigners had complete control. In each concession the law was the law of the foreign country, not of China. From these bases the foreigners carried on their lucrative exploitation of Chinese commerce, industry, and natural resources.

The Tianjin Number Two Municipal Guest House (now the *Heping Hotel*) where I first lived in China, was built as the luxurious mansion of a high French official. In fact, as I've bicycled around Tianjin I've frequently come across buildings in various European styles which were part of the concession areas. There must be hundreds of them.

I have two maps of Tianjin from those times, one showing the city in 1917, one in 1932. In the 1917 map the British, French, German, and Japanese concessions are each of them larger than the Chinese old city, and smaller areas are held by Italy, Russia, and the Austro-Hungarian Empire.

The effects of the First World War soon made that 1917 map obsolete. In the 1932 map, the former German concession has been taken over by the British, and the Austro-Hungarian by the Italians. The USSR revoked the Russian claims; their territory has been taken over partly by Belgium; part of it is shown as one of three "Special Districts" in which foreign powers seem to have cooperated. The presence of the United States, which forced China to give it the same rights granted to other countries, is seen there. Here, on the 1932 map, the streets are still named "Alexandra", "Tomsky", "Crimea", and so on, but here the Standard Oil compound is located at the corner of Baikal Road and the Russian Bund. The map also shows a "Woodrow Wilson Boulevard."

The street names on this map are fascinating. The British concession has London Meadows Road and streets named Victoria, Windsor, Greenwich, Oxford, Wellington. The river front here is called the British Bund. The French have Marschal Foch Avenue and 14 Juillet Street, and their river front is called Quai de France. The Italians have Vitorio Emanuel and Fiume Streets, and their river front is the Banchia d'Italia. The Japanese have streets named Mitsushima, Fuykoshima, Kotobuki.

I got my strongest feeling about the concessions when I stood on Liberation Street (*Jiefang Lu*), which the British called Victoria Avenue, and looked at the old British Bank building, now the Bank of China. That imposing flight of granite steps, those massive Greek columns and entablature, that whole solid granite mass, gave me the clue: those bloody British expected to be here for a thousand years! You get something of the same effect from the elaborate country club and race course the British maintained for themselves south of the city.

It was hatred of those foreign invaders, and of the horse-trading in Chinese territory among the European victors of World War One that gave birth to the patriotic May Fourth Movement, beginning May 4, 1919.

In Tianjin, the concession era ended with the Japanese invasion of 1937. For eight years the Japanese occupied the city, a key centre in their brutal attempts to subdue China by terror. After the Japanese surrender in 1945, and during the following civil war between the Communist and Nationalist (*Guomindang*) armies, the American influence grew strong. The Americans, as they have often done elsewhere, supported a corrupt and brutal regime against a popular movement, placing their bets on Chiang Kaishek. They turned over to Chiang huge amounts of war material left over from the Pacific campaign, supported him with huge grants, sent him many American advisors. US Army and Marine forces were based in Tianjin. After the Japanese surrender, it was from Tianjin that American planes ferried large units of Nationalist troops into north-east China to help them seize control of that key area before the Communists could— an effort which failed.

The Nationalist army holding Tianjin surrendered to the Communists in January 1949. On October 1 that year Mao Zedong stood on the rostrum over Beijing's Tiananmen ("The Gate of Heavenly Peace") and announced that China had "stood up" and the long wars were over.

Thereafter, Tianjin was one of the centres of the campaigns of the socialist era: the Anti-Rightist Campaign, the Great Leap Forward, the Cultural Revolution. During the Cultural Revolution Tianjin's universities and most of its high schools were shut down for years and thousands of their students were sent to the countryside.

In the Deng Xiaoping era, the 1980s, Tianjin prospered and is now a bustling centre of foreign trade, with large industrial parks for the foreigners' factories. Foreign businessmen are common now in Tianjin and there are expensive Western hotels to serve them. (A factory worker, if he could get in at all, would have to spend three or four months' wages to sleep there for one night.)

There's an irony to all this. The old concessions are gone, but the same kind of foreigners are back, this time with handshakes rather than guns. Like the foreigners of the old concessions, they are in China to take out profits for the companies back home.

In Guangzhou in 1985, while I was waiting for my luggage after a flight from Xiamen, I heard an American businessman say loudly, "They've got a real hotel in Xiamen now. Fifteen stories. Real Western food. Jacuzzis, saunas, everything. We'll put our junior executives there when we start business in the fall."

"Will there be an American school for their children?" a European asked him, perhaps ironically.

"Children? We wouldn't send people with children to a place like this!"

I don't imply, of course, that all foreign businessmen are barbarians. One semester while I was living at the Tianjin Friendship Hotel I met an American, the manager of a new joint-venture making cosmetics for sale in China as well as for export. I kidded him a lot, saying Chinese young women, who have naturally beautiful complexions, would never go for cosmetics. He counted on their loving them when they got the chance. He was right; I was wrong. In the big cities now all the young women and many little girls are wearing make-up and his company is booming. But I must say for this man that he had a real faith in his products, telling me how careful his company was not to use anything harmful and how good his products were for sun-burned or chapped skin. He was also very knowledgeable about China and really hoping to make it prosper. He spent a lot of time exploring Tianjin by bicycle.

In general, though, I'd say that whether the foreign businessmen are good guys or bad guys is not the point; the point is that they are there to take money out of China for the companies back home. A more ominous point is that the Chinese seem to be welcoming them with open arms. "But it's different this time," they tell me. "This time we Chinese are making the rules." Well, we'll see.

I remember that on October 1, 1984, the 35th anniversary of Liberation and the founding of the socialist State, I was invited to the Tianjin government's National Day banquet. One thing that amazed me at this formal occasion was that in all the speeches, in the elaborate souvenir booklets, in all the publicity, in the songs sung by famous entertainers, there was no mention at all of socialism or of the Revolution. It was purely a celebration of the new economic prosperity, and most of the invited foreigners were executives of big foreign companies doing business in Tianjin.

I sat next to one of them, a large pleasant-mannered Texan. His company was busy in Tianjin's oilfields, and he told me that where he lived, in the Tangu port fifty kilometres downstream, there was a large fenced-off area where the executives and other foreigners and their families lived in air-conditioned houses, "just like home", with TVs, luxurious bathrooms, big refrigerators, where they also had Western schools for the children. I wonder if it shows up on modern maps, and has streets with American names.

Chairman Mao advised, "Take what is good from the West, and leave the bad." Excellent advice, but to tell which is which is not always easy. And there's an old saying in China: "The young calf does not fear the tiger."

I seem to be in a small minority in China to think this way about the foreigners and the business boom they are part of. But there are other problems in the midst of the prosperity. One is a bitter feeling among some Chinese (I have no way of knowing how many—they certainly do not include political or economic leaders or the people who control the mass media) that the ideals of socialism are being shoved aside by selfish materialism. "We used to say `Xiang qian kan`," they tell me, quoting an old socialist slogan: "Look to the future!" "Now we still say `Xiang qian kan`," but they rub their fingertips with their thumbs in an international gesture. The bitter pun is based on the fact that the word for "future" or "forward" and the word for "money" have the same sound in Chinese, so the slogan now means "Look for the money!"

Of course, these problems are national, not just problems of Tianjin. So is inflation. So is unemployment. So is the slipping position of women in society. All these I must evaluate later, in other chapters.

I must keep until later, too, one of the most crucial events of recent Tianjin history (as of China's): that is, the student demonstrations of 1989 and the smashing of that movement. Tianjin was one of the centres—but that movement must have a chapter of its own.

Whenever I talk about social problems in China, even the most severe ones, I should remember to put them in context against the background of the peaceful and gratifying daily life which makes my own memories of China pleasant. There's inconsistency for you! I miss China like crazy, and the same goes specifically for noisy polluted old Tianjin. I think of how the huge sprawling city divides itself into neighbourhoods, each with its own stores, open-air markets, parks, and interesting sights, its own balance between ancient and modern, its own atmosphere. To explore Tianjin by bicycle (before the streets were crowded by trucks and autos—that is to say before about 1996)—that was a never-ending adventure.

I think, too, of the way Tianjin people enjoy the few weeks each winter when it is cold enough to freeze the lakes. They haul out their skates and come by the hundreds to the Water Park and the smaller ponds in parks and on campuses. And on every pond and canal and even large puddle throughout the city little kids ride tiny short sleds, sitting on them cross-legged and propelling themselves by two metal rods, scooting about on the ice like water-bugs.

I think of exhibits at the Art Museum, and ballets and plays at the theatres, especially one time in the early 1980s, when foreigners were few, when the Tianjin Drama Company invited me to see a play about San Francisco's Chinatown which they had written and staged. They spent over two hours talking about it with me backstage, asking what errors they had made in representing a country none of them had seen. And there was the time I had a bit part in a movie, in a street scene which had to be filmed at four o'clock in the morning so the street would not be full of people staring at us. And the puppet company I spent a lot of time with one year, photographing the whole process from making the puppets through rehearsals to the final performance. And the kite-flying contest in a large soccer field, and the Museum of Natural History with its splendid dinosaur exhibits, and the many times I've enjoyed watching the kids in the Children's Palace practice their dancing, singing, playing music, painting, gymnastics; and the Museum of the Dramatic Arts in an old theatre where years ago Sun Yat Sen used to preach reform.

I remember going to the Water Park with my students, where we rowed on the lake, had picnics, strolled through the zoo. I remember with special delight the hospitality in the homes of those of my students who lived in Tianjin.

In general I don't like big cities any more, having lived in them quite enough of my life, but if only they could get rid of the air pollution and let us see a few stars at night, I think I could live happily in Tianjin.

7
Places: Xiamen

In Xiamen, on the south-east coast of China, I sat on the little porch of my apartment one lovely sunny afternoon in February 1991, sipping the famous Fujian tea and enjoying the view and the sweet fresh air. I lived in one of a small cluster of apartment buildings appropriately called *Ling Feng*, or "High Peak", high on the steep hill which overlooks Xiamen University. To get here from the centre of the campus, I bicycled on an upsloping street for about five minutes, then got off and pushed, where the street suddenly became steeper, for another five minutes. That brought me to the foot of a very steep flight of granite steps: ninety-one steps in all, as I painfully counted them the first few times.

Most of the foreigners preferred to stay in the Foreign Teachers Guest House, where they not only were closer to the classroom buildings but also had maid service and telephones and a dining hall. But a few of us chose to live in apartments and do our own shopping and housekeeping.

It took me about a week to be able to come up those steps without stopping for breath halfway, and without gasping at the top, but soon I was quite casual about it—as I was about the five flights of stairs to my classroom in the new Foreign Languages Building, and the seven flights I climbed to visit my students in their new dorm. (No elevators in these buildings.)

And how could I have complained, anyhow, when I saw the old retired people who lived in *Ling Feng* coming up those ninety-one steps with loads of groceries, who never paused or stopped chattering to each other and never out of breath? And I know why, when the university offered to move some of those old people to the new apartments down on the beach road, they refused to go. *Ling Feng* is special. We all feel that, up there, and it gives us a bond which made it easy for me to make friends among my neighbours.

The first family I became acquainted with was the Wangs, who lived two floors above me. They were the only people in China, I think, who did not know how to hang clothes on horizontal bamboo poles: theirs kept falling off and I'd find a quilt on my doorstep or the baby's diaper-cloths in the garden. I hung them on the clothesline in my garden, and sooner or later one of the Wangs would come for them and we'd get into a conversation. Next door to me lived Professor He and his wife. He is a professor of fish research, specializing in what colours will attract what species of fish. He's also a famous collector of stamps. His collection fills one room of their apartment, and includes, he boasts, almost every stamp ever issued by the USSR, and an almost complete collection of Chinese stamps, and, since his field is fish research, a wonderful collection of stamps with pictures of fish, from dozens of countries. Professor He reads English with no problem, but his spoken English consists of a few phrases. He practiced these phrases on me every day with enthusiasm. His wife, a modest and retiring woman, kept an eye on me and shyly brought me cooked dishes (not quite believing a man could cook for himself), and urged me to use their washing machine. Good people, and good neighbours.

My apartment was on the ground floor of a five-floor building. I had a small porch and a flower garden to hoe and weed in. I was shaded by a huge Longing-for-Her-Lover tree, with leaves the shape of the eyebrows of the classical Chinese beauty, and small golden buttons of flowers which are said to resemble her tears. There was also a flowering peach tree, a pomegranate, a papaya, and against a wall twelve-foot-high clumps of poinsettias (which grow wild here), and a bush called *ye lai xiang*, or "Night Comes Fragrant", which lived up to its name.

Behind us was the forest, and above that the granite crags of *Wulao Shan*, or "Five Old Men Peaks". There were many birds, though I never learned their names because my neighbours and students didn't know, either. Their songs mingled with the sound of little kids' voices from the kindergarten near the foot of those ninety-one steps.

The air was a pleasure to breathe, for this is one of the few places I've been in China with unpolluted air. There was the scent of the ocean in it, and of the forest behind us and the flowers which are everywhere in Xiamen.

But what people who visited me exclaimed about, after catching their breaths, was the view. *Ling Feng* overlooks the campus of Xiamen University, which is built on the slope from the peaks to the ocean. The campus is shaded by banyan trees and eucalyptus trees and *mumian shu*, or kapok trees, (with their strange, fleshy, red flowers) and palm trees and lichee trees and longyan trees, interspersed with banana plants and beds of flowers. Among the trees are glimpses of the old campus buildings, of soft red brick with upturned eaves in the old style, and downhill from them the landscaped park with a pretty pond, and beyond that the square new classroom buildings, then a row of old buildings and the athletic field, and then the campus swimming beach on the ocean.

My view was down across this campus, and across a wide stretch of water which is the entrance to Xiamen harbour, the open ocean to my left and the harbour out of sight to my right. Many ships came and went, from new container ships to old junks, and there were always about fifty small fishing boats anchored here and there. Beyond that were the harbour islands, then the mountains of the mainland, behind which I watched the setting sun.

You can see why I usually brought out my meals and ate on the little patio. And I could do this through the winter months, too, because there is no winter in Xiamen. Oh, they call it winter and complain about the cold, but it never comes close to freezing and there are always birds and flowers.

That day in February, as I sat drinking tea, I had a sudden insight. Not very deep or unusual, I guess; everybody must experience it. It struck me that we see things in an oddly contradictory way. For one thing, this was a solid scene, which could be caught in paint or by photograph. It had a solid sensory reality. As I sat there, I felt outside of time, as if all this had always been here and always would be. But at the same time I had a deep sense of the fact that nothing in this world is timeless. Everything is always changing, flowing, in flux, even these solid granite hills.

I started thinking that way because I realized that in spite of my comfortable feeling of timelessness almost everything I could see from that hill represented changes which even I had seen in my brief time in China, or lay before me saturated in a history of which even I, a stranger, had been made aware.

The most obvious change was the number of new buildings since I taught classes here eight years ago. A little to the right, down near the ocean, I can see a row of old two-storey buildings. I know they are quietly sinking into the ground, their floors sometimes invaded by seeping water. There, eight years ago, was the office of the Foreign Languages Department, the classrooms of which were scattered among several buildings. Now, directly in front of me, mirrored in the central pond, is a big five-storey building, in the box-like modern style, which is the new Foreign Languages Building. Near it are the new chemistry and physics buildings, and the new library. In the mid-distance, this side of the pond, a huge new building is going up which will be both a hotel and the new "Guest House" for foreign teachers. (Remind me to stay out of that!)

To the left, overlooking the beach, is the new graduate women's dorm, seven stories high, intelligently designed with the open-air corridors and stairways all on the landward side. The ocean side is all windows, and every room in this dorm has incredible views of the ocean and islands, and lovely sea breezes in Xiamen's hot summers.

Nearby is the new beachside residential area where a number of my friends have new apartments. Even the *Ling Feng* buildings up here on the hill are all new since I was here before.

If you scramble up over the Five Old Men Peaks behind us, you come on the other side to a wonderful large botanical garden, both a park and a research institute. Here new restaurants, new pagodas, new display buildings are all going up. Looking downhill from the botanical gardens you see the crowded city centre, with at least a dozen sets of cranes and scaffolds where new high-rise buildings, including four international hotels, are rising like mushrooms. Beyond the city, beside the harbour, is the new Huli Development Area, in which you can smell the wet cement as buildings rise on all sides even before the streets are paved.

In 1982, to get to Xiamen from Beijing, I had to fly to Shanghai, overnight there, then take a thirty-hour train ride looping through the mountains before reaching Xiamen. This time, eight years later, I flew from Beijing two hours to the new Xiamen airport. As we came in for a landing I looked down on rows of new factories like a set of Monopoly, where eight years before I had visited a prosperous commune farm.

As for the harbour, the big container ships I can see from my porch remind me that the harbour facilities are now three times as large as they were then, and still expanding.

All over China I've seen the cranes and scaffolds of new construction, but never so frantic as here. There's a story behind that.

For many years Fujian Province was getting the least development money of any part of China. And *that's* because back then this was a sensitive military zone and nobody wanted to develop an area that might at any moment be smashed by an invasion from Taiwan.

When I was here in 1982 I could hear the cannon practicing in the mountains at night. There were signs in many places, in Chinese, Russian, and English: "No foreigners permitted past this point!" No foreigners were allowed on the beach at night, and no cameras at any time. The only time I have met hostility in Xiamen was once when I was photographing some old buildings near the shore and people thought I was sneaking pictures of the beach area.

Not all of this was hysteria. My students showed me where the last Nationalist shell fell on Xiamen University in 1979, thirty years after the general cessation of hostilities. In the hills above us are many solid, ugly concrete pillboxes with machinegun slits, many of which have bullet scars on the outside. There's a similar pillbox just inside the main gate of the campus

And once when I was able to get tacit permission to go past the "No Foreigners" sign with a Chinese friend and bicycle along the coast for about ten kilometres, we passed many pillboxes carved right out of the cliff beside the road, and we stopped at a fortified beach with landing-boat traps in the water and anti-tank traps and lines of barbed wire on the beach, and looked across the water at the island of Da Dan, still held by the Nationalists. There was a military airport there, my friend said, from which warplanes could be over Xiamen in less than a minute. We saw no planes, but we heard incessant loudspeakers from there. I asked my friend to translate, since the speakers were using the local *Minnan* language, not Mandarin. They were saying that the Communist leaders in Beijing were drunkards and womanizers, living in decadence while ordinary people worked hard for little food, but that on Taiwan everybody had a good job, a house, an automobile, and complete freedom of speech. (That last was ironic, since on that same day the editor of the only opposition newspaper had been arrested.) The program ended with a shout: "Thank you, Guomindang, for leading us into the future!"

I wondered what effect this propaganda was having on the local peasants, but they probably tuned it out after a while. And I was amused to see that they had stolen strands of the barbed wire from the beach to hold up their grapevines.

Back in 1949, of course, such things had been no joke. Here in Xiamen there had been ferocious fighting as the Communist armies tried to smash the last of the Nationalist forces, and the Nationalists fought a rearguard action to protect their evacuation as Chiang Kaishek's army, defeated on the mainland, retreated to Taiwan. The Communist forces might have gone on to take Taiwan and finish the job, but US President Truman sent the US Seventh Fleet into the Taiwan Straits to protect Chiang.

In an odd way it was appropriate that the last battle between the Communists and the Nationalists should have been fought here. In the mountains of western Fujian and neighbouring Jiangxi, in the 1920s and 1930s the Communists built some of their strongest bases. Chiang, with his airforce and heavy equipment and foreign advisers, routed them from there, and it was from there that the Communists began the famous Long March, all the way west to the borders of Tibet, then all the way north to the mountains of Ningxia, harassed by Chiang's army and warplanes all the way. Things came full circle here in Fujian Province at the end of the 1945-1949 Civil War, when the

Communist armies forced Chiang and the remnants of his armies to flee from here to Taiwan.

For years after that it was the policy of the Communists that they must take Taiwan, and it was the policy of Chiang that there would certainly be an anti-Communist uprising on the mainland if he could just stage a convincing invasion. The Communists periodically shelled the Nationalist islands near the mainland, and the Nationalists shelled Fujian Province.

Now both sides have quietly decided that there can be no military solution. The mainland Chinese are hoping for a peaceful reunion. There's a billboard by the beach road showing a woman and a girl holding their arms out to each other, with a body of water separating them, and the slogan "Let her come home!"

And now that the military threat is apparently over, the Chinese government has decided it's safe to invest in Fujian and the whole province is buzzing to make up for lost time. Xiamen has been declared a New Economic Zone with the power to deal directly with foreign investors, and is booming, largely with money from Taiwanese.

The military pillbox just inside the campus gate is now hidden by banks of flowers.

Other things I notice from my hillside reflect changes in ideology. The most obvious is that pond and the flowery park around it where students lie on the grass and read or talk or flirt before going to class. None of that was there eight years ago. It *had* been there in the 1950s, I'm told, but during the Cultural Revolution it was embarrassing, being a frivolous waste of productive space. Peasants moved in from the countryside, drained the pond, and turned the whole area into farm fields. About fifteen years later, in 1982, I saw them working those fields as I went to my classes. It took many years for the university to persuade the peasants to let them have the area back. You couldn't just chase peasants off their fields; it could be done only by promising many of them jobs. (*An aside*: That's why our mail delivery is all bollixed up. Several of the peasants got jobs in the university post office, and since they know no English and most are illiterate in any language, mail often goes to the wrong places.)

If I look down to the right, in the mid-distance I see the main gate, overtopped by phoenix trees with bright red flowers. Just outside that gate is an area where the buses from the city end their run, an area which is also the entrance to the internationally famous *Nanputuo* Buddhist temple. In 1982 some people set up a fruit stand in that area, selling fruit which they had bought in town. A theoretical controversy was raging: were these people performing a needed social service by making fruit available, or were they rotten capitalist roaders making profits just by moving fruit from one place to another? Also, on special religious days vendors set up tables along the road to the temple, selling incense sticks, paper money to burn for the dead, and religious souvenirs. Everyone was uneasy about this, too, and when I started to photograph them there was a shout and the vendors all turned their backs to me.

Today, there are many such fruit stands, and alongside the street is a row of new small buildings owned by the university but leased to stores selling groceries, household goods, antiques, and computer software, and a dozen little restaurants of all levels of price and cuisine. There are many people selling religious things every day on the road to the temple, and they'll let you photograph them—though they may ask you to pay for the privilege. Business is booming everywhere, and nobody worries about its ideological implications any more.

But I, old grump that I am, find myself thinking about the trade-off. The new prosperity is obvious, and mostly admirable.

When I criticize, remember that I'm delighted by the rise in living standards. And I greatly enjoy eating lunch in one of those small restaurants, the "Shandong Jiaozi", where I sit at a sidewalk table and watch the people go by or look up the hill at the upturned eaves of the new temple buildings among the trees. A smart youngster brings me my lunch with a smile. (She knows what I want: ten steamed *jiaozi* and ten fried *jiaozi*, and lots of soy sauce.) If she's not too busy she asks me about life in Canada. It's very pleasant.

But society has paid a price. If people are not concerned with ideology, is that necessarily a blessing? Nobody seems to question anything as long as it makes money.

Nobody seems to notice that the type of person the new commercialism encourages is the brash newly rich young men with leather jackets and long sideburns who roar up on their motorcycles to see how their stores are doing and swagger and spit on the floor and boss the help around. Nobody seems to notice that the help, especially in the restaurants, includes a lot of girls who ought to be in school.

In the little free market down a side street, where I buy "sesame flower" buns for breakfast, everything is put into flimsy plastic bags now, instead of the customers' shopping bags. Nobody seems to notice how the plastic litter is piling up everywhere.

In the centre of town there are expensive restaurants where ordinary people can't afford to go. Most of them would be fearful of even trying to walk through the doors of such places. There you see the new rich of China showing off. In the "old days" of a few years ago, everyone I knew took lunchboxes when they went to a restaurant, to bring home leftovers, but the new style is to order more than you can eat and mess it around and walk away from it, to show how rich you are.

One of my Xiamen students, herself a teacher in a workers' evening school, told me that she went to have her hair done in a downtown beauty parlour and found herself attended by the owner. She got talking to this woman, who said, "I come from a poor family in the hills. We didn't even have any shoes when we were kids. At fourteen I came to town and worked as a maid with a family that treated me very badly. Then I got a job in a beauty parlour and found out I have a real knack for doing hair. So I started my own business, and worked mighty hard at it, until now it's the biggest one in Xiamen."

My student asked how much she was making, which is a perfectly polite question in China. The hairdresser said, "Five thousand a month." That was a shocker, at a time when the average factory worker was making between one and two thousand yuan a *year*. My student said, "That's wrong! I'm a teacher, which is more useful to society than hairdressing, and I make 250 a month."

"Well," the woman replied, "you're an intellectual. You have books and intellectual friends, and ideas. Me, I have nothing but money. Without money I'm nobody. Because I have money, my husband doesn't dare raise a fist to me. Because I have money I can walk into any restaurant in town and they come running to welcome me. Without money, I'm *nothing*!"

As my student says, the woman has a point. But the huge spread in income is a huge problem, which the government refuses to see as a problem. Such people are "pioneers", Deng Xiaoping says, leading the whole country into prosperity.

Well, maybe. But I note that in Shenzhen, the first New Economic Zone, the most prosperous area of China these days, Chinese money is not accepted—even Chinese people must have Hong Kong or American dollars. For Chinese people to dress in Chinese style clothes or wear their hair in Chinese style makes them a laughing stock. And smuggling, prostitution, gambling, economic crime are, the newspapers say, "rampant".

The beach road which I can see from up here on *Ling Feng* leads along the shore around the central mass of hills into the city. I used to bicycle slowly along there just to enjoy the scene. It was a sleepy narrow road, with lots to see. Just outside the university is a hospital where I go for acupuncture. You might see a group of people by the door, but you couldn't tell by looking at them which are doctors, or nurses, or orderlies—they all wear the same white medical gowns and caps. They all come to work on bicycles, too.

Beyond that I come to big logs laid out beside the road, some of them four feet in diameter. Girls from the Hui'an commune up the coast are cutting them into planks with long two-person saws. These girls, about fourteen to eighteen years old, come to work in the city, giving half their wages to the commune and keeping the rest for their dowry. They all wear the same kind of wide-brimmed straw hat, fastened on tightly, and pretty long-sleeved shirts that are so short they show a three-inch band of bare waist, and wide blue pants, and sandals. They stick together and want nothing to do with city ways. They won't talk to me, and they are fiercely determined not to be photographed—they'll down tools and go away if you persist. They do a lot of the heaviest construction work in Xiamen, carrying enormous loads on carrying-poles.

When the Nanputuo temple built new pagodas and altars among the trees on its steep hillside, I saw Hui'an girls coming up the steep paths with loads of bricks and cement on their carrying poles—loads I couldn't even pick up. (I tried!) I think of these girls when people tell me women can't do heavy work.

The planks these girls were cutting beside the road were for the shipyard I come to next, where on three slips traditional wooden junks are being made. Next I come to the stonecutters' yard, where workers cut tombstones for export and the Hui'an girls, in pairs, carry heavy blocks of stone slung from a pole, the stone swinging perilously close to their sandalled feet.

Xiamen Island is really just a big chunk of granite with a thin overlay of soil, and the sound of hammers on granite is everywhere. In Xiamen they make chicken-coops and toolsheds of granite, and long fences are made by setting hand-chiselled granite posts tightly side by side. Bicycling along the road, you often see a group of young boys, each squatting on a granite block and reaching down below his feet to "face", or finish, the surface with his hammer.

Beyond the stonecutters' yard I come to a small harbour where the fishing boats come in at high tide and slump on their sides in the mud at low tide. Beyond that, it's the ropewalk, where rope is made. Sometimes they have a job too big for their long shed, so they lay the strands for three or four blocks along the street and tie the end to a lamppost and use their hand-power machine to twist them together, while people patiently step over or lift their bikes over.

Then there are blocks of little stores, and apartment buildings three floors high, the top two stories jutting out to make arcades of the sidewalks. (Sidewalks themselves are a rare sight in China outside of big cities.) In the shade of the arcades people live a large part of their lives outdoors: women washing their babies in tubs of water; little kids sitting on the curb eating, the bowls close to their faces and their eyes staring over the bowls at the passing foreigner; old men sitting on stools smoking long-stemmed pipes; a group of girls sorting red peppers and chatting in high voices; women scrubbing clothes on granite scrubbing-boards built right into the curbs (which are also granite), an old woman splitting firewood with a cleaver.

There's a fine little free market further along this road, taking up the space so completely that you must get off your bike and push it slowly through the crowd. There, all kinds of foods and handicrafts are set out on tables or just on cloths on the road. There the teahouse man wanders, with his portable teahouse: a carrying pole with a little table at one end already set with cups, and at the other end a steaming kettle. He'll set the table down anywhere you want to squat by it and drink. Sometimes there's a crowd around a man with a performing monkey. Sometimes a class of little schoolchildren, their faces made up like actors, sing to the crowd to celebrate some holiday or the end of a school term.

Beyond all this I come to a row of factories from which long lines of carters strain to pull loads of soy sauce, canned lichees, and other such products down to the harbour. Where the road rises abruptly to cross some railroad tracks, the carters take turns helping each other get the heavy loads up the steep place.

I come to the harbour finally, at the centre of town, where freighters are moored right alongside the street to receive the goods from the factories. I used to stand watching the busy water traffic of ships and ferries and little sculled boats darting around like waterbugs.

And what has all this to do with the subject of trade-offs? Well, you see, it's all gone now. The hospital is still there, I mean, and the stonecutters and the shipyard, though the shipyard is making metal ships now, not wooden junks. But all the rest is gone. Recently I bicycled along that street for old times' sake, but now it's heavy truck traffic, almost bumper to bumper. The exhaust fumes are dreadful, and there's no room or peace or breathable air for the activities that made the old street so fascinating. The people are presumably staying indoors. The free market and the ropewalk have gone elsewhere. If you bicycle along that road now you must keep your eye on the traffic every second; there's no time to look at things—and nothing left to look at along there anyhow.

There are big changes, too, where that road ends in the city centre, where Zhongshan Lu, Xiamen's main street, comes down to the water. Eight years ago, if you turned up Zhongshan Lu you'd find several blocks of sleepy stores, with various kinds of goods. People sometimes followed the old foreigner into stores then, to see what I would buy, and sometimes an old Chinese man or woman would astonish the bystanders by talking to me in rusty half-forgotten English, learned in the missionary schools long ago. Now the scene is almost unrecognizable: the blare of ghetto-blasters from the new music stores, the bleating of horns from buses and taxis, the brash young men who shout at me in English, "Hello! Change-a money!"—openly working the black market in currency; the rush of people in and out of the new department store, the billboards and other advertisements everywhere—it's all different. I swear to you that the people are even walking faster along the street.

Another casualty of modernization is the sounds of street peddlers I used to hear, on campus and off. In 1982 I used to listen for them. The earliest each morning was the milkman, pedaling his flat-bed tricycle stacked with crates of bottled milk. He blew a whistle to alert his customers and they came running out of apartment buildings and dormitories carrying jugs or bowls. They didn't get the bottles, you see; the milkman poured the milk into their bowls and kept the bottles. The soy sauce man, with a large jar of sauce at each end of his carrying-pole, used to come shouting his wares. The pots and pans mender announced his coming by clashing strips of metal. The popped-rice man with his firepot, the knife-sharpener, the rags and bottles man, all came with their loud chants. Down among the new apartments by the shore a young fisherman came dripping from the ocean carrying his casting net and a basket of fish, shouting, "Buy fish ah!" and peasants with loads of rice called out "Trade for rice ah!" offering to trade the new crop of rice (which they could legally sell only to the State) for ration coupons. Almost all of them are gone now, as people prefer to buy what they need in the new private-enterprise stores.

Another thing I miss is the big signs that used to be prominent on every athletic field, saying "Friendship first! Competition second!" Why did they have to take those down?

My students sometimes accuse me of being an old fuddy-duddy in love with the past. (They don't put it that bluntly, of course.) I plead "guilty with extenuating circumstances." I really have trouble sorting out my own feelings. Certainly trucks are better than carters straining frantically to pull heavy loads. Certainly the new apartment buildings, the new university library, the new student dorms, like the new availability of food, clothes, and so on, are all very good things. I wouldn't deny any of that.

But I do miss some of the old ways, yes. More important, I do worry sometimes about the price society pays for these good things, and wonder whether that price was necessary.

All this while I'm sitting on my hillside sipping Fujian tea and thinking about these things, remember? And speaking of good new things, there's that fine new graduate women students' dorm down there on the left. A lot of implications suggested by that seven-storey building. Plain history, for one thing, because that new dorm's dining hall replaces a dismal one. I eat there frequently with my students, both for their company and for the food. I stand in line and get my noodles or rice and then have my choice of over twenty dishes, of meats and vegetables, all fresh and well-cooked. Imagine that! My students complain about the food, and I tell them that's an inalienable right of students everywhere but they should count their blessings.

This class of second-year graduate students in 1990 consisted of twelve students, eleven of whom were women. They were excellent students, one of the best classes I've had the pleasure of teaching anywhere. As often happens with my best Chinese students, they were full of energy and eager to be friends, without any sense of apple-polishing.

When I moved into this apartment on the hill from the Foreign Teachers Guest House, they came to help, and when the truck was late in coming they just picked up my suitcases and boxes of books and carried them, coming chattering up those steep stairs like a flock of cheerful birds. Before I knew it they were washing the windows of my apartment, moving the furniture around, checking the stove, making the bed, hanging the mosquito net. Later, every now and then they'd come up the hill and we'd have a feast in my apartment, when the lone male, an excellent cook, came into his own.

At Mid-Autumn Moon Festival, we all went down to the beach in the evening and dug holes in the sand to put candles where the wind wouldn't blow them out, and ate mooncakes and watched the huge full moon rise slowly out of the ocean, and talked about our homes. Another time, we spent a very long day bicycling all the way around Xiamen Island (the "No Foreigners" signs are all gone now), stopping off at fishing villages along the way.

Have I mentioned the fact that they were also excellent students, bright, eager, hard-working?

Do you wonder that I miss China?

But paradoxically enough these excellent students represent a crisis in Xiamen and in most other Chinese universities.

It's connected to the economic boom, which is at its most intense here in Xiamen. I've just read that Fujian, Guangdong, and Hainan Provinces together make up the fastest-growing economic area in the world. These are the New Economic Zones which are the pride of Deng Xiaoping. In March 1992, at the age of eighty-seven and in very poor health, Deng would come out of retirement to come here and make a speech urging that the economic reforms must proceed even faster. (We assume he did that to head off the old guard who since Tiananmen have been trying to slow down or reverse this development.)

How does all that affect the universities? Well, the universities are no longer the only road to advancement. A competent and enterprising young man who is fluent in English can get a job with one of the hundreds of new foreign companies, with the excitement of being "on the growing edge" of things, with a far larger salary than any university professor's and chances of rising in the company as it expands.

So fewer and fewer of the best young men are coming to the university. Of those who do, fewer and fewer stay on to be graduate students and opt for an academic career. The fact that I'm saying "men" here is accurate reporting: everybody wants men in the new companies, not women—or women only in subordinate positions. So it's the men, the best qualified men, who are missing now in the universities.

The women, having fewer outside opportunities, are more likely to stay on as graduate students. That means, of course, that more and more of the top students in my classes are women. The men students tend to come in two kinds: those few great students who have a real calling for scholarship, and incompetents who couldn't make it in the marketplace but hope that by sticking out the MA program they can go out and try their luck again.

Even from Beijing University, that Mecca of academics, the absolute tops in China, a Chinese friend writes me, "The most brilliant students do not go on to graduate schools these days."

Xiamen, here where the economic boom is frantic, is having trouble finding enough graduate students to keep the system going. So they are lowering admission standards, and for the Foreign Languages Department, where women outnumber men, they are lowering admission standards for men even more. (I suggested to a vice-president that in science and engineering, where men outnumber women, the women's exam should be easier, but he thought I was joking.)

One result of these trends fascinates me. That is, that girls from the countryside who are smart and capable and are lucky enough to have good schools now stand a better chance of getting into university. Half of my great class came from the countryside, and four of them were the first people from their counties (of either sex) ever to get to university graduate school.

For some reason the same doesn't seem to be true of men from the countryside. I think perhaps new economic possibilities in the countryside give them more options at home than the women have. In any case, a number of the men who come to Xiamen from the countryside are very low in academic achievement and in incentive. They come not because they want the education but in hopes that an MA will let them achieve their one overriding objective: never to go back to the countryside again. They never flunk out of the university. Nobody does. I have failed some of them, in more than one university, and have discovered that their grades were changed as soon as I have left. One of the ironies of Chinese universities is that although factory workers have lost their "iron rice bowls", that is, guaranteed employment, students have kept theirs, so poor students and good get shoved up the line together. I know no more depressing fact about Chinese universities than this. And I feel very fortunate that almost all the students in almost all my classes have been eager and hardworking and competent.

Well, you see why I sit here and look down at that new dorm building and think with pride of my class, and still am reminded by them that universities in China are in crisis.

My thoughts don't often turn to such troubling things when I sit and drink tea or eat a meal on my porch. Most of the time, the feeling of this place is peace. That's one reason I like it so much.

And yet, you know, even this place has its ups and downs. Not every day gives me a clear view of the ships or the mountains beyond. Some days are quite foggy down there on the water. And there have been some days when I wouldn't have wanted to sit here at all. In 1990, I came here in August, coming early to teach a short summer class before the regular semester. That's typhoon season in these parts, and before the middle of September we had been hit by six typhoons. Fortunately (for us), the island of Taiwan takes the brunt of the storms, shielding Xiamen from severe damage, but we got rain, in all-day downpours heavier than anything I had ever imagined, and very strong winds.

And heaven knows Xiamen has had its share of the social equivalent of typhoons. The name *Xia Men* means "Gateway to China", or "China's door". (The old name *Amoy*, I'm told, means the same in the local Minnan language.) It suggests two functions that were very important for centuries: to open the door to trade, and to close the door to the pirates who terrorized this coast.

By the time Marco Polo came to Fujian in the 13th Century, the province was booming with trade, especially with the Arab countries but even down the east coast of Africa. The city of Quanzhou, up the coast from Xiamen, which Marco Polo knew as *Zaitan*, was one of the world's great trading ports. Marco tells us (though you must not put too much faith in his numbers) that there were over a hundred thousand Arab traders based there.

The trade, and the fisheries, were under the protection of a goddess, Mazu, who is still honoured here and in Taiwan. When I first managed to get past the "No Foreigners" signs in 1982, my companion and I stopped at an outdoor festival in her honour. Her bronze statue was petitioned by means of prayers written on cloth streamers and hung up before her altar, and peasants were taking vegetables and other food from their bags, passing them back and forth in the incense smoke while muttering prayers, and putting them back in their bags.

In 1990, on my bike ride around the island with my students, we came to a small temple overlooking a beach where fishing boats come in. The temple was open to the east, to the ocean and the sunrise, and the fishermen told us it was the temple of the Goddess of the Sea, that is, Mazu.

One reason Mazu fascinates me is that she is so similar to the Mayan goddess Ix Chel, whose temples, also open to the sea and the sunrise, I found on the island of Cosumel, in Mexico. In both cases, the goddess, in contrast to her male counterparts, was peaceful. And I suspect that Mazu, like Ix Chel, is goddess not only of the sea, and of peaceful trade, but also of fertility and thus of farming and of childbirth.

In the 17th Century, a local warlord named Koxinga (Zhen Chengong) ruled the Xiamen area. He is remembered as a hero, and there are statues and a museum in his honour on Xiamen's Gulanyu Island. His claim to fame is that he took a fleet to Taiwan and drove out the Dutch, and held the island as a last bastion for the overthrown Ming emperor. His recent acclaim was at its height when the Chinese took it for granted that they must capture Taiwan from the Nationalists; it seems to have dwindled now that the idea of military conquest has been shelved.

In the 19th Century Xiamen was one of the treaty ports forced upon China in the Opium Wars with Great Britain. Then, Gulanyu Island, in Xiamen's harbour, was reserved for the foreigners. No Chinese were permitted to live there (though they could come and work there by day as servants to the invaders.) Now, Gulanyu is a peaceful and attractive resort area, where no motor vehicles or horsecarts or bicycles are permitted. Its restaurants are fashionable places for expensive, noisy wedding banquets. Its beautiful beaches are very popular. So is its Sunlight Rock, the high point of the island, from which you get spectacular views of Xiamen and the harbour islands and the ocean—and, nearer at hand, some of the old foreign buildings, solid buildings which those foreigners must have expected would be theirs for centuries.

In 1938, the Japanese army stormed ashore, and occupied Xiamen brutally for seven years. There is still a roadway from the university through the hills to Xiamen City, paved with blocks of granite by conscript labour—the old Japanese military road.

From 1945 through 1948, Chiang Kaishek's Nationalist army held Xiamen, until they were driven out in savage fighting by the Communists.

So—this peaceful scene from my hillside apartment has not always been peaceful!

There have been pleasanter moments in Xiamen's history. One that I like is the story of Tan Kah Kee, who in the late 19th Century emigrated from Xiamen to South-east Asia and thus became a *huaqiao*, or overseas Chinese. Many thousands of others had done that, all the way back to the 16th Century, but Tan Kah Kee was special.

The overseas Chinese have kept up the tradition of "once Chinese, always Chinese." Over the centuries, many of them have sent back money and most of them seem to have dreamed of coming home with a fortune. Of course, most of them never made a fortune. Hundreds of them died, for one example, building the railroads in the United States. But those few who did make good came home in triumph, if only for short visits. So *huaqiao*, in the minds of most Chinese, means a wealthy person who comes back with lots of money and expensive presents and word of how much better life is anywhere else but China.

Many come back to Fujian Province to swagger and show off. You see pictures of them in the newspapers, in their poverty-stricken home villages, sitting like kings surrounded by awe-struck peasants. (Their example is embarrassing for those who come back from abroad without a lot of money. Some of my friends in Canada, students from Fujian who are completing their studies, are worried about going home because they can't possibly afford the presents they know families and friends will expect.)

But it would be unfair to leave it at that. Many other overseas Chinese have used their good fortune to help China. There's an "Overseas Kindergarten" in Xiamen, a model school, open to all the children of the area but financed by overseas Chinese. Overseas Chinese have funded many businesses in Xiamen, and many have come home to Fujian to retire.

But of all the *huaqiao*, my favourite is Tan Kah Kee. He made a fortune in rubber and brought back his wealth to do something for his country. And he knew what the country needed. In 1920, he bought this picturesque hillside I overlook, and he built Xiamen University on it.

They tell me he was a strong-willed man, who oversaw every detail of the construction of his university, snooping around to see that each mason was doing his job properly. The pleasant old dormitories on campus, of soft red brick, with up-turned eaves, are his buildings.

When the university was built, he turned it over to the government. Then he went to Jimei, on the mainland nearest Xiamen Island, and there built primary schools, high schools, and seven specialized research institutes.

He also designed his own memorial, the column of which is a landmark in Jimei. He decided what decorations should be around the base of the column: encircling rows of pictures carved in stone, which are an encyclopedia of general knowledge. Here are dozens of plants, with their names and uses. The same with animals. The same for various machines and inventions. The same for various occupations of mankind. On the base of the column itself are stone pictures teaching children good behavior: how to brush their teeth, how to make their beds, how to have good posture, how to eat properly, even how to use the toilet.

He spent his whole fortune this way, then lived a very simple life for twenty years.

They say he was a crusty old character, and hard to get along with. I try not to think of the rubber workers on whose backs he accumulated his fortune. But for what he did with that fortune he has my admiration. It's not everybody in this world who dedicates his success to the enrichment of society.

A different kind of thing I remember Xiamen for is the food. Southern Chinese pay a lot more attention to their food than northerners, and the climate indulges them in this. In Xiamen there are always fresh vegetables in the market, and the fruits come into season in succession: bananas, lichees, longyans, persimmons, sweet little pineapples, papayas, tangerines, jackfruit (*boluomi,* literally "pineapple honey.") Xiamen is, understandably, a favourite place for northerners to hold conventions during the winter. (That's one reason for the big hotel going up down there in mid-campus). When the northerners leave for home, they carry large net bags bulging with Xiamen fruit.

There are always fresh fish, of many kinds, and Xiamen is famous for delicious tiny oysters, as big as the end joint of your little finger. And there are razor clams, and shrimp—oh, many kinds of seafood, all fresh.

There are very few chickens here, but many ducks, and the local people know how to cook them to perfection. And they like duck eggs: if you go to the market looking for eggs you'll have to look hard among all the duck eggs to find anyone selling chicken eggs.

Two of my favourite dishes in Xiamen: First, what they call *hailijian*, or fried oyster patties. Start with those tiny fresh oysters, add sweet-potato flour, fry them until almost done, then stir in a couple of eggs and a chopped-up aromatic local green vegetable, push them into patties, and serve them piping hot. Wonderful!

Second, there's a dish they call *chunjuan*, or "spring roll", which is different from spring rolls anywhere else. They bring the ingredients to the table and you make your own. Start with a thin crepe. Add some plum sauce. Pile up on it a chopped, cooked mixture of shrimp, oysters, and many other fine things. Add two kinds of seaweed fried crisp. Roll it up, tuck in the ends. Devour. Oh, my goodness! Don't get me going on Chinese food!

Another thing southern Chinese love more than northerners do is fireworks. I don't mean the kind governments use in great public displays. I'm thinking of the delight with which the southerners use firecrackers. The opening of a new building, or even the completion of one storey of a building, is announced by firecrackers. The start of a wedding feast is announced by a wild burst of firecrackers outside the door of the restaurant, and the end of the feast by another.

As far as possible, people plan their weddings to fall on auspicious days. One year there was a day on which the numbers of day, month, year, in both the solar calendar and the old lunar calendar, added up to lucky numbers. There were so many weddings that day, and so many firecrackers, that next morning the streets were littered with the paper remains.

On holidays, too, firecrackers are heard everywhere. The Chinese have far fewer holidays than Westerners, and they work six days a week, so when a holiday comes it is enthusiastically celebrated. Recently, they have taken over the idea of Christmas, on the excuse that they don't want foreigners to feel homesick. It's not religious with them—it's an excuse for a big party. At Christmas in 1990, I was persuaded by one of my students to join him in an act at the Christmas party—a comic dialogue in Chinese. *That* kind of party.

Chinese New Year is tied to the lunar calendar, like our Easter. Their traditional year begins some time in February or March with Spring Festival, a sort of combination of Thanksgiving, Christmas, New Year and Easter rolled into one— by far the most important Chinese holiday. It's a family holiday, and everyone who can possibly make it home for the big day (and the big family dinner) gets there. The trains and buses are jammed—one of my friends spent three days and nights standing up in a crowded train to get home for Spring Festival.

The week before, everybody is busy cleaning house. The wives are scrubbing, throwing out rubbish, washing walls. The husbands are washing windows. The daughters are airing out quilts and mattresses. Teenage sons are sneaking away to get out of work. Everyone goes to the stores and buys new clothes and lots of presents and a huge supply of food.

The first day is at-home family day. The second day, traditionally, is for visiting the husband's parents, the third day visiting the wife's parents, and thereafter several days for visiting friends and colleagues. People came up my hill dressed as if for a royal ball and loaded with presents, to visit the retired people here on *Ling Feng*.

I'm remembering one solar New Year—I mean January first—the first one I spent up here on the hill. All through the year children and adults alike had been saving pennies and getting in stocks of firecrackers. I sat on my porch waiting for midnight, but even so I was unprepared. At exactly midnight, every person in Xiamen, it seemed, set off strings of firecrackers all together. The smell and smoke of gunpowder came rolling up the hill.

I took it as a whopping affirmation: We may have problems, but we're still here, and don't you forget it! Bang! Bang! Bang! Bang!

8

Places: Ningxia

In the spring of 1983, while I was teaching at Nankai, came an invitation from Ningxia University, in the Ningxia Hui Autonomous Region, to give a survey course in American literature during the summer.

That was exciting to me for many reasons. Ningxia is on the edge of the Gobi Desert, in China's north-west, an area I had not yet seen. The Hui are a large ethnic group, scattered throughout eastern China, but in Ningxia they are so numerous and concentrated that they have their own Autonomous Region, on a par with the provinces. They are Muslims, and I hadn't visited a Muslim area. Ningxia was then a closed area, not open to foreigners except those with work permits, so it might be untouched by the newness, and I wanted to see as much of old China as possible while it was still there. And it was said to be one of the poorest areas in China, so it would certainly be beyond the showplaces China wants tourists to see.

My Nankai students didn't want me to go. Like most Chinese, they were quite ignorant about what life is like in other parts of China. Until recently, Chinese people didn't travel. There were exceptions, of course: some of my students had traveled during the Cultural Revolution as Red Guards with free passes on the railroads; a generation of young people had been sent to the countryside to work during the late 1960s and early 1970s, though they saw only the locality they were sent to; university students saw only the areas of the universities that had admitted them. Chinese government officials, like those elsewhere, love to go to pleasant places for conferences, so they probably traveled most.

But the mass of people were ignorant of anything but their own small region. That's changing now, as television shows them the world (superficially, of course) and the most audacious young women even as far away as Lhasa imitate the latest fashions of Beijing. Newlyweds are beginning to take honeymoon trips and come back with lots of colour photos. And more and more people are moving around on business, or looking for work, or just staying ahead of the police. But in "the old days" of a few years ago, my students shared the general ignorance of their own country. They worried about me. There would be sand storms, they said. In that poor area there would not be enough for me to eat. Living accommodations would be crude, and the people uncouth.

All of which made me perversely more eager to see that part of the country.

At the beginning of July a young teacher from Ningxia University showed up to escort me. I used to resent this custom, as implying that I was incompetent to travel by myself, but the Chinese look on it as a courtesy. And I realized that my escort would have an opportunity he might never have again, of seeing Beijing, the capital city, on his way to meet me in Tianjin.

It's a long two-day train ride from Beijing to Yinchuan, the capital of Ningxia. We traveled "soft berth", in a compartment with two padded benches, one on each side of a table, and a sleeping shelf above each bench. There were four people to a compartment. By day, they sat on the benches. At night one slept on each bench, the others on the sleeping shelves, all of which made comfortable beds. I must say I like Chinese trains for long distance travel. The roadbeds are smooth, and the roll and clack of the train is soothing at night.

After a long day and a night, in the first light of the second day, I climbed down from my bed-shelf and looked out the window. Sure enough we were running alongside the Yellow River, through sagebrush country much like parts of Colorado. We were rolling through western Inner Mongolia.

All during that long day the train ran quickly beside the Yellow River, through areas very sparsely populated (for though we think of China as densely populated, that's true only of the fertile eastern part of the country—the west is mostly mountains and deserts.) Soon we left the sagebrush country and rolled through what I think of as real desert, with high shifting sand dunes and the great river running through. It's very odd to see one of the world's major rivers running among pure sand hills with not as much as a blade of grass anywhere and no signs of human beings—not even boats on the river.

I kept my face to the window all day. I get excited by places that are strange to me, and this was nothing I'd ever seen. Rarely, we shot past a place where the river water was being used for irrigation and there were trees and rows of crops and clusters of boats on the river banks—but then we were in the empty desert again.

A fine dust came in around the windows. When I wiped my sweaty forehead my handkerchief came away with dark streaks. About once an hour the young women attendants came through with damp cloths and wiped the windowsill and the table. They brought hot water for tea, too, and stopped to chat a while. Other attendants brought menus so we could pre-order our dining car meals.

The two men who shared our compartment, government officials of Ningxia coming back from a trip to Beijing, were puzzled by my staring out the window, where they saw nothing worth looking at. Most of the day they sprawled on their bench, leaning against each other and snoring, having got, I suppose, little sleep in the capital.

As the long day drew to a close the green areas grew more frequent, the background changed to mountains, and suddenly, as darkness was beginning, we shot into a place that looked like south China: many canals, bordered by willows and spanned by moon bridges, many tall trees, old buildings with up-turned eaves, crowds of people. It was Yinchuan, where a delegation waited to give me such a warm welcome it felt like a homecoming.

The railroad is the way to come to Ningxia. It gives you a feeling for that most important geographical fact: the great river flowing through, making life possible in the desert. The Yellow River flows north here, just east of the line of mountains called *Helan Shan*. It is turned eastward and then southward by a horse-shoe curve of mountains, and so on its long journey to the east coast. In the northward section of that long curve, an area protected from sandstorms by the mountains, the river brings life to Ningxia just as the Nile does to Egypt.

The river has been supporting life here since ancient times. In the Tang Dynasty (A.D. 618-907) this whole area, including present Ningxia and western Gansu, was a flourishing part of China, an important trading centre on the old Silk Road, with several cities. The famous cave murals near Lanzhou and a few pagodas in Ningxia are reminders of that era. During the Song Dynasty (A.D. 960-1279) the area was taken over by Tangut tribes from the Tibetan plateau, who established the Xia kingdom, cutting off the Silk Road access to the Middle East and Europe.

In time, the Xia kingdom assimilated a great deal of the Chinese culture and became, culturally if not politically, part of the Chinese empire. It's hard to know many details about its particular culture because it was completely wiped out by

Genghis Khan in the 13th Century. As was his custom, any city that resisted his army was exterminated, the people slaughtered and the city demolished. As one of the standard histories of China puts it:

> [Genghis Khan] fell upon the kingdom of Hsia, which was utterly destroyed. According to . . . Chinese history not more than one-hundredth of the population survived, the countryside was covered with human bones, the cities left desolate. Many of the border cities were never re-occupied, and have been invaded by the drifting sands of the desert. The irrigation works fell into decay from lack of attention, and the country reverted to steppe. A region which in T'ang times had been wealthy and cultured, as the Buddhist sculptures and cave monasteries prove, became a semi-desert, the poorest and most backward part of the Chinese empire. (C.P.Fitzgerald, *China*, 4th Ed., 1976, p.433)

I dwell on this gruesome event because if what I've been told is true it leads up to an extreme example of irony: it seems that it was Genghis Khan who gave the region the name *Ning Xia*, or "Peaceful Xia".

I thought about my eastern students' warning of the poverty of Ningxia when I saw where I was to live. The dormitories were closed for the summer, so I had been put in the city's Number One Welcome Guest House. (*Di Yi Zhao Dai Suo*)

This was an elegant old-fashioned compound, surrounded by a high wall, with a gatekeeper at the entrance to certify that I was indeed a welcome guest. Inside the compound I found myself among gardens, with roses, dahlias, snapdragons, and many other flowers in profuse bloom, and the pleasant small noise of fountains. There was peace and quiet here, and the air was fresh and cool after the pollution and blistering heat of Beijing. Walkways with ornately painted ceilings connected a number of three-storey buildings among the flowers. A wonderfully fragrant, cool, and peaceful place! If the Chinese were smart, they'd build guest houses like this for tourists, instead of high-rise hotels just like luxury hotels everywhere.

In my building I had a three-room suite on the second floor, with a huge comfortable bed, and a large sitting-room. In late afternoons teachers and government officials gathered there to tell me their plans for the development of the region. The Responsibility System of farming had been implemented, they said, but they couldn't wait to take advantage of the New Economic Policy for industry. Even here, clearly, the spirit of newness was getting people excited.

The young woman who kept my rooms neat, Xiao Ren (that is, "Young Ren", "Ren" being her family name) looked about seventeen—a healthy, cheerful youngster with her hair in two long braids, a fashion I like though big-city Chinese now consider it hopelessly old-fashioned. She did her work in the best Chinese style, working well but in a relaxed, friendly way. Whenever I entered my building she came from behind the desk, with a shy smile, to unlock the door of my suite. (In the old Chinese tradition, guests shouldn't have to bother with keys.)

I was tempted to write back to my Nankai students and tell them that the accommodations here were so civilized and the people so healthy and interesting, that I might never return to the east.

It was a pleasant time I spent in Yinchuan. Every morning I lectured, to a class of over a hundred which included teachers, students, and people from other units. A good class; after each session they kept me answering questions for a long time.

At the Guest House, every morning just before six, there would be a gentle knock at my door. Cao Ren had come for me so we could go to the park together. Cao Ren was a high official in the Ningxia government, in charge of education, a tall, quiet, friendly man. We would walk half a block to a large park, *Zhongshan Gongyuan*, named after Sun Yat Sen, "the father of modern China"—the leader of the movement that overthrew the Qing Dynasty in 1911. One of his names was "Zhongshan", and there are as many parks, streets, and places named after him as there are "Washingtons" in the United States. (The main street of Xiamen, you remember, is Zhongshan Road.)

The park is spacious, with groves of trees, sports fields, a large lake on which people row boats, and pagodas, formal gardens, exhibit halls, a zoo, and amusement-park rides for the kids. The park opens at 5:30 in the morning; there were always a hundred or so people waiting to pay their five *fen* and go in. (Five *fen*, about two cents Canadian, was the standard price for admission to parks.)

Cao and I spent about an hour in the park every morning, first doing *tai ji quan* exercises and then walking around. (Everyone seemed to know Cao; many of them greeted him by name, and he stopped and talked to a lot of them. A striking difference from most of the high office-holders in the east, who isolate themselves from commoners.)

Many people were there each morning, some running, some doing exercises, some playing badminton. A group of eight young women passed us at the same place every morning, running seriously, waving but not stopping, training for races. An old man who seemed to have had a stroke shuffled by in a halting kind of jogging. A couple and their young son ran past us each morning. At the zoo, old men had brought out their pet birds in fancy bamboo cages, and hung the cages from the branches of trees near the zoo's outdoor aviary. Zoo birds and cage birds sang together while the old men smoked long-stemmed pipes and watched the young women run past.

There were always several groups learning *wushu* arts and traditional Chinese exercises, each taught by a man or woman who demonstrated the movements—some so gracefully that I had to stand and watch. (These teachers volunteer their time just to help people, and keep their arts alive.) We saw boys and girls in amazing *kungfu* leaps and turns, young men sweating and grunting in Mongolian wrestling, a group of middle-aged women swinging red-tasseled swords in unison, people of all ages in a quiet walled-in area doing slow deep-breathing *qigong* with their eyes shut while the teacher chanted instructions.

On the shores of the lake singers practiced scales. On benches under the willows students hunched over books. One girl taught the English alphabet song to her little sister, waving her finger to keep time: "A B C D, E F G . . . "

I did *tai ji quan* faithfully each morning in a large pagoda. Usually someone good at *tai ji* would watch, and frown, and correct the position of my hands or improve my styling. One of them brought me a gift, a manual of *tai ji quan* with illustrations of the positions.

All this took place before breakfast, which for most Chinese is a small meal snatched before leaving for work, or on the way to work. Just outside Zhongshan Park an enterprising family had set up a stand where people could pause as they came out of the park, to buy twisty deep-fried bread (*youtiao*), and hot soy milk—the same breakfast many of my Nankai students had every day.

In the afternoons I wandered around the city. Near the Guest House was a busy street, with a constant stream of people, many of them orthodox Muslims with white skull caps. Many of the men had narrow faces and wispy beards, and looked more like Middle Eastern Jews or Arabs than like the Han Chinese. The traffic was people walking or bicycling, and lots of two-wheeled carts pulled by tiny donkeys trotting briskly along pulling big loads.

I found a Hui bakery, where no animal fat is used and the buns, sweet rolls, cookies, and cakes are very tasty. Only bakeries have ovens in China—the many kinds of bread cooked at home or on sale in the markets here are all either deep-fried or fried in heavy skillets. (Once when I visited a Hui family they offered me a dozen kinds of bread: flat, twisted, puffy—all made without ovens.)

Off the main streets I soon saw that Yinchuan was not like Tianjin. Most of the side streets were not paved. The one-storey houses were made of sun-dried brick stuccoed with a mixture of straw and mud, so the warm brown colour of the local mud is also the colour of the houses. The roofs were flat, with rafters sticking out past the walls; the rooftops were used for storage, or for drying grain. The buildings got fewer as I walked away from main streets, and there were small herds of lean sheep, both black and white, or single donkeys, all grazing on the sparse roadside grass, and watched over by children.

To get to the university each morning, I went by car. My driver was both chauffeur and mechanic: he carried spare gas and spare parts in the trunk. (At that time there were almost no gas stations in China, and no gas station mechanics at all.) He washed and polished his car frequently, and every time he parked it he dusted it all over with a long duster made of chicken feathers.

This driver was a good example of the breezy Western spirit. He joined in conversations as an equal with whoever was in his car, and when teachers and officials met in my rooms to talk, he came too, pulled up a chair, and took part.

One morning as we drove towards the university, with farm fields on one side and the buildings of the city on the other, I saw people sitting next to piles of watermelons and suggested we should buy one. On the way back from my lectures, we did stop. The vendor was a man of about forty, stocky and muscular, with a dark weather-beaten face. He wore patched old clothes— his jacket needed still another patch at the torn elbow. He was sitting cross-legged on the ground, smoking a pipe with a tiny brass bowl and a stem so long that he held the bowl in his lap. He told us calmly that his melons were the best and freshest to be found anywhere, grown without chemical fertilizers. Then, having made his pitch, he puffed on his pipe and stared off into space as if it were beneath him to care whether we bought or not.

Ningxia people boast that theirs are the best watermelons in China and perhaps in the world—better than Xinjiang, they say. Just then it was the small round melons that were ripe (one of the university teachers told me he could eat hundreds of them in one season.) There were many varieties: even I could see that some were darker than others, some smooth, some mottled. I'm told there are sixteen kinds grown locally, some originating in Yunnan, some in Iran, some in Pakistan. The driver selected five melons carefully, holding each one to his ear and giving it a twisting squeeze to be sure it was ripe. I selected two. When I said we had too many, he waved his hand deprecatingly. "Wait till you taste them!" He handed one to the peasant, who took up a villainous-looking rag from the ground, shook the dust off it, gave his knife a ceremonious wiping and cut the melon, which split ahead of the knife. Inside, it was so red and juicy, and proved so delicious, that I forgave him the rag and we stood there eating, spitting out seeds.

Watermelons are popular in China: the papers say that in watermelon season Beijing's garbage doubles. But these were truly the best I've tasted anywhere. I asked the peasant where he grew them, and he pointed across the road. I asked if we could go there, and he called something over his shoulder. Then I saw that there was a boy of about twelve sitting silently under a tree watching us. He came slowly, and his father told him to take us to the fields. He was a country boy, with unkempt hair, ragged pants, an unbuttoned dirty old denim jacket and no shirt. His feet were bare. He was acutely shy, and didn't answer when I spoke to him.

We walked up a dirt road, and soon the noises of the main road died out behind us, leaving us in the great silence which for me is part of the beauty of farm fields. The air was clear and fresh. The sun was warm. The earth had a good moist smell.

It had rained off and on for three days, a rare occurrence in Ningxia, and there were mud puddles everywhere, some of them being explored by noisy ducks. We overtook a peasant with a heavily-loaded two-wheeled cart that was stuck in a deep mud hole in the middle of the road. Although it was drawn by two large horses rather than the usual small donkey, the horses were straining and churning the mud without success. The driver stood in mud halfway up his calves and shouted orders, and finally with a great scramble the horses pulled the cart clear and stood heavily panting. The horses' legs and bellies, the cart's wheels, the man's legs were all shiny with the brown liquid mud.

As frequently happens to me in China, I wondered about the significance of things. Why was such a big hole in the road unrepaired? Obviously the new Responsibility System of farming was being practiced here or that peasant could not have been selling melons beside the road. I had heard that ever since the communes were wiped out by Deng Xiaoping and people no longer worked in large teams but each individual or family or small group leased land from the villages and worked at what was profitable for themselves, public things such as irrigation systems and roads and schools were being neglected. So I had to ask: are the roads worse and worse now? Or is this a new hole which will soon be fixed? The teamster didn't linger to talk; he was already hurrying his horses to make up for lost time. My driver was uninterested and only shrugged. So I had to shrug too, and leave it unanswered.

In the fields, I could see at once the changes from the commune system. Instead of large fields of one crop, with lines of people—men and women, young and old—working side by side — now the fields were chopped up into small units and were a patchwork of different crops: beans growing up bamboo pyramids here, rows of Chinese cabbage there; rows of spinach, plots of corn (planted very close together), many fields of watermelons. People were working one or two to a field. At the edges of many fields were small roofed-over platforms where the peasants kept watch by night to prevent their crops being stolen. Everything has its price in this world, and the new emphasis on individual initiative, which resulted in a spurt of increase in production, makes farming much less sociable than it had been.

We came to our farmer's melon field. Two people were standing on the narrow path: a boy of about seven and a pathetic old woman. The woman was extremely thin and ragged. She suffered from cataracts, I think, for she tilted her head way back to look at us, and felt her way with a stick. She stood still as we passed. None of the Chinese spoke to her, and I could learn nothing about her. The little boy wore a dirty shirt, torn at the shoulder, and short pants. He was barefoot and his legs were muddy. His hair was stiff with dust. But he was a stocky, healthy-looking kid. He led us out into the field and showed us a ripe melon, which we split open and ate on the spot, offering a slice to the boy, who took it politely, gave us a big smile, and ate and spat seeds like the rest of us.

On the other side of the path, in the next field, three barefoot girls in thin, simple dresses were hoeing a plot, preparing it for the next crop. They used the heavy, clumsy-looking Chinese hoe which is swung overhead like a pickaxe and turns up the soil like a spade. I had tried swinging one, and had to admire the way these girls worked. The nearest was about twelve or thirteen, muddy, cheerful, strong, with a shy smile for the foreigner. It was summer and school was out, but I wasn't sure any of these kids would get to school in the fall. Now that the communes are gone many parents in the countryside all over China are keeping their kids out of school to work in the family fields.

That's part of the trade-off. The farmers now have much more control over their own lives. Certainly they work hard now, and you can see them in the fields at all hours. But there are prices for the new individualism and the surge in productivity.

For one thing, this matter of the children. Farmers want more children now, to work in the fields, so the population policy, which was always shaky in the countryside, is slipping badly. And children are kept out of school, especially girls (84% of children not in school are girls, according to the Women's Federation).

Another thing I wonder about: I look at this farm scene with its great peace and apparent prosperity, and I have to notice that the plots are very small. I see one clump of corn, planted very close together. But that's not the efficient way to grow corn. You get a much better crop per unit of land if you grow it in large fields where the wind can blow the pollen from stalk to stalk—in a small plot a lot of it just blows away.

And all these plots are so small they can only be worked by hoes. There are places where this is inevitable, such as small hillside terraces where machinery can't get in. But here was a flat plain going on for kilometres. Surely they'd get better crops with tractors. How can the yield be increased beyond the ability of hoe agriculture except by machines? But the paths between plots here are so narrow that no tractor could get in, and the plots so small it would be foolish to use tractors anyhow.

At Liberation, the peasants had been given small plots of land, then discovered it was more efficient to work together in Mutual Aid Teams, then in cooperatives, and finally in communes. Are we starting the cycle all over again? Or will enterprising individuals solve the problem (as they are beginning to in some places) by buying up the contracts for many plots of land, combining them into large holdings, and hiring the peasants to work for them? If this happens, China's countryside will "progress" back into something ominously like the old landlord system.

And thinking back to that big hole in the road, I have to wonder about another trade-off. In the communes, in off-seasons everyone worked on community things such as roads, terraces, irrigation canals. Now these things are deteriorating. The government is in some places paying farmers in grain to do such work, but that seems a partial and temporary expedient.

And how about that skinny old woman with the bad eyes whom nobody paid any attention to? In the commune she'd have had medical attention—not the best, certainly, but what medical care there was. Why was she so neglected that we (including me, I'm pained to remember) never even offered her a share of our melon?

My companions were not interested in such questions. It's a strange situation. On the one hand, those platforms where farmers protect their crops from each other. On the other hand, memories of the days when they worked together. Well, Chinese peasants are ignorant of a lot of things city folks know, but they aren't stupid. They got together in the 1950s to form Mutual Aid Teams and cooperatives without anyone shoving them. I have to hope they'll go that road again.

We kept going along the path, heading back to our car by another side road. We passed a cluster of flat-roofed houses, their walls the same light brown as the fields and the muddy legs of farm kids. As in so many parts of the world, mud and dust are alternating facts of life here. There were puddles beside the road: in the largest one two tiny girls were playing, stark naked kids about two years old. They were the same colour as the muddy water they played in. They splashed each other and squealed and paid no attention to us.

Back at the car, the driver looked at his watch. He had to hurry to get me home for lunch. That afternoon, when teachers and officials came to talk to me, there was a watermelon feast, and the desk was soon covered with juice and seeds, and the wastebaskets overflowed with rinds. Poor Xiao Ren had a mess to clean up that day while we were off sightseeing.

By the time things were organized for sightseeing, my son Aaron had arrived. He was backpacking his way around the world and couldn't resist coming to see me in this closed area, which he could do as the son of one here on a work permit.

Aaron's arrival was eventful. He had intended to join me in Beijing, but while he was in Hong Kong his money was stolen from an inner jacket pocket by one of Hong Kong's famous pickpockets and he had to wait for his brother in Canada to send more money.

Aaron had developed an effective way of getting around China without knowing more than a few words of the language. He's six foot three and obviously not Chinese, so he stands out in a crowd. In Hong Kong he bought a ticket to Guangzhou, using English. In Guangzhou, he got off the train and just stood there, and sure enough a young man came up to him, a student at the Guangzhou Foreign Languages Institute, looking for somebody to practice his English on. When it was time to move on, Aaron gave this new friend the money to buy a ticket for him to the next city—and thus, city by city, made his way across the country. But since the tickets were purchased by Chinese nobody thought to ask if the traveler had the permits necessary for foreigners, so Aaron arrived in a closed area without a permit.

He had sent a telegram saying which train he'd arrive on, so Cao Ren and I went to meet him at the station. Like all Chinese trains this one was long—more than thirty cars, all crowded— and there was a mob on the platform. There was only one first-class car, the conductor of which told us there were no foreigners on the train. We hurried down the line asking the other conductors, and finally one said, "We did have a foreigner, but the police have got him."

We hurried into the station, and there on a bench between two large policemen was Aaron, looking disheveled from five days in crowded hard-seat cars with no bed, or bath, or change of clothes—and very happy to see us.

The police released him in the custody of Cao Ren, and early next morning we went to the police station. There the first thing we were told was that the penalty for entering a closed area was two years in jail. Two policemen talked to us. One, who spoke a few words of English, was young and menacing. The other was an older man, bald and stout. After a few moments, the older one launched into a long speech. "This old man," he said, motioning to me, "has come all the way from Canada, like Dr. Norman Bethune, just to help China. We should support him in every way. This young man was only trying to join his father. We must take a lenient line with him."

He had hardly started this speech when the young policeman suddenly jerked around and stared at him. It had hit him, at the same time it hit me, that somebody in authority had been telling the older policeman to cool it. I glanced at Cao Ren, but he was looking at the ceiling. The young policeman, though angry, had to make out a travel permit and give it to Aaron, first shaking it in his face and saying, "Okay this time. No okay next time!"

The irony of all this was that a month after we left Ningxia it was proclaimed an open area and the whole system was relaxed. Now, my Ningxia friends write to tell me, there are many tourists and the tourist bureau is organizing camel rides, boat-rides on the river, trips to the crumbling western end of the Great Wall—and trying to devise other ways of amusing the travelers. With the influx of high-spending foreigners, all prices are shooting up rapidly.

As for our own sightseeing, which we did in company with Cao Ren and university officials, first we went to see the old Xia pagodas and temples, then the splendid new mosque, where we were welcomed by the two directors. We took off our shoes and entered the main room of the mosque, a large empty space with a great many prayer rugs on the floor, all facing a closed door. (This, they told us, is a symbolic door, suggesting the door in our hearts which must be opened to God.)

In a meeting room we had tea—the special Ningxia kind, made of tea leaves, sesame seeds, dried dates, dried longyan and other fruits, walnuts, and wolfberries. It's served in cups of local design, with saucers attached. You move the lid of the cup just far enough to drink, while it holds back the fruit and seeds.

These directors (and later the Hui governor of the Autonomous Region) told me about the exciting plans for future development, which indeed everybody was talking about. Since this is a Muslim area, its lines of contact should be with Muslim countries, they said. Several leaders, including the governor, had made the pilgrimage to Mecca, and now many more were going. Arabic, which had been only a religious ceremonial language, was now being taught in crash courses as a practical language for merchants, industrialists and government officials.

A delegation had just returned from Saudi Arabia with the exciting news that the Saudis would invest heavily in joint ventures to develop the Ningxia economy. To begin with, they would help develop the manufacture of products from local

wool and leather for export, and the export of herbal medicines
and the mining of minerals.

There was no longer any tension between religion and
communism in Ningxia, obviously. Instead of the Cultural
Revolution's warfare between Red Guards trying to destroy
religion and Muslims fanatically determined to keep it, now
the Red Guards are history, and government and religious leaders
join in the excitement of economic opportunity. Being Muslim
now just gives a special way to be part of China's modernization.

In this spirit, my hosts wanted me to see the new things,
the New Economic Policy things: the new shoe factory, the
blanket and rug factories. But I wanted to see the old things,
the local things: a desert reclamation project, a market town,
the homes of local people. We compromised by jamming it all
in.

First, to the factories, where the smell of new concrete
reminded me of Xiamen. At the shoe factory there were still
piles of odds and ends from construction, and we reached the
building by boards laid down in the mud and debris. Most of
the interior space was empty, awaiting the machines. But the
managers and workers were bubbling with enthusiasm. The
newness! It vibrates in China these days, even out here on the
edge of the Gobi Desert. They took Aaron's foot measurements
and in a few days presented him a fine new pair of shoes.

The blanket factory was turning out splendid blankets of
the local wool. I was given one as a parting gift—it still comforts
me in Saskatchewan winters.

The carpet factory, which also uses local wool, was already
turning out several models, some with designs standard
throughout China, others, the striking and interesting ones, of
traditional local designs.

Though I was personally more interested in the old things,
I couldn't help catching some of the excitement of these new
factories. Ningxia really is a poor section of China, and these

new projects will raise a standard of living that needs raising. Probably, indeed, here in the minority areas where the old cultures are strong the New Economic Policy will work best. The standard of living will rise but old ways will not be thrown overboard in the scramble for the dollar, Western fads will not be worshipped, and society will stay on an even keel. Ningxia is not Shenzhen or Beijing. (Friends of mine doing research among the Bai people of Dali, in Yunnan Province, by the way, have come to the same optimistic conclusion about that area.) But I still think it odd that there's so much excitement about the modernization of industry and trade, and so little about modernizing agriculture.

Among the things I wanted to see were the desert reclamation projects. China attracts world attention for its methods of reclamation, even though it still loses more land to deserts each year than it regains. I was told that projects in reclamation of the pure sand desert were too far away but we could see some projects on the loess plateau. (Loess is made up of wind-blown dust which over thousands of years has built up a high plateau on which almost nothing grows. It's easier to reclaim than the sand deserts, needing only water and protection from strong winds to be productive.)

Meanwhile, Aaron and I were shown a movie about a model project. It wasn't a well-made film—there were too many shots of officials and experts getting on and off buses and sitting in conference rooms. But the desert shots were exciting. They showed workers putting down over several acres of sand dunes a kind of net made of thick straw rope, the interstices about a foot square. In the interstices they planted desert grasses, and, as those took hold, young trees.

I suspect the reason we didn't see anything like this outside of that movie is that such projects are too expensive to be anything but rare. But we did see a most impressive one that looked quite practical, up on the dry loess plateau.

We traveled by car, coming by switchbacks up out of the canals and willows country onto the plateau. After a dusty ride we came to a gate, where our host, the director of the project, was waiting for us with the courtesy we had learned to expect in China. Soon we were seated around a table, and while young women filled our teacups the host explained this project.

We were in the Yinchuan Orchard and Forestry Plantation, in which seven hundred workers were developing orchards and tree nurseries on this dry plateau, and producing fruits and seedlings for Yinchuan City. There was a residential village here, and nursery schools and a primary school for the children. Here were 4000 mu (666.66 acres) of orchards, 6000 mu (1000 acres) of tree nurseries, and another 4000 of desert in the initial stages of reclamation.

It was raining lightly when we finished the briefing and set out. The rain we had had in the past few days was quite unusual in this arid region, and our hosts and the workers and some children we passed all seemed to enjoy walking in it. We drove down narrow lanes between lines of very tall poplars set close together. Now and then we got out and walked around to see the orchards, which were worth getting wet to see.

Each unit of orchard was a field about 100 by 50 yards, surrounded by tall poplars as windbreaks. In all the fields ran lines of irrigation ditches. In some of these fields were grapevines; in others, pears; and in others, apples. I was amazed at the healthy trees and vines and the fruits looking like pictures in garden catalogues.

We munched bunches of sweet green grapes. We munched juicy pears. We stood admiring the prize apple tree, bearing, they said, over 800 apples. I bit into a delicious apple—one I couldn't put a name to—with green skin and juicy, crunchy meat. The seven hundred workers obviously knew what they were doing.

As I stood in this splendid orchard, the workers around me beamed, and reminded me that twenty years ago the ground I was standing on had been loess desert, with not a growing thing in sight.

We brought back a load of fruit, and offered some to Xiao Ren. She would accept only one apple—but I'm sure she was delighted that we had brought apples, pears, and grapes instead of watermelons.

Sometimes we spent a whole day seeing the country, leaving early and getting home for a late supper. Once we drove twenty miles up river, leaving the green trees and canals, traveling up the deep valley which the river has cut out over centuries. This Yellow River, I'm told, carries more sediment than any other river in the world. A lot of it originates here as the loess is eroded out.

We came to a large dam spanning the broad river, a dramatic sight in the otherwise empty landscape. We stood on the top of the dam and looked upstream at the lake which wound out of sight up the valley, then on the other side looked down the steep drop at the turbulent brown waters roaring out, some from the turbines, some over the spillway. We went down inside the dam to see the turbines in action. The whole mass of concrete was humming and vibrating to the whirling of the huge machines.

This dam creates enough power to bring electricity to the whole Ningxia Autonomous Region with some left over to sell to Inner Mongolia. It's the power from this dam which makes possible the burgeoning of industry in Yinchuan. It's part of the reason for the confidence in great changes.

From the dam, symbol of the future, we drove into the past—to a small village that looked as if nothing had changed here for hundreds of years: dusty unpaved streets, mud-brick buildings, crowds of people on foot, brisk donkeys pulling two-wheeled carts. In the market, a peasant had unhitched his donkey and tied it to a wheel of the cart, and it was eating from a basket on the ground while the peasant set out his vegetables for sale. In the cart a small girl and a small boy stared with apprehension at the foreigner. Their faces were dirty, their hair dusty, their feet bare. But the little girl wore a fancy bracelet and necklace that looked like silver, and they both were eating large pieces of fried bread while watching me.

We had lunch in a small restaurant in this town, in an area separated from the street only by a lattice, and while we ate onlookers jammed up against the lattice and watched our every move. They didn't look hungry—people seemed poor here, and obviously didn't have enough water to bathe or wash clothes too often, but they did look healthy. They were just curious about the strange creatures that had come to town. Later, when we sat in our minibus for a while waiting for the driver, there were faces flattened against the windows just inches from our faces. Among the onlookers but not crowding forward, I noticed a hauntingly beautiful Hui girl of twelve or thirteen standing with a baby brother on her hip and just staring at us.

From that village we had a long drive to see a popular market which draws people from many villages and towns. There were thousands of people there; it was by far the largest market I've ever seen in China. We wandered through a maze of lanes lined with large dark tents festooned with streamers and flapping banners. It looked quite medieval. In one line of tents merchants were selling cloths of many kinds, and clothing, and jewelry. In one area were lots of restaurants—well, stoves, anyhow, where sweating cooks were turning out a lot of wonderful-smelling food. Customers bought bowls of food, then squatted just anywhere (with heels flat, as all Chinese seem able to do effortlessly) to eat. In a large area horses, donkeys, and sheep were for sale. In another, wagons were being repaired—a blacksmith was fitting a red-hot new iron tire to a wagon wheel and immersing the wheel in a large tub of water, making great clouds of steam. There were places with vegetables and other foods for sale, including lots of spices and herbs, and lines of tents where you could buy cooking-pots, bowls, and other houseware. Here and there were fortune-tellers, and one young man had a photography tent where a young couple were having their picture taken sitting behind a cardboard cut-out of an automobile, the photographer carefully arranging them so it would look real, and trying to keep the bystanders far enough away so they wouldn't be in the picture.

I could have stayed there for hours, but our friends were looking at their watches and saying we had another stop before heading home, so off we went. That last stop was a visit to a Hui farmer's home, since I had asked to see how people lived. Our host was a stocky man with a weather-beaten face and an easy smile, who met us at the gate. He wore the white Muslim skullcap, and a bright clean embroidered coat. (That was impressive; it's not easy to keep clothes clean in this arid and dusty area. I was flattered.)

He showed us around with pride; he was prospering under the Responsibility System, he said, and had just moved his family into this new house. It was an impressive homestead, laid out as a square around a courtyard in the old style. On one side was the house, a single-storey building of sun-dried bricks covered with stucco then painted white. The farmer insisted I should take a picture of the power lines coming into the building, for he was benefiting from the power dam, and had electricity. Along another side of the square courtyard were sheds, and pens with a few sheep and donkeys in them. On another side were workshops and a storehouse. The fourth side was a wall, against which were piled stacks of hay. In the centre of the yard was a well, capped by a hand pump of exactly the kind I remembered from childhood—the kind you have to prime before it will bring up water. This courtyard was of unpaved dirt, but swept clean—everything was clean and in order here.

Entering the house we were in a large main room, with the *kang*, or heated brick sleeping shelf, all along one wall. We were introduced to the farmer's large family, which included his wife and children and his brother and *his* wife and children, and a few others whose relationship I didn't catch. One girl, about ten years old, urged me to come and see her baby ducks, so I went back out to the courtyard and watched her round up a dozen or so very small ducklings and herd them towards me. When she noticed that I was photographing her, she cried, "No! No! the ducks!" so I got some nice shots of them, too. But ducks are ducks anywhere—she, with her excited smiles, was what I wanted to remember.

Back in the house, the table was loaded with cups of Ningxia tea and a dozen kinds of bread—all cooked without an oven, on top of the stove, and all tasty.

This family's prosperity must not be taken as average or commonplace. When I asked to see how the people lived, I had in mind the common lot—but of course my friends were showing off the most prosperous homestead around. They insisted that it was evidence of the correctness of the Responsibility System, which here and everywhere had replaced the communes.

It was certainly evidence of the way the Han and the Hui are getting along together in Ningxia these days. The governor was a Hui, and Hui and Han people mingled everywhere I went—in the streets, in the university, in government. That was not always true—far from it.

The Han (the ethnic group we think of as "the Chinese") make up 92 per cent of China's population. The other fifty-five recognized ethnic peoples total only 8 per cent. The Han, like every other group I've heard of that outnumbers other ethnic groups in their midst, have over the centuries tended to consider those others as barbarians, at best as primitives who may someday become as civilized as "us". The reason so many of the fifty-five ethnic peoples live in remote or mountainous areas is that over the generations before socialism the Han pushed them out of better farming and hunting areas.

There have been, in fact, many times of ethnic violence in Chinese history. Considering only the Hui and their fellow Muslims for the moment, the great Muslim uprisings of 1862-1873 were caused by Han oppression and the resulting tensions. Jonathan Spence, in his *The Search for Modern China*, tells us that "Discriminatory legislation protected Chinese [*sic*: He means Han] involved in violence with Muslims, and religious riots and feuds were commonplace." (p. 189) He also tells us that the incident which sparked the great Muslim uprising was an argument over the price of some bamboo poles, as a result of which bands of Han destroyed a number of Muslim villages. The relationship, in short, was as senseless and brutal as that between ethnic groups in various parts of the world today.

The violence, as is usual in such cases, was not one-sided. During the Long March, when the Red Army went through areas inhabited by various minorities, the locals usually fled, and rolled rocks down the mountains at the Han whom they had historical reason to fear and hate.

The Red Army's worst disaster of the Long March was inflicted on it by Muslims, near present-day Ningxia. Zhang Guatao, the erratic commander who aspired to replace Mao at the top, split the Red Army, taking his Fourth Army north-west and crossing the Yellow River north of Lanzhou. There, a Nationalist army waited until half of the Fourth was across the river, then attacked, annihilating the half that had crossed. A major unit of the Nationalists was the Muslim cavalry, which destroyed, among others, a regiment of women soldiers of the Red Army. Harrison Salisbury tells us in *The Long March*, "The Muslims wiped out the women's regiment. The two thousand women were killed, tortured, raped, sold in the local slave markets." (p. 320)

Against this grim and bloody background, credit must be given to Mao Zedong and the Communists, who when they seized power in China made a strong effort to end the hostilities and bring the minorities into the national "family". Teams of Han were sent by the government into minority areas, where they learned the languages, encouraged the people to develop their own culture, devised written languages for those that had none, helped develop schools taught in the local languages, and brought technical help to develop local economies. There's a fascinating account of one such project, in an old culture based rigidly on slavery, in Alan Winnington's *Slaves of the Cool Mountains*.

The government set a policy that wherever minority people were a sufficiently large proportion of the population there should be autonomous regions, politically equal to provinces, in which the minority people control the government, designate the official language to be used in courts and government and schools, and so on. There are five such autonomous regions: Inner Mongolia, Tibet, Xinjiang, Guangxi, and Ningxia. Smaller concentrations of minorities have similar rights over autonomous areas, prefectures, and counties.

When I visited Inner Mongolia University in the spring of 1979, I was told that the central government had set it up for the benefit of the Mongolians. They brought together from all over the country a group of scholars of Mongolian history, language and culture to form a key department—instantly the most important centre of Mongolian studies in the world. They specified that as Mongolians became qualified for university entrance, or for teaching positions, they should have priority.

There's a catch, and a big one it is: when push comes to shove, it's the central government and the Communist Party that make the final, binding decisions. While minority people fill the top positions in government in their areas, the Party, which keeps ultimate power, is controlled by Han. And central government decisions override minority decisions. For example, overall educational policy, including what languages shall be taught at which grades, is set (and often changed, to the irritation of the minorities) by the central government. In Inner Mongolia, the national law that any Chinese citizen can live in any area of China has resulted in such an influx of Han settlers that the Mongolians, who used to be a large majority of the population, now constitute about ten per cent, and falling. One result is that there have been Han protests at the university against the policy favouring Mongolian student admissions.

Worst of all, the whole concept of the "Minorities Policy" was set aside during the Cultural Revolution. Gangs of Red Guards went into minority areas and destroyed temples, put monks in "Education Through Labour" camps, and forbade local customs. I once met a Mongolian woman who was traveling through southern China as a Chinese-English interpreter with a group of foreigners, who told me, "Yes, I'm a Mongolian, but I can't ride a horse and I can't speak Mongolian. It was forbidden when I was growing up." Far out on the grasslands of Inner Mongolia, I met an old herdsman who said he would never go off the grasslands to live in a city, where his children would be put in schools and taught Mandarin. He was keeping as far away from the Han as possible. And you remember that when I went to the Institute for the Minorities in Beijing, a Tibetan student told me that in his hometown there was a saying: "Never use a rock for a pillow or a Han for a friend."

Against this turbulent background it seems to me all the more praiseworthy that today in Ningxia the Hui and the Han get along together as well as they certainly seem to. Many areas of the world where there are problems of ethnic hostility could take lessons from Ningxia.

When it came time to leave Ningxia, we had seats booked on the plane to Xi'an, for Aaron had never been there and anyone who comes to China must see the Qin emperor's tomb and its terracotta army. At the last minute, because it had rained, the airport runway was nothing but mud and the planes couldn't take off. Cao Ren said he'd get us train tickets to Lanzhou, in Gansu Province, where we could change to the train to Xi'an, but again at the last minute there was a landslide on the line and rail traffic was halted.

Because of these unforeseen hitches, as it turned out, we had a most welcome opportunity. The Ningxia government provided a car, with a driver, a guide-interpreter, and a companionable man named Xue, the director of the university president's office, and we drove right down the middle of Ningxia, where the only foreigners before us had been a few oil prospectors.

Early in the morning we came up out of canal country by a switchback road onto the loess plateau, and for a very long day we drove south across it. The scene, even for me and for Aaron, coming from the prairies of Saskatchewan, seemed remarkably flat. Most of what we saw was sky, the land lying flat beneath it out to a distant horizon. There were extremely rare bunches of grass, and small lonely bushes. The space was so empty, cut only by the straight line of our gravel road, that when a truck came towards us from the opposite direction we saw it approaching for half an hour.

Sometimes we crossed dry gullies on bridges, gullies cut by the infrequent rain. Whenever it did rain, the loose soil was quickly cut into patterns like the veins of a leaf. When dry, this loose soil gets picked up by the wind and carried east, causing dust-storms in far-off Beijing and Tianjin and even, as a Japanese airline pilot once told me, reaching Japan in the form of very fine yellowish dust which the Japanese call "Yellow snow".

Perhaps six trucks passed us all that long day, and for the first half of the day we saw no other sign of human life. Three times we saw herds of wild camels running in the middle distance. What did they eat? Where did they find water?

About noon we came to the first of a series of villages of a remarkable kind. Unfortunately, although we had stopped whenever I wanted to take pictures of the landscape, I couldn't persuade Xue to let us visit these villages. It was quite enough, obviously, that we had permission to traverse this forbidden area at all; to go visiting was out of the question. Too bad!

These were new villages, made possible by using electricity from the new dam to pump water from the Yellow River up onto the loess plateau and into irrigation canals. Here, the government had settled people from very poor mountain villages.

The first sign that we were coming to one of these was a long, high earth wall stretching east and west across our way. As we passed through the gap in each wall we could see that it was quite thick, and that the north side sloped upwards to deflect north winds from the village. These walls were eloquent to Aaron and me. Coming from Saskatchewan, we know what prairie winds can do, especially in the winter when at low temperatures they can quickly freeze people—and here, it seemed, the intensity of such winds might be even more severe.

Beyond the wall the row-houses appeared, also stretching east and west. Their north walls were all blank, and probably also quite thick for protection from wind and cold. To us, coming to these villages from the north, they looked like encampments in Antarctica. But when we passed them (with Xue sometimes bending the rules enough to stop the car and let us look) what a change! The south sides of the houses were mostly lattice-and-glass windows. In the courtyards were flowers, vegetable gardens, fruit trees. Near the road were giant sunflowers. Beyond each such village was the life-giving canal and beyond that fields in which wheat and barley were almost ready to harvest.

These people came, I was told, from areas in the mountains so poor that they couldn't raise enough food to feed themselves, and had to depend on government relief supplies. Here, obviously, they lived in comparative plenty. They were woefully isolated, but surely they were used to that. A bigger problem, I'm guessing, was psychological. Mountain people and prairie people, as we well know in western Canada, are two different breeds. A prairie person who had moved to the mountains once complained to me that there was nothing to see: "The damned mountains shut out the view!" And mountain people shrink into themselves on the prairies. I wondered if any of the villagers had refused to come and were still eking out a near-starvation existence in their mountains. How I wished we could stop and talk!

As the day wore on, the land began to rise in a long gradual slope towards the Six Turn Mountains (*Liupan Shan*), and began to seem more habitable, with scattered bushes and patches of grass. Here we began to see herds of sheep, always tended by children. We stopped to talk to some of the shepherds, boys about twelve years old with ragged clothes and dusty hair—but healthy-looking, with bright eyes, their smiles showing healthy teeth. They told us proudly that they didn't go to school because their work was needed. Their sheep, like the boys, looked lean but healthy. Some were white, some black, and many had curved horns. When the boys looked up from talking to us and realized that their sheep were going in the wrong direction, they set out running with whoops and yells to head them off, running faster than the sheep.

Most of these shepherds were boys, but we saw one group of three girls, herding about twenty sheep quickly along a dry riverbed, too far off for us to talk to them. They were striding along, looking over their shoulders at us but not slowing down. Each of them had a cloth bundle slung over her shoulder, perhaps their dinner.

Soon we began to pass groups of peasants walking or riding donkey-carts along the road in the direction we were going in, obviously headed for some special event, for they were all scrubbed clean and wore clean, bright clothes, the smaller girls with huge hair-ribbons.

We came to a side road (the first one all day) and saw that the people were turning into that road, and we could see flags and a crowd of people, and heard music. But Xue was adamant— his orders would not let us take any side roads or do any exploring. For a mile or two we passed groups coming from the opposite direction, to the festival we had to miss.

Well, at least all this gave me food for thought. Perhaps the ragged and dusty clothes we had been seeing were simply work clothes. Perhaps most people had another set of clothes for festive occasions, and enough water to wash up then. These people, I'm sure, are not poor in the same sense as the poor people of Shanxi before the Revolution (and some of them still), constantly on the edge of starvation. They were not like the wretched beggars I had seen in Harbin, sitting in filthy rags and beating their foreheads on the pavement to appeal to charity.

As evening drew on, we came to an actual town, though a small one, a county seat named *Gu Yuan*. Here we were to spend the night. We were asked not to go outside the hotel compound, and I gather there was some attempt to keep quiet about the fact that we were there. If so, it failed, for a crowd quickly gathered at the gate of the compound, people standing patiently hoping to get a glimpse of the foreigners. Here we were not taken for Americans, for just as in Harbin I heard some people saying, "*Sulian ren! Sulian ren!*" that is, "Russians!"

This hotel was the kind I like best in China: small, backward, with no modern conveniences, but with a most friendly spirit and with good food, clean comfortable beds, and a great quietness. Our bath water was carried to our rooms in buckets by lines of young women. The waitresses in the dining hall were friendly and talkative, and two of them patiently showed Aaron how to fold a napkin into the shape of a phoenix, the way they do for guests at banquets.

The next day we got off early again, and were soon in the foothills of the Six Turn Mountains. Water was more abundant here. The road crossed over some actual brooks, and in places rills of water ran beside the road. There were cows in the fields. There was traffic on the road: people walking, donkey-carts, even a couple of small tractors.

As we got up into the mountains, we had beautiful views of wide valleys, with corn in shocks, and further off, fields of buckwheat in flower making patterns of soft pale violet. Beside the road, at the edge of the fields, we sometimes saw a cluster of a dozen or so beehives, and among them the tent of the itinerant beekeeper, who moves his hives by truck or by train following the seasons of the flowers.

The mountains became rocky and rugged. This was the area where the Red Army came at the end of its Long March, before they developed their headquarters in Yan'an further east. Here at last they were safe from the warfare and awful hardships of that ordeal. I was near the end of that incredible march which had started in the mountains of Jiangxi and Fujian, near where I lived in Xiamen.

I kept looking for some signs of the Red Army, some abandoned encampment or even a Western-style historical marker, but they had left behind only the memories of those heroic days.

The Six Turn Mountains, though we had approached them on a long gentle rise all day long from the north, slope steeply to the south, and we came down a lot of scary hairpin turns before finding ourselves in Gansu Province. Gansu wraps around the southern part of Ningxia. Further west it opens up into cowboy country, where the film "The Herdsman" (*Muma Ren*) was made. This was a populous area, and we passed through many towns and villages. At one point we passed a steep cliff close to the road, and saw that a temple had been carved out inside it; there were rows of windows in the cliff face, and over each window a fancy small roof with up-turned eaves and tinkling windchimes. This is said to have been in ancient times one of the homes of Sun Wu Kong, the Monkey King, a chief actor in one of the most popular of Chinese legends, the folk epic *Journey to the West*.

Finally, towards evening, we crossed into Shaanxi Province and soon were in the city of Xi'an. We felt like seasoned travelers, like desert rats, even, getting out of the car slowly, with muscles stiff from the long drive, and looking with rustic wonder at the tall buildings and heavy traffic. It took a long hot bath in a hotel suite for me to realize that this was, after all, the familiar world we had started from, the world of Tianjin and Beijing.

I knew we were back in tourist country when we were charged, for a very skimpy supper, more than twice as much as a huge supper and breakfast together had cost in Gu Yuan. Odd, to pay more for food where it's plentiful than where it's relatively scarce. And I was irritated by the brusque, impatient service in the big city hotel. I had become used to better things in the Ningxia my Eastern students had thought would be such an awful place for me.

9

Events: The Communes Come And Go

Why is it almost impossible to solve the big social problems of Latin American countries (and many other countries)? Why is the best that seems possible in Chiapas a stand-off? Because two to five per cent of the people own eighty-five to ninety-five per cent of the land, as they have for centuries. To broaden the base, and give everyone some share of the country's assets, it would be necessary to break the monopoly of those at the top, and especially their monopoly of the land and its products. Until the land is re-distributed, there will be no end to the pattern of a few very rich people and a mass of very poor ones. But as long as those few at the top own the government, the army, and the police, and as long as they, quite humanly, refuse to give up power, it remains practically impossible to re-distribute the land. The history of many countries, therefore, is punctuated by the brutal repression of popular movements— whether they are peaceful attempts at change or violent uprisings. (See Eduardo Galeano's *Open Veins of Latin America*.)

This old pattern suits the purposes of the big transnational companies. They can help the few at the top retain their power, and in return they can get strangleholds on the countries' economies and natural resources. Those with local power see their best interests in cooperating with the big transnational companies, against the interests of the impoverished lower classes.

I mention this classic situation in order to point out that the Chinese revolution broke the pattern. One of Mao Zedong's crucial contributions to the success of the revolution was his persuading the other leaders that in China, where some 85 per cent of the people were peasants, the revolution had to be based on the peasants, and on the re-distribution of land. It was this that made peasants run off to join the revolutionary army. And it was the peasant armies, and the peasant villagers who supported them, fed them, hid them, sent their young people to join them, that made the revolution possible. As Mao said, the army lived among the people the way fish live in water.

When the Red Army liberated a village, the soldiers called the people together to confront the landlord in "speak bitterness" sessions, and to oversee the "turning over" of the village society. Traditionally, the landlords had prepared for hard times by hoarding large amounts of rice and grain, which were now brought out and distributed to the peasant families. Then the land itself was distributed by peasant committees, in such a way that each family got a fair share. If the landlord submitted to the new system, he was given an equal share. If he refused, he either ran away to the city, or resisted and was overpowered. Many were killed. As Mao Zedong has admitted, it was not a tea party.

But the distribution of the land to the families of the village was only the beginning of the new system. China at that time was one of the world's poorest countries, and the population was already huge, so nobody got a very large area on which to make a living, or very much in the way of farm implements and supplies. It was soon obvious that if families worked together they'd be better off. At first working together meant the spontaneous formation of "mutual aid teams", which could be as simple as four families sharing ownership of an ox or a plowhorse which none could afford by themselves. It could mean cooperating in seeding and harvesting, for example, or many other ways of working together while each family kept control of its own land. Later, peasants united to form cooperatives, some being simply larger mutual aid teams, and some involving pooling the land. Cooperatives were nothing new: Mao Zedong when young traveled through the south seeing the lives and problems of the peasants, and saw places where the peasants had on their own initiative taken land away from landlords and formed cooperatives. I suspect it was this that gave Mao his basic ideas about how to change rural society.

Later still, the cooperatives were united into communes. Was this, also, a spontaneous and voluntary development? In some places, yes—especially in the liberated areas of north China while the civil war was still raging further south. But when the revolution had been won, and the new society was being set up, it was decided by the leaders in Beijing that the commune was to be the standard form of organization in the whole countryside, and there were certainly many peasants who were forced into that organization against their will. As I've said many times, when socialism is a matter of grassroots decisions within an overall framework, it gets the enthusiasm which makes success possible. When socialism is decisions made at the top and enforced on everyone, it becomes "commandism" and is resented.

The word *commune* has different meanings in China and in North America. During the 1960s, especially, we thought of communes as groups of young people—say a dozen or more—who went off in the woods and worked out a way of living together as "intentional families". In China, the communes were a way of organizing rural society. There could be a few thousand or as many as fifty thousand people in one commune, divided up into villages (then called "production brigades"). Each production brigade, which might consist of a few hundred people, had control over its own affairs at the local level. Things the village could not provide for itself were provided by the commune as a whole, acting through its headquarters—things such as electricity, high schools, agricultural research institutes, large machines such as threshers which could make the rounds of all the villages in turn, fertilizer factories, brick factories, factories making small farm machines such as compost shredders, factories making irrigation pumps.

In those days there was very little money in circulation. I think the system of dealing with this in the communes was ingenious. Everyone was assigned "work points"—so many points for a day's work in the fields, so many for teaching school, so many for keeping the commune's account books, and so on. When the harvest was all in, the people turned to digging irrigation ditches, building aqueducts, terracing hillsides, repairing roads, and so on—all this for work points. Whatever work was needed was paid in work points. At the end of the year, the year's income, in money and in grain and so on, was divided up according to each person's work points. Schools were free for the children of commune members. Medical attention was free. (Such as it was, it was available to everybody.)

Getting medical services to 500,000,000 people was a huge problem. Western medicine was available only in certain hospitals in the big cities, and only to people with money or influence. Traditional medicine, in the villages, was a strange mixture of folk wisdom and superstition—ranging from acupuncture and a sophisticated knowledge and use of herbs to such shamanistic practices as beating the patient to drive out the illness. What was to be done? It was all very well to enlarge the system of "teaching hospitals" to train doctors and nurses, but for that to reach all the people would take decades. Before that could be adequate, there was an ingenious quickly-organized system, called "barefoot doctors".

In the first barefoot doctor clinic I visited, the young woman "doctor" held up her foot and said with a laugh, "You see, we do wear shoes! 'Barefoot doctor' is only a name." In her tiny clinic, she had simple medicines and other first-aid supplies. On the wall was a chart of the acupuncture points on the human body, also a chart showing which women in her area were taking contraceptive pills, and a calendar with notes reminding her when to tell each of them to come in for her free pills.

One of my Xiamen students, who had spent seven years in the countryside, had been a barefoot doctor in a commune, and told me a lot about what that involved. She had six months of training in a hospital, learning how to monitor the local water supply, how to give first aid, how to diagnose the common diseases of her area, how to give simple acupuncture treatments. Then she went back to her commune, and worked in the fields alongside the other commune members, but had regular hours in her clinic and was always on call for emergencies. She had a telephone to call the county hospital for anything she could not handle. When a roving team of doctors visited her area, as they did regularly, she had time off from her farm work to accompany them on their rounds and learn from them. In turn, she told them about local traditional use of herbs for various ailments, and gave them samples of the herbs and notes on their use. The doctors told her that those herbs were then studied in laboratories back in the city, and that over 400 items had been added to the Chinese pharmacopoeia in this way.

She remembers having a mixture of feelings about her work. There was pride in the extent to which the system was working, and there was despair at not knowing more, not being more useful. Her work as barefoot doctor was financed, by the way, like all other work in the commune—she received work points for her medical work just as she did for her farm work.

(The classic description of this whole revolutionary change-over from the old landlord system to the communes is William Hinton's *Fanshen: A Documentary of Revolution in a Chinese Village.*)

When Deng Xiaoping came into power, one of the big changes he made was the disbanding of the communes. He and Mao Zedong had very different ideas about how society should be organized, and about what motivates people to work hard. So the question of how successful the communes were is largely a political question. Bill Hinton, in conversations with me and in his book *The Great Reversal*, cites a 1980 study done by the government which reported that 30 per cent of the communes were doing very well, 30 per cent were doing badly, and the other 40 per cent were getting along but had problems. As Hinton points out, that means that about 200,000,000 people were getting along or doing very well in communes, which suggests that while there were problems that needed to be dealt with, the system as a whole was proving itself.

It seems ironic to me—and another example of my thesis that "commandism" is a threat to socialism—that under Mao, everyone was organized into communes, like it or not, and that under Deng all the communes were disbanded, like it or not. (Though Hinton describes a few communes which were stubborn enough to refuse to disband, and are still prospering.)

Communes that did not work well were likely to be in places that were already getting along well without them, especially in the south where the climate permits three crops a year and there is plenty of water. It is significant that the movement to do away with communes started in the south, in Sichuan Province. And wherever there were dictatorial, inept, or corrupt leaders in charge of a commune, of course there was resentment of the system. But the major cause of resentment was that the peasants, who had been given land at Liberation, found their individual plots taken away from them and merged into the communes, in which they were no longer either free agents or individual owners.

One of my friends tells me of a commune where she lived, in which everything was decided by leaders, and the peasants were little more than agricultural labour. In the morning, her work team would assemble slowly, waiting for the late-comers to show up. Then the team leader would tell them what was to be done that day—perhaps weeding plot number 7. They would stroll over to plot number 7. There the team members would sit around and talk or have a smoke, and by perhaps ten o'clock the first hoe would hit the ground. Clearly, their powerlessness in the affairs of that commune, together with memories of owning their own land, meant that they had no motivation to make the commune succeed. The revolution had given them land; the commune had taken it away.

On the other hand, I have seen communes which were certainly successful, their success built on all working hard together. One of the first I saw was high in the Shandong mountains, in one of China's poorest areas. Most of this commune's territory was nothing but steep mountainsides. When I visited in the spring of 1980, the hillsides had been terraced, with stone walls holding up strip-fields, one above another all the way up the mountain. The crop here was sweet potatoes, which they harvested, dried, ground into flour, and made into noodles as their basic food. To get a head-start on the season, the workers had buried pipes under the terrace fields. At one end of each strip, there was a firepit, with people tending the fires. The heat and smoke went through the pipes, and at the other end, smoke was coming out—all up the mountain, at one end of each strip. A strange sight! In this way, the fields were warmed enough to plant the sweet potato tubers as much as a month early.

These peasants were mountain people, who carried heavy loads up steep paths while talking to each other. The children came scampering up or down the paths to see the foreigner. The people took time to be friendly, explaining what they were doing, and smiling and waving when we left. It made me ache to think of the work involved in making those terraces, and laying those pipes. I couldn't imagine anything comparable being done by individual owners of small plots. But at least, now that the terraces were in place, it would take only routine repairs in off seasons to maintain them, and commune workers would get work points for that.

Later, in the far south, in the Guangxi Zhuang Autonomous Region, I visited a commune which specialized in growing cane, refining it, and selling sugar. Actually, I hadn't planned to visit this commune—I was in a car with a driver and a guide from the city of Nanning, on my way to see the area where the Taiping Revolution had started—but we passed fields where lines of workers were cutting sugar cane, and others gathering it up and loading it onto trucks. We followed the trucks to the sugar refinery, and I saw the cane fed into a big machine that rolled and squeezed it and dropped the juice into evaporation pans, and I followed the whole process, to the warehouse where bags of sugar were being piled up ready to go to market. Here, too, the people seemed both hardworking and friendly. And here, too, it was hard to see how such things could be done, even cooperatively, by owners of small plots.

In the autumn of 1979, I visited the Houheyu village (oops—I mean "production brigade") in a commune near Tianjin. Here I found almost five hundred people living on the equivalent of a quarter section of land. (For non-Canadians: that means about 160 acres or 65 hectares.)

The leaders showed me their little historical museum, with black-and-white photographs of the area before and after Liberation, and told me the story of their "turning over" in the 1950s.

Before Liberation this area had been owned by three feuding landlords, each with his own private army of retainers, and was frequently raided by bandits. The landlords neglected the soil, which became poorer and poorer, but they raised the tax rates year by year, and collected taxes for as much as sixty years in advance. There were frequent floods and famines. In bad years many people died of starvation; many others wandered off to the city hoping to survive as beggars.

Then came Liberation. The power of the landlords was broken. In time, a commune was organized and their village became this "production brigade". They set out to re-make their land.

"Over there," they said, pointing across the small river that runs through their area, "was a hill that used to divert flood waters every year to the low fields on this side. So the first thing we did was to bring all the dirt from that hill over here and level everything out." Sure enough, the land is level now, though in the museum I saw old photos of the hill. Now, all is fields on both sides of the river, with low dikes bordering each field so they can be selectively flooded. The tops of the dikes are also the narrow pathways along which people walk.

"Then the commune brought in electricity and gave us electric pumps, so now we pump water out of the river and bring it in ditches to all the fields. And you can see we diked the banks of the river so it doesn't flood anymore."

"Wait a minute," I said. "What kind of machines did you have to move all that dirt?"

They laughed. "Machines? Carrying poles and baskets, hoes, and strong backs—those were our machines. Everybody worked—men, women, children, peasants and leaders—we all worked, sometimes sixteen hours a day. And we came home singing." Seeing my amazement, one old woman explained: "It was our own fields."

Standing among their crops of wheat, corn, potatoes, squash, cabbages, tomatoes, beans; looking at their many chickens and the flock of ducks in the river watched over by youngsters with long bamboo poles, seeing the rows of sties in which a few hundred pigs were being raised, for food, for sale, and as a source of fertilizer; looking around at the brick houses, the concrete threshing floor, the hall where meetings are held and movies are shown; seeing neatly-dressed kids coming home from school; looking around me at the peoples' smiles as they watched me taking it all in, I felt a touch of that "turning over" spirit myself.

Now I must hasten to put all this in perspective. The Houheyu production brigade was one of the best, one of the most fortunate. They had good land to work with, and plenty of water—many other villages had only those steep mountainsides, or saline or rocky soil, or semi-desert. They were close to the big city of Tianjin, where they could easily sell their pigs and vegetables and get the leavings of breweries to feed the pigs. Most villages across China are isolated, in many cases not even having any roads to connect them with other places. And the Houheyu was more fortunate than a lot of other villages in having wise, energetic leaders and in getting good help from the commune. I'm not suggesting that all villages in China were so successful!

Today, China has trucks, tractors, sophisticated construction machinery, so big projects no longer depend on endless lines of workers with carrying poles, each carrying two baskets of dirt. The need is not the same, but of course neither is the spirit. Today people think of those mass labour projects as old-fashioned, even quaint. But the Houheyu is there, after all, with its memories of the revolutionary spirit and what it could accomplish.

When you talk about communes, sooner or later you must talk about Dazhai, a famous commune in the very poor province of Shanxi. It was singled out by Mao Zedong as a model of what revolutionary spirit and self-reliance could accomplish, and all over China we saw the motto "In agriculture learn from Dazhai!" It was on posters in towns and was scrawled on village walls everywhere.

What was special about Dazhai? Under the charismatic leadership of the commune head, the people in an eroded, mountainous, drought-prone area worked together to terrace their hillsides, build irrigation ditches, set up a noodle factory and other enterprises, and prospered. There were houses for all its families, schools for the children, food and social services for all. And they did this without external help, relying on themselves. That, at least, is the picture I get not only from official reports, but also from people who have visited the commune, and others who have lived and worked there. (Members of Bill Hinton's family worked in the noodle factory.)

When Deng Xiaoping came to power, one of the first things he did was to discredit, and finally eliminate, the communes. It was expedient, as part of his campaign, to discredit Mao's favourite commune, so under Deng we got stories suggesting that Dazhai was a propaganda ploy by Mao, and was really not self-sufficient at all, but had been secretly supported with grants and with the labour of army units. But when the edict went out to cancel the communes and lease the land in individual plots to families or mutual aid groups, no one in Dazhai could be found willing to oversee such a change, so the central government had to send in directors from outside to enforce the reforms.

I'll have more to say about Deng and his decade later, but here I have to mention what I have myself seen as some of the results of doing away with the communes.

The big change was eliminating the commune as a political, social, and economic structure. Ownership of the land reverted to the government, meaning, practically, local government. The use of the land was contracted out to individuals or families or small groups. For example, one farmer might contract to grow rice in a certain field, guaranteeing to give the village ten per cent more rice than it had been getting, and keeping any surplus as his own, to sell to the government or on the open market. Another might contract to grow apple trees on a barren hillside. At first, this reform enlisted great enthusiasm. As I traveled around China, I could see families working in their fields early in the morning or until darkness at night. And agricultural production boomed—at least for the first few years.

But many problems followed. For one thing, the problem of how the local government was to maintain control of the land which it owned was resolved by limiting contracts to three years. But it was quickly realized that this gave the farmer no incentive to preserve the fertility of the soil—when you build fertility, you build for the future. So the term of the lease was lengthened—at first, to ten years, then to fifteen years, and now, in most places to fifty years with the right of the family to inherit the lease if the farmer dies. But as Marx and Mao have both commented, "ownership" is a tricky question. Marx said that whoever gets to make the decisions about how the land is to be used is, practically speaking, the owner. More and more these days, farmers speak of "their" land and so do journalists and researchers when referring to the farmers.

Another problem was that there was now no "work point" system to pay people for maintaining the roads, terraces, irrigation canals, and so on, or for teaching school, or for providing medical care, or for paying local officials. All these must now be based on money, and where is the money to come from? So roads are not kept up. Terraces are not kept in repair. Parents must pay for their children's schooling, and many decide that the kids would be more use and less expense working in the family fields. Many villages these days are without any medical services. There is not the support there used to be for old or disabled or otherwise disadvantaged people. Local officials levy taxes for their own salaries and for road repairs and such basic services—but also have got into the habit of levying miscellaneous taxes, fees, and "voluntary" contributions at such a rate that a reporter found sixty-seven different such demands on the farmers in one area. There have been riots in some places in anger at these charges, and although the central government has been saying for many years now that such charges must not total more than 5 per cent of the farmers' income, continual stories in the newspapers show that the problem is far from solved.

More serious than these problems, in the long run, is that farmers have found that they can make more money by raising non-food crops such as cotton than by raising grain; some have even left their contracted fields unfarmed and gone into the trucking business or other business, buying the grain they owe the village instead of raising it, and keeping the land as only an emergency place to fall back on if things go bad. That helps the peasant, but does nothing to increase the country's overall grain crop, so it is becoming harder to keep up the production of grain, China's basic food.

Another long-range problem is that the revolutionary spirit of community and cooperation has tended to give way to a spirit of self-interest. Remember the fields I saw in Ningxia? Small plots, hoe agriculture, lookout platforms to keep "my" crops from being stolen. Replacing communes with self-interest has been part of a general change in Chinese lives. It is linked to the modern materialism, and the spread of irresponsible degradation of the environment, and the spread of crime and corruption. To take only one example, the awful floods of the summer of 1998, as many Chinese newspaper articles and editorials pointed out, were caused not only by heavy rains, but by the clear-cutting of the upstream forests, the shoddy building of some dikes and neglect of others, and the general neglect of the common good in the scramble for personal wealth. (The forest cover in the upper reaches of the Yangtze River, the papers say, was reduced from 75 per cent to 5 per cent in the ten years before the floods.)

These days, China is in flux, in these matters as well as many others. I notice two tendencies pulling in opposite directions. One is the trend of people with money buying up the leases of many others, then hiring those others to work the land for them. This tendency heads us back towards the landlord system. The other trend is farmers coming together in various forms of cooperation—which heads us towards mutuality. Neither of these trends will take us precisely back to any previous stage of history. As people say in many languages, "You can't step in the same river twice." Whatever develops next will, of course, build on the past in its own ways. As with so many other things in China these days, I hope to be around long enough to see where it comes out.

10

Events: The Cultural Revolution Comes And Goes

I've mentioned the Cultural Revolution frequently throughout this book, but that movement was so complex, and lasted so long, and shook China so deeply, that it really should have its own chapter, to pull things together and draw some conclusions.

That's not easy, though. It's a complex subject, and the evidence is not all in—largely because China has not yet been willing to look at all the evidence and come to terms with it. The general view in China seems to be that the Cultural Revolution was simply a time when society went crazy. But that means shutting the door, refusing to look at it (and shutting off any opportunity of learning from it, so that if it was some kind of disaster they might think about how to prevent such disasters in the future). No, it's too early for the history of the movement to be written in China.

And when I look for help from Western historians, I find one expert saying "This movement defies simple classification." (J. D. Spence, *The Search for Modern China*, p.603) and another saying "Its full history is still far from known or written." (J. K. Fairbank, *China: A New History*, p. 383) This in spite of the fact that Spence's book was published in 1990, fourteen years after the end of the Cultural Revolution, and Fairbank's two years after that.

So I give you fair warning: I know what I saw and what I was told by people who lived through it. I know what conclusions I have drawn. But I make no claim to the last word. We'll be hearing about this for many years as the evidence accumulates, I think; meanwhile I present my own ideas.

There are, it's clear to me, two sides to the story: the good things that happened then, some of which I saw at the time and others I heard about, and on the other hand the horror stories I was told and read about later. And it's not a simple matter of which is correct—both aspects were there and need to be comprehended.

First, I remind you of the things I saw and heard when I was in China in 1976, during what was then called "The Glorious Proletarian Cultural Revolution". You remember how moved I was by my talks with the teachers of the Hunan Number One Teachers College in Changsha and their attempts to change the post-secondary school system from an elitist middle-class institution to one which would serve the whole society. They did away with the whole grading system in order to encourage students to concentrate on learning, not on competitive scores. And they found ways to keep the college in touch with the public which its graduates served, and to respond to that public's needs. They did away with entrance examinations in order to give opportunity to those students, especially the children of workers and peasants, who were capable of doing well but had neither the money nor the academic preparation to get into traditional universities. (Fu Feiying, that great guide on my 1976 study tour, was a product of this system. She came from a worker family: her mother worked in an embroidery factory; her father was a mechanic. After high school, she worked on a commune farm for two years, then was admitted to the Beijing Foreign Languages Institute as a "Worker-Soldier-Peasant" student.)

Their whole approach delighted me; it dealt with aspects of education which I have found frustrating in my own teaching in the US and Canada. But it was needed even more in China than in the West, because the traditional system in China was even more elitist than ours.

You remember Feiying's account of how her class solved the problem of learning English while uniting theory with practice, thus trying in their way to make the classroom less isolated from society as a whole.

You remember the skipping-song dance of the high school girls which exemplified the principle of grassroots socialism, and the debate in the commune over men's and women's workpoints which was another example of the same thing.

You remember the Tianjin kite factory, and the East is Red Tractor Factory, good examples of what a socialist factory should be.

All of these were part of the Cultural Revolution's struggle to change elements of China's society from the old feudalist tradition to a new socialist one which would spread the benefits of the whole system to as many people as possible.

On the other hand, those horror stories. You remember that when I started my teaching at Nankai University in 1979, I was told there would be no classes the following Tuesday because of a memorial service for the dean who during the Cultural Revolution had been beaten to death by students.

When Deng Xiaoping came to power in 1980, one of the first things he did was to declare that the Cultural Revolution had been a ten-year disaster. In fact, I'm told, he demanded that all government workers at high levels must sign a statement to that effect or lose their jobs. I'll talk about Deng in a separate chapter, but note here that so many people agreed with him that they welcomed the period of his leadership as a relief from the violence and disorders of the previous period, that is, precisely, of the Cultural Revolution.

I asked a woman I know in Tianjin what the Cultural Revolution had been all about, but all she could say was "The Cultural Revolution was *evil*, from beginning to end!" When I asked an old professor at Nankai what was the theory of the Cultural Revolution, he said, "Theory? What theory? We heard nothing about any theory. All we knew was we were herded into mass meetings where we waved the Red Book and shouted slogans after the leaders. There was no theory!"

You remember that the managers of the Tianjin Generator Factory which I visited in 1979 called the Cultural Revolution a time of chaos disrupting production. They said that the politics which took up most of their time was "empty": mass meetings ending with raised fist salutes and shouting of slogans, but no study, no discussion, no understanding of the issues.

It goes back to my theme of "commandism", doesn't it?

I remember the time at Nankai when many of us joined a tree-planting campaign. I told the old teacher working with me how good it felt to be working all together on such a project. He stood and thought for a moment, then said, "Yes, the Party says plant trees, so we plant trees. And next week if the Party says cut down trees, we'll cut them all down again."

Add to all this the senseless violence of the movement.

One of my Xiamen students told me that when he was in high school Red Guards came and urged all the students to rebel against old ideas and overthrow old ways. His class went back to their school room and beat up the teacher and broke the windows and tore out the pages of their textbooks and threw them in the air like confetti. Another high school student, the daughter of friends of mine, came home from a rally, and took a hammer and smashed a three-generation collection of carved jade.

Once in Xiamen I was walking with an old colleague past a bare, empty space. Here, he told me, there was once a lovely garden park, famous throughout the south, with flowers, pagodas, willows beside lotus ponds. "During the Cultural Revolution, we were organized into teams and we had to destroy the whole thing—cut down the trees and bushes and throw them in the ponds, burn the pagodas." He, too, had tears running down his face as he told me about it.

Another Xiamen teacher told me that he had spent years and all his spare money building up a famous collection of Bibles, in several languages. He showed me one—a large German edition with metal hasps, interspersed with colour reproductions of famous paintings. This was all that was left of his collection. "They came three times," he said. "They even dug up the yard to see if they had missed anything I might be hiding. They took all my books, and burned them. I have only this one left—it was hidden for me by my brother in his house. And they 'struggled' me."

One of my Nankai students told me, with tears running down her face, how when she was a child, she had been held by two men at the front of a mass meeting and forced to watch while her father, on the platform, was displayed with a dunce cap on his head, and beaten and forced into the painful "airplane position" while the crowd shouted insults at him. (She had no explanation for it, only the dreadful memory).

In 1982, I asked my Xiamen University graduate students to write poems modeled on Walt Whitman's "There Was A Child Went Forth", keeping the opening and close and putting their own memories of childhood in between. One student wrote this:

> There was a child went forth every day,
> And the first object he looked upon, that object he became
> And that object became part of him for the day or a part of
>   the day,

Or for many years or stretching cycles of years.
The morning sunshine became part of that child,
And buildings tall and short, red and blue and white
And green trees along the streets waking up in the breeze,
And buses, cars and bikes passing speedily by,
Workers and clerks all in a hurry,
Shops and stores opening doors
And boys and girls hand in hand heading for school,
Their red scarves and gay shirts and skirts became part of
    him.
The deafening cheerful streets became part of him,
A sea of flags waving and moving, and firecrackers
And loudspeakers on cars sending shouts of delight and songs
    of power,
And unlucky men and women marched by Red Guards
(Down their children's cheeks run tears of hunger and fright)
Full of confusion they dodge, stumble and fall.
Blows fall on the clothes that cover their cold bodies,
Their painful cries and the laughs of the Red Guards became
    part of him.
The moon was high, and fires in the street were bright.
Books of science or foreign kind were thrown down, burning
    like branches of pine.
Spectacles of scholars were flung to the ground;
Broken pieces glittered to the stars.
These became part of that child who went forth every day
And who now goes and will always go forth every day.

Thousands of young people, including about thirty who later became my students, were sent to the countryside to live and work among the peasants. They were to broaden their knowledge of society by experiencing for themselves the hardships of the lives of peasants, and they were to share their skills and knowledge with the peasants. Some of my students got back from the countryside after two or three years; others were there as long as seven years. (I told one of my classes that I, as their teacher of literature, found that they brought to their reading a much deeper knowledge of life than students straight from high school. One student replied, "Yes, we learned a lot about life. But it needn't have taken seven years. I could have learned all that in one year!")

Thousands of intellectuals who were government or Party officials were sent to "May Seventh Cadre Schools", which were another way of experiencing the hard life of poor peasants. Some were sent to far-off parts of the country, such as Tibet and Xinjiang and the mountains of Yunnan, and one couple I know about didn't get home for fourteen years.

Once in a Beijing hotel I talked to the man cleaning my room, who said, "I hate Mao Zedong! If he hadn't interfered, I would be a doctor now, doing important work. By the time I got back from the countryside, it was too late, and I'll spend the rest of my life changing beds in hotels."

Before I get into the history of the movement, and then into my own conclusions, let me give you a clue from these examples, a key to understanding the contradictions. The Cultural Revolution, like the whole socialist movement, was a class struggle. That was true of the breaking of the landlord culture during the Revolution, and was equally true of the Cultural Revolution. Those who benefited most were young people like Fu from workers' families, and those from poor peasant families. For the first time in China's history, it became possible for such people to go through school and university and become intellectual workers, either going back with their knowledge to the countryside or staying in a big city to work. Remember my friend who had been a barefoot girl in the

Shandong mountains, who became one of the directors of a big research institute?

Those who suffered most from the Cultural Revolution were middle-class intellectuals or were (by the standards of that time and place) wealthy. Look at the examples above. The woman who could only say that the Cultural Revolution was evil told me as part of her grievances that she had owned seven rental houses in Beijing (at a time when anyone who owned a bicycle, a wristwatch, and a transistor radio was called "rich". Most of the people I knew lived in tiny apartments—she was the only one I've met who owned whole houses.) Six of her rental houses had been taken away from her, leaving her with one rental house and the house she lived in. The aggrieved teachers were part of the old elitist universities. Notice the contrast between the university professor who said there was no theory, and the teachers of the Hunan Teachers College who had a very clear theoretical idea of what they were doing and why. There was, indeed, theory behind the conditions and activities I admired in 1976—the theory excited me as much as the activities.

Be aware, too, that the people I lived and worked among and heard from in China were for the most part intellectuals, the elite class that included my student who asked what he could learn from "stinking peasants". That class was targeted by the Cultural Revolution, and suffered most. It was from them that I heard nothing but grievances about the Cultural Revolution. (Well, I think of three teachers who talked about good things happening then, but only three, in the years I taught in Chinese universities.)

When I asked the students in one of my English-language conversation groups to explain the class structure of Chinese society, they said it was a non-subject. "There's no such thing as class in modern China." Wow! Perhaps that's a clue to why they see the Cultural Revolution as simply a time when society went crazy—they see the suffering, which for their class was real and dreadful—but they don't make any sense out of the movement.

After the Cultural Revolution was over, stories began to be published, fiction and autobiography, about suffering during that period. These quickly swelled into a widespread movement called "The Literature of the Wounded" (*Shanghen Wenxue*, literally "Scar Literature"). I have a collection of some of these stories: *The Wounded: New Stories of the Cultural Revolution*, 77-78, published in Hong Kong in 1979. A number of "Wounded" stories were made into moving pictures during the 1980s. Among the best, I think, were A Small Town Called Hibiscus (*Furong Zheng*), which had the audacity to suggest that corrupt leaders of the Cultural Revolution days were still in power several years later, and The Blue Kite (*Lan Fengzheng*). In the West, a number of books about suffering during the Cultural Revolution appeared, of which the best known is Nien Cheng's *Life and Death in Shanghai*.

However, none of the writings I've seen, and none of the accounts of the Cultural Revolution I heard from my university colleagues, explain why wildly different things could be happening at the same time, in the name of the same movement. The "Wounded" stories were written by and about people who suffered, but apparently without any understanding of what was happening or why. Most of these accounts seem to me authentic and very painful, but I keep thinking that the same kind of book might have been written about the French Revolution by a member of the aristocracy whose loved ones had died on the guillotine—full of genuine pain, but not otherwise enlightening.

So, what was it all about?

The Cultural Revolution was not a unique happening in the history of socialist China: it was the last, the longest-lasting, and the most violent of a series of mass movements, all of which were attempts to popularize class struggle as the key to the ongoing socialist revolution.

From the start, there had been many different reasons for people to join the Communists in an uprising against Old China. Many people simply ran away from intolerable situations in their villages. Some were middle-class supporters of Sun Yat Sen, opposed to the Chiang Kaishek regime which had kept the name of Sun's movement but had turned it into a dictatorship. Some were Communists, others liberal intellectuals, others refugees from oppression, others simply peasants who wanted land, others youngsters who followed the vague but shining light of their ideals. The pressures of warfare could hold them together, but with peace it became obvious that they had not all been fighting for the same goals. The Communists postponed the inevitable ruptures as long as possible by pushing the idea of a united front, but sooner or later the tensions had to come to a head.

There had been factions within the Red Armies from the start. In the third month of the famous Long March, a time of constant danger that their whole movement might be wiped out by Chiang Kaishek's superior military power, the leaders took time out for an important debate about their goals and methods. This debate was between those who insisted that revolution must be based on the urban proletariat and must therefore focus on attacking the cities, and others, led by Mao Zedong, who pointed out that by following that theory the Communists had already lost several crucial battles, with great losses, and pointed out, too, that the strength of China was not in its infinitesimal urban proletariat but in the peasants who were the big majority of the nation. Mao won this debate—the first of many such debates that he and the Party would face.

At the end of the Long March, in the Communist base in Yan'an, there was again a need to decide such questions as what their goals were, what their tactics must be, and who was in charge. In 1942, in Yan'an, there was the first of several mass movements, a "Rectification Campaign" which established the primacy of the Party, and of Mao as leader. It was as part of this campaign that Mao issued his famous speech on the relationship between art (especially writing) and revolution, stating that all literature is based on class and that for the purposes of fighting the revolution all literature must be based on the needs of the masses and the needs of the revolution. *Talks At The Yenan Forum on Literature and Art* has been published in many editions. It would be a distraction to report it in detail here, but it is essential reading for anyone who wants to know what Mao stood for. There's no time here, either, to go into the perplexed question of how far he was talking about a fierce revolutionary struggle and what writers should contribute to it, and how far he was setting up rules for writers and their role in society after socialism had been achieved.)

After the revolution had been won, there were many questions about what exactly the new socialist China should be. In 1957, the Party under Mao issued a call for discussion and criticism, under the slogan, "Let a hundred flowers blossom and a hundred schools contend." The response was an outpouring of criticism and demands for reform and change of direction. Either this outpouring surprised and dismayed the leaders, so that they decided to crack down on dissent, or the call for criticism had been all along a cute ploy by Mao to get dissent out in the open where he could smash it. In either case, what followed was the "Anti-rightist Campaign" of attacks on dissenters, especially writers. Many writers were denounced in mass meetings, and sent to the countryside to "learn from the peasants", and were forbidden to publish—some for as long as twenty years.

In 1958 came the "Great Leap Forward", a mass campaign to develop agriculture and industry—one goal of which was to outstrip the United Kingdom in industry within fifteen years. Some of my older friends tell me that there were many good achievements of this movement, but I think it will be remembered for two failures: the attempt to produce iron and steel in "backyard smelters", and the famine of 1959-1961.

One of my friends at Nankai University recalls that she became engaged, in the year of the "Great Leap", to a university teacher who came from a village in Hebei Province. She went home with him to meet his parents, and on the way he told her what a beautiful village it was, surrounded by orchards and made cool by shade trees. When they got there they found a treeless village baking in the hot sun of the plains. Every tree had been cut down to fuel the backyard smelters, which however had produced nothing but mounds of useless low-grade iron that still cluttered the village.

Why did they do it? Certainly common sense told them that their prosperity depended on the orchards? It brings up a basic question about such campaigns, including the Cultural Revolution, doesn't it? How could people bring themselves to do such stupid and destructive things? I suspect that some people were afraid to stand out as dissenters, considering what had happened to dissenters in the past. Others trusted Mao Zedong to know better than they did about what the country needed. Add to that the fact that local leaders, eager to report their energetic compliance with Party orders, would push everyone to comply, whether it made sense or not.

One of my friends, a girl in those times, remembers that in her village the rice crop was so great one year that they left a lot of it to rot in the fields. They were certain, in the excitement of socialism and the Great Leap Forward, that next year would produce an even bigger crop, and the following year bigger still.

But in the next two years the rains did not come. So there were three years of famine, blamed by many on the errors of the Great Leap campaign and by others on natural disasters—my own guess is that it was a disastrous combination.

Then there was the Great Proletarian Cultural Revolution. It started in 1966, seventeen years after the founding of socialist China. Many things were coming to a head in that year. Two opposing factions had become politically powerful: A Beijing group supporting Liu Shaoqi and Deng Xiaoping took the position that Mao's theory of class struggle was theoretically and tactically wrong. (Few people would dare to come right out and say that—in traditional Chinese fashion, they expressed these convictions obliquely, in their defense of a current style of literature and in a generalized call for pluralism and the relaxing of rigid controls.) The other group, centred in Shanghai and led by Mao's third wife, Jiang Qing, and by Lin Biao, attacked other current literary trends as part of their demands for class struggle and for holding to Mao Zedong's version of revolutionary socialism.

(Several books have been written about Jiang Qing, mostly exposing her fanaticism. Some day, I hope, someone will write a balanced biography of Lin Biao, a more complex and to me a more interesting person. In his twenties, during the Long March, he was already one of the Communists' most brilliant generals, his name, they say, striking fear into opposing armies. During the anti-Japanese war, Lin was consistently a brilliant general. After the Japanese surrendered, it was under Lin's command that the Communists defeated the Nationalists' campaign to seize and hold the crucial northeast, and did this in spite of massive aid given to the Nationalists by the United States. Lin was one of the generals whose armies then swept South and overwhelmed the Nationalists. He commanded the attack on

Chiang Kaishek's rear-guard army protecting the retreat from Xiamen to Taiwan. In 1959, when Mao quarreled with Marshal Peng Dehuai, Lin became Minister of Defense in Peng's place. During the Cultural Revolution, Lin made the army into a political power for the left, and used his prestige and power to idolize Mao Zedong. He was the editor of the famous *Little Red Book* of quotations from Mao, and it was he who established the habit of calling Mao equal to Marx and Lenin, and of referring to him as "The great leader and great helmsman". [English doesn't catch the emphatic meaning of that Chinese *da*, which in this context should be translated as "greatest", since there could be only one "great leader."] In 1976, I often heard people refer to Mao this way; "As our great leader Mao Zedong says . . ."

Lin was officially designated as Mao Zedong's successor as leader of the Communist Party, the top job in China. But it all came apart in a big hurry. Some people told me that Lin became impatient and plotted to kill Mao and take control of the country. He was said to have planned to have Mao's train blown up. Western historians have suggested that Mao was made very uneasy about the way the army under Lin was taking a political role in the country's affairs. The official story is that Lin plotted to overthrow Mao, was betrayed by one of his associates, and escaped in a small plane which then crashed in a remote area of the Republic of Mongolia, killing all aboard.)

I have a 1968 booklet entitled *Summary of the Forum on the Work in Literature and Art in the Armed Forces with which Comrade Lin Piao Entrusted Comrade Chiang Ching*. It shows that Lin first called in Jiang Qing to reform the performances of the army's entertainment sector; after that, he and she were able to move onto the broader national stage and reform the opera (a very popular art form in China). Another booklet I have is called *On the Revolution of Peking Opera*, by Chiang

Ching (Don't let the variations in the spelling of names put you off. The romanized spelling has now been standardized in the form called *pinyin*, which is what I am using consistently except where I'm quoting.)

Jiang was an extremist. She made opera so doctrinaire that the only themes permitted were those celebrating the triumph of liberation from Old China and the glories of socialist China. In Luoyang in 1976, I saw an opera called "The Liberation of the Miao People by the People's Liberation Army in the Year 1952". (It was really an old traditional melodrama made over hastily into revolutionary propaganda—the audience of workers and peasants loved it, though whether they loved the familiar melodrama or the political message I leave you to guess.) Eventually, Jiang forbade all but eight approved operas for public performance.

Jiang was the leader of the radical Shanghai group. With Mao's active support, this group won its struggle against the moderate Beijing group. But Mao himself gave Jiang and her associates the name "Gang of Four", an expression that became popular all over China. That group, and especially Jiang herself, was hated in China, not only for her repressive ultra-left policies but for what they believed to be her outrageous hypocrisy. I'm told that while she imposed a puritanical lifestyle on the Chinese people, she herself lived in luxury. They say that although she drastically restricted what operas, plays, and movies the people could see, she herself had a private collection of American movies which she often watched. They say that after the great earthquake of 1976, she refused to let a relief train take precedence over her own private train. They say that at one time she talked about becoming Mao's successor, and later even aspired to be empress of China. They say that when she was finally arrested, the rejoicing was so great that all the wine was bought off the shelves of wine stores for the celebrations. They say that the happiest people then were the young women who had been forced to wait on her hand and foot.

I emphasize "they say", to indicate that my evidence is only what I heard, and to bring up my own suspicion that regardless of how well-founded these accusations might be, the people were also making her a scapegoat for Chairman Mao—they could revile her, but for a long time they did not dare attack him, or even his memory after he died.

Back in 1966, besides these factions, there were other pressures. Seventeen years of mass campaigns and authoritative controls, of sleepy traditional teaching and oppressive administration in the schools, and a great deal of oppression by corrupt local officials, had built up a resentment that was ready to break out. The very term "Cultural Revolution" suggested that while the military and economic revolutions had been won, there was still a lot in society that needed to be revolutionized.

Mao himself seems to have had a great impatience for the way things were going. He was disgruntled by the way the nation was losing its revolutionary fervour and settling down, and the way corruption was spreading in the ranks of the bureaucracy and the Party. It was time for a new mass campaign. He was getting on in age—he was seventy-three in 1966—and he must have felt that time was running out.

Also, he seems to have sensed that other leaders were edging him out of control. That may have been true, but it also seems clear that for some time Mao had gradually become paranoid. (See the ending of Harrison Salisbury's *The Long March*. Salisbury retraced the route of the Long March with old generals and other officers who had made the march, and heard their stories about that campaign and about what had happened since then. In the last section of his book he lists all the leaders who for one reason or another had been sidetracked or discredited or in some cases killed—in Salisbury's opinion, because Mao saw them as threats to his rule.) It has been asserted that Mao towards the end of his life suffered from Parkinson's disease, and that his paranoia was one of the symptoms.

In the spring of 1966, in Beijing's prestigious Beijing University a professor of philosophy put up a wall poster sharply criticizing the university's administration. This, the first of the "big character posters," struck a spark, and a wave of rebellion against the administrations and curricula spread through the universities of the city, and soon through the universities of the whole country. Mao Zedong expressed his admiration of that first poster, and predicted that it was the start of a popular revolt against stultified thinking. He appealed directly to university students and other young people to save the revolution from apathy and from its enemies. He put up his own big character poster, calling on the people to "bombard the headquarters," that is, to attack the leaders—of the universities, but also of government and even of the Party. The reaction was swift. Big character posters went up all over. (I saw new ones still being posted in 1976.)

By the summer of 1966 the rebellion spread to Beijing's high schools, and students were organized into groups and issued red armbands and started calling themselves "Red Guards" (*Hongwei bing*).

What happened after that is very confusing. Certainly in many places the Red Guards attacked office-holders at higher and higher levels, and displayed them in street marches or mass assemblies where they were shouted at and beaten. Many intellectuals were beaten to death, and some used so badly that they committed suicide—including the famous writer Lao She, author of Rickshaw Boy (*Luotuo Xiangzi*).

In Beijing, Mao Zedong addressed big rallies of Red Guards in Tiananmen Square and urged them to attack the "olds". There seems to have been no central or overall control of the Red Guards, and various groups of them had such different ideas that in many places they were fighting against each other, even with guns. A friend of mine from Yunnan Province tells me that there, where the Red Army had liberated the area without a shot being fired, divergent Red Guard groups now fought each other with rifles and machine guns seized in raids on army arsenals. In my university, Nankai, in Tianjin, no classes were taught for four years and two factions fought each other with guns until a group of workers and peasants came onto the campus and restored order. Most schools, I gather, all across China, were shut down, and the students either organized themselves into Red Guard units or were sent to the countryside to "learn from the peasants".

The worst excesses of the Cultural Revolution took place in the areas of China's minorities. There are fifty-five recognized minority nationalities in China, with their own languages, costumes, folkways, religions, and traditional territories. At Liberation, Mao Zedong developed an enlightened policy—on paper, I think it's surely one of the best minorities policies in the world. He sent teams of researchers into the minority areas, to learn the languages and record the folkways, and to help the minorities develop economically. The minorities were encouraged to respect their own cultures and histories, and to run their own local governments.

But among the Han (the group that we recognize as "the Chinese"—some 92 per cent of the population) there has always been a strong prejudice against the minorities. I remember watching a Chinese movie in which a Han man falls in love with a Tibetan woman and brings her home to meet his parents. His mother immediately welcomes the girl with a big hug—at which the whole audience burst out laughing.

During the Cultural Revolution, teams of Red Guards went into the minority areas and tried to put down the local religions and customs. Hundreds of temples were destroyed. Thousands of priests were herded into "learn through labour" camps. People were beaten for praying in public. Schools were forbidden to teach the local languages. A Mongolian I've talked to in Canada claims that in Inner Mongolia alone thousands of people were killed.

It was surely partly on account of this kind of mayhem that the Red Guard movement lost its mandate. Even in just military terms, it was stupid to make enemies of the minorities, most of whom live in the border regions, with ethnic cousins just across the border. Religion is central to the culture of many minorities, and the attack on their religions fueled a hatred of the Han which it will take generations to overcome, a hatred which has fed underground separatist movements in at least four parts of China.

The army, under Lin Biao's command, had been ordered to stay neutral, but eventually things got so out of hand that it had to intervene and restore order, which in some places it did by literally battling the Red Guards. Mao Zedong himself accused the Red Guards of having gone too far, and of betraying the whole purpose of the Cultural Revolution. Many thousands of them were sent off to the countryside to live and work among the poor peasants. (I learned about this from some of my students who had been Red Guards, and who, although they had managed to return from the countryside and get into university, and eventually into my graduate classes, were still angry at what they saw as being used and thrown away.)

Two basic questions bothered me more and more, as I heard the accounts of violence and disorder: Where were the police? Where were the courts? Did the victims of Red Guards have no legal recourse? And why, in a society which I personally have found moderate and non-violent, did such widespread, cruel, vindictive violence flourish? A third question, which still bothers me, is how to keep any sense of proportion—was the turmoil universal in China? Did it interrupt ordinary life for everybody? Were there no islands of sanity?

Well, I think two points must be made which help us understand what happened. One point is the question of law. You must remember that for thousands of years Chinese society was ruled by authority, not by law. The idea of law as binding on everybody, even officials, is a recent idea in China. (Before you call that weird, remember that the idea of law is not an old one in Western society, either. Think of the case of King Solomon and the two women who claimed the same baby. There's no question of law in that story. Solomon decided the case by his own personal wisdom and authority. For most of recorded history, famous judges have been famous for their wisdom, not for the upholding of law.) So in China when people in power said this or that shall be done, there was no law to appeal to— whatever authority decided, was the law.

Another thing to keep in mind is that after years of bitter fighting, after the wars of liberation were won, the idea of bitter struggle against unscrupulous enemies was carried over into peace time. Think of that when you read about China's lack of tolerance for dissent and dissenters. One of the basic tenets of the Cultural Revolution was that anyone who opposed the policy of the Great Leader was not just a dissenter but an enemy. Enemies threaten the whole system. Enemies have no rights. For generations (going back long before socialism, but unfortunately continuing under socialism) the Chinese had been taught that dissent, or criticism, is taboo. I saw this even in my classes, where it took a determined effort to persuade my students that I was really interested in their own ideas, not just there to expound my own "correct" ideas.

The stifling of dissent can never create a stable society—the need for expressing dissenting opinions is always there, and given opportunity will break out—and if the stifling has been severe, the outbreak may have an equal and opposite severity. (I don't mean to lecture the Chinese. The lessons I see in this aspect of Chinese history are just as important for the West as for China, and for all aspects of society, not just politics.)

The other question—was the turmoil universal, or were there islands of sanity—is one that cannot be answered yet. I hope historians will investigate it while there are still people alive who can testify. One thing I hope they can clarify is how many people were dedicated to making the reforms succeed, and how many were just going along with things, waving the Little Red Book but not trying to understand what it was all about. The Chinese are good at making an appearance of complying with conditions they can't reject. One of the reasons I like the movie "A Small Town Called Hibiscus" is that it shows this clearly—it was necessary to comply with orders to search out "bad elements", but they identified only a few people, and brought them out to display when necessary. Hard on the few, yes—the movie makes that very clear. But a way of token compliance, while the majority went on with their lives.

Other ways of surviving the reforms were developed by people in power who were not about to lie down and be reconstructed. One trick was to jump in as a champion of reform and wave the *Little Red Book* more vigorously than anyone else. Another was to deflect the attention of Red Guards onto someone else. Youthful idealism can sometimes be fanned into fanaticism, which is very convenient for those who know how to direct that fanaticism against their own rivals.

The movement broke down into local factional struggles and chaos, with factions also at the top changing the direction of the campaign abruptly. One of my Chinese friends, writing to me about those times, says, "When Deng announced the shift from class struggle to modernization as the agenda, people welcomed it wholeheartedly. For we were so sick of endless struggle against so-called enemies who might have been comrades yesterday and might change back to comrades tomorrow."

To add to the confusion, it's also clear to me that different things were happening in different places. My students at Xiamen University all remembered their high schools being shut down, but the high school I visited in Zhengzhou, where I saw the elastic skipping dance, was functioning very well. Though Qinghua and Beijing Universities and others, including my base, Nankai University, were shut down, still the institute which taught Fu Feiying so well was functioning, as were the Shaanxi Teachers University, the Hunan Number One Normal College, the Central Institute for the Minorities, and many workers colleges, technical institutes, high schools, primary schools and kindergartens, all of which we visited.

Minorities were widely forbidden to follow their traditions, but in the Central Institute for the Minorities we found minority students in traditional dress studying their own languages and customs, eating their traditional foods in the dining halls, talking to us freely about the historic enmity between their ethnic groups and the Han.

During the Cultural Revolution, public markets were shut down and peasants who tried to sell things which they had grown on their private plots were called "tails of capitalism which must be cut off." In the story "A Corner Forsaken by Love", written later but set during the Cultural Revolution, a peasant woman says, "If I take the eggs we've saved to sell in the street, I risk being driven from one place to another." And yet, in my journal for May 11, 1976, is a detailed description of a large market fair we drove through outside of Luoyang, going very slowly because of the great press of people. There we saw hundreds of peasants selling all kinds of things, including lines of old women sitting by the road, each with her basket of eggs.

At the Thousand Buddha Hill in Shandong I saw that all the statues had had their heads knocked off, and the pagodas had been burned down. But the Wild Goose Pagoda in Xi'an was not only intact but kept in excellent repair. So were the thousands of statues in the Longman Caves near Luoyang, and the temples and parks of Beijing and many other places I visited.

During the Cultural Revolution, to read foreign books or study foreign languages was to lay yourself open to persecution. One of the teachers of English at Nankai was sent to the countryside charged with reading too many foreign books. But there was Comrade Fu with her excellent English, after all, and the local guides who joined us in each city we came to, and the English classes we visited in several institutes and high schools. A dozen of my Xiamen students who had been sent to the countryside had been able to continue their study of English by the aid of English classes broadcast by the Guangzhou radio station.

You can see how hard it is to sum up.

One thing certain is that the Cultural Revolution failed to reach its objectives. It erupted into such violence that the following generation repudiated all theories and ideologies. It tried to change the elitism of intellectuals by beating them, humiliating them, sending them to feed pigs in the countryside—the result of which was an even more rigid sense of class and a hatred of all aspects of socialism. The irony is that those reforms which the Cultural Revolution was most determined to accomplish were finally not accomplished.

What happened? Well, for one thing, Mao died and Deng came into power and turned off the tap. He swept away the communes, and the reforms—including those reforms in the schools which so excited me at the Hunan Normal College. But I think that Deng or no Deng, the things which the Cultural Revolution set out to change were too deeply entrenched to be overthrown by such a mass movement.

Take the universities as a clear example. The universities were the first target of the Cultural Revolution, the places where it started. Many changes were experimented with. Think of teachers and students not only working hard in class but exercising together outside of class, and getting in the wheat together, to break down the hierarchal gap between teacher and student. Think of competition replaced by students and teachers working together to bring the whole class to a high level of competence and achievement. (One teacher said to me, "Why do you fail students, in the West? If you take them in, why don't you teach them?")

But it was breathtaking, once the Cultural Revolution was repudiated, to see how quickly the universities bounced right back to the old patterns. The experiments sank without trace. Chinese universities today are run on the same pattern as old traditional Western ones, and have adopted the same standards, the same degrees—everything. Some of us are nostalgic for "the old days", and for the great students of those days. That nostalgia is about all that's left.

Or is it? Are the teachers turned out by the Hunan Normal College not having an effect on their schools? Are my great students who came through those years in the countryside full of experience and strength not having an effect?

I've noticed three different kinds of people who came back from their years in the countryside. One: cynical uneducated unskilled people who form the drifting perpetrators of small crimes—breaking and entering, picking pockets, swaggering, going in small groups or in gangs, carrying knives which they use to defend each other—victims and victimizers. The second:

artists, especially the makers of movies, who came back with a new knowledge of the extent to which the country people had been left out and ignored, and with detailed knowledge of the hard lives of the peasants. They produced, for example, those great movies of the 1980s which won prizes at world festivals— "Yellow Earth", "Old Well", "Red Sorghum", "Hunan girl", "Border Town". They brought the neglected country people to the world's attention—and in doing so, made the Chinese government very uneasy. The third group: those great students of mine, smart, eager, worldly-wise but idealistic—the best students a teacher could hope for.

Well, that those were great students doesn't justify the violence and suffering, any more than advances in technology in time of war justify war. Finally, all I can fall back on is the fact that good things really did happen then, alongside the horror—and my hope that eventually society will learn how to make social progress without violence and chaos. There are some signs of progress, after all. When one dynasty succeeded another, in China's long history, it was by conquest, with disruption and violence and suffering and chaos—but Hua succeeded Mao, Deng succeeded Hua and Jiang succeeded Deng quite calmly (whatever power struggles went on backstage.) That may not be enough to call a trend yet, but we can hope.

11

The Eighties: Deng Xiaoping, "Capitalist Roader"

In August 1979, when I started living and working in China, China's Premier was Hua Guofeng, and the pictures of Mao which had been everywhere had been replaced by a picture of Hua sitting next to Chairman Mao. Mao is touching Hua's knee and saying to him, "With you in charge, I am at ease." But Hua's attempts to wear Mao's mantle were not working. Few people knew who he was before these pictures appeared, and some of them told me they wondered if Mao had ever really said that or had ever patted Hua's knee. Similarly, one of Hua's pronouncements—"Whatever Mao Zedong said and whatever Mao Zedong did must be taken as correct"—was not popular at a time when people were just beginning to feel free to criticize Mao. (It started obliquely. When I mentioned the Gang of Four to a hotel worker in Beijing, he said, "Oh, yes, the Gang of Four." But he held up *five* fingers.)

There was a feeling of impending change in the air. On January 1, 1979, China and the United States had "normalized diplomatic relations". In August, when I arrived to live in China, there was still no sign of change, but everyone knew it was coming. Everyone knew that the person who was increasingly important in China's leadership was Deng Xiaoping, the Vice-Premier. And sure enough, in 1980, Hua Guofeng was quietly set aside and Deng became Premier. Mao Zedong was dead and ceremoniously entombed. Hua Guofeng, that shadow of Mao, had been set aside, and Deng Xiaoping was telling the world that the Cultural Revolution had been a ten-year disaster. It was obviously the beginning of new times in China.

I remembered with irony that in 1976, when I asked commune leaders what problems they had, the first thing they said was, "We are struggling against right-wing attempts to overthrow previous correct decisions." When I said that those words didn't mean anything to me, they said, "We are struggling against the false ideas of the number two capitalist-roader in power." And when I asked them to be more specific, they said, "We are opposing the false ideas of Deng Xiaoping." Now, in 1980, we were beginning a decade of Deng's leadership, a decade which would develop according to Deng Xiaoping's ideas.

Deng was born in 1904 (so he was ten years older than I was). When still a teenager, he was one of a group of Chinese who went to study in France, and joined the Chinese Communist Party there. (Zhou Enlai was one of that group, and Zhou did not forget him.)

In the 1930s, Deng joined Mao Zedong in the organization of Soviets in Fujian and Jiangxi Provinces. He was one of the leaders of the Long March, apparently as an organizer and administrator. After Liberation, Chairman Mao put Deng in charge of the huge project of moving factories and other possible targets of US bombing from the coastal areas to the West, a job he accomplished so efficiently that Mao singled him out for praise.

But in 1958, Deng was strongly opposed to the excesses of the Great Leap Forward, and by implication he opposed Mao's theory of ongoing class struggle. Mao became disillusioned with him. He began to be mentioned as one of the "capitalist-roaders in power". During the Cultural Revolution he was dismissed from office, put under house arrest, and set to work in a factory.

After Mao's death, Premier Zhou Enlai brought him back into the top leadership and made him, in effect, Zhou's successor. (Zhou himself was dying of cancer.) When Zhou died, and the people covered the monument to heroes in Tiananmen Square with flowers and memorial poems in his honour, the Gang of Four had all the flowers and poems removed, and then blamed Deng for the ensuing riot. So he was again removed from power. With the arrest of the Gang of Four, he was called back into the leadership once more. He became Vice-Premier under Hua, and in 1980 succeeded Hua as Premier.

This immediately signaled a new period for China. Deng announced that the Cultural Revolution had been a ten-year disaster. He called for an end to the ideological wars with his slogan, "Black cat, white cat, what does it matter so long as it catches mice?" (I heard that repeated frequently, and always with approval.) Deng announced that it was time to get back to work building up China, launching a campaign for the "Four Modernizations"—that is, the modernization of agriculture, industry, the army, and science and technology.

Two big popular changes were quickly obvious in people's lives: the ideological campaigns were over, and there began to be an increase in consumer goods, more and more year by year. Deng was credited with these changes—not entirely accurately. Mao Zedong had said back in 1963, "If in the decades to come we don't completely change the situation in which our economy and technology lag far behind those of imperialist countries, it will be impossible for us to avoid being pushed around again." And it was Zhou Enlai who had proposed the slogan "Four Modernizations" and urged a campaign to accomplish them. But it was unmistakably Deng who brought the campaign about, and established modernization rather than class struggle as the agenda for China.

Under Mao the nation had built up the infrastructure and the economy that made an outpouring of consumer goods finally possible. To cite just one example, China under Mao developed the fertilizers that made agricultural modernization possible, and the new fertilizer factories went into production just in time for Deng to come along and get the credit. But still, unmistakably, he was the leader of the modernization campaign, the leader who replaced class struggle with building up the economy.

One of the most important changes Deng advocated, the one which in the long run will perhaps have the most important effect on Chinese lives, was his demand that China should be ruled by law— not by the fiat of people in authority. For thousands of years China had been ruled by authority. In some dynasties there had been complex systems of law, but it was understood that these were simply the codification of the decisions of those in power. Whatever people in power said, was the law. The Constitution of China, unlike the Constitution of the United States, is not binding on the government. Any government in power can change it. The idea of law as binding on everybody, even officials, goes against a tradition of thousands of years. It will take a long time to be generally accepted—it will be especially hard work to convince officials that the law binds them, too.

I remember the case of the mayor of a town outside of Tianjin. He was returning from Tianjin in a mini-van with some of his town officials. On the new tollroad, he refused to pay the toll. When the toll-taker refused to let him pass, he ordered his men to seize her, and they took her with them to his town. The next day, to his great surprise, soldiers and police came and arrested him, and he was taken back to Tianjin and thrown in jail. The Tianjin newspaper had a photo of him in a cell, holding the bars and staring out as if he thought the whole world had suddenly gone crazy.

One of the hardest things to change in China is just this. For many generations anyone in power, at any level, took it for granted that the position carried the right to do whatever he wanted. If there was trouble, he had only to appeal to higher powers, who would 'of course' uphold the ancient principle. In the movie "A Small Town Called Hibiscus", the story of which takes place during the Cultural Revolution, an arrogant woman is able to ride roughshod over the whole village because she is protected by an uncle in the provincial power structure.

In another popular movie set in the Cultural Revolution, "At Middle Age", a minister of state needs a cataract operation. His wife throws her weight around to get the best doctor. She assumes that the doctor in charge is not the best, simply because she is a woman. When she finds out that the woman really is the expert, she tries to make friends with her. She tells her she should eat a certain fruit to keep up her health, and when the doctor says that kind of fruit is not available, she says, "We have lots of it. I'll get you some." She offers the use of a government car. Finally, she says, "Are you a Party member, dear comrade?" When the doctor says no, she adds, "Well, if you do a good job on this operation, you will be." A gasp went through the movie audience at this. Outside the theatre afterwards one of my friends said to me, "We HATE them!" without having to tell me whom she meant. (It was this hatred, ultimately due to the corruption which comes from rule by authority, that later brought masses of people out to support the students demonstrating in Tiananmen Square against corruption in high places.)

I'm sure it was the Cultural Revolution (in which he had been hurled out of high office twice, and had lived for years under house arrest, working in a factory, denounced as a "capitalist roader") that made Deng determined to do away with emotional mass campaigns and put the country under rule by law. As part of his campaign, he renounced the worship of leaders. When the ubiquitous pictures and statues of Mao Zedong disappeared, and those of Hua followed them into oblivion, they were not replaced by pictures or statues of Deng. In many cities the huge public squares where charismatic leaders had whipped up the emotions of massed crowds were broken up into smaller spaces, separated by fountains and raised flower beds.

All these changes made Deng popular. When Deng was on the reviewing stand of the National Day parade in Beijing, October 1, 1980, some students in that parade suddenly unfurled a banner saying "*Xiaoping, nin hao!*" (The closest equivalent I can suggest in English is "Hi, there, Xiaoping!" It was an impudent use of his personal name—tempered, I was amused to note, by *nin*, which is the formal way of saying "you"). It would have been hard to predict, on that day, that at the end of the decade students would march with the banner, "*Xiaoping, xia tai!*" ("Xiaoping, resign!")

For years now—under Deng and after Deng—the government has pushed a public campaign for the rule of law. But the change will not be easy. I think it will take many years. To show you how far the campaign still has to go, these days newspapers often quote some official as saying that anyone who breaks a certain law "ought to be punished", as if there were some question about it. It is common for a local or regional police force to announce that for the next three or four months it will enforce such and such a law which was already on the books.

In the November 12, 1998 issue of *China Daily*, China's English-language newspaper, is an article with these passages:

> Qu said that his committee has reached consensus with the Supreme People's Court to tighten 'rule by law.' The action

aims to arouse public awareness of 'rule by law'. . . . Between
1990 and 1997, the country uncovered more than 320,000
violations of State laws on water conservation and water-
pollution control, and another 3.78 million cases against
State Forest Protection Law. . . . Due to ignorance of 'rule
by law', a number of laws are not well enforced, said Qu,
adding that publicity and education must be expanded to
encourage people to follow laws.

The indications are that the battle is gradually being won,
but it will take a long struggle. The influence of foreigners doing
business in China has been strong, with their insistence on the
enforcement of contracts, on copyright and patent protection,
and on laws setting the rules of the economic game in general.

The current Premier is Zhu Rongji, who is called China's
economic tsar. He is pushing the campaign step by step, making
law, and enforcement of law, cover more and more sectors of the
society. (But even he is too politically astute to try to make the
law apply to the top leaders and their families.)

The eighties were a decade of steadily rising standards of living,
which I watched with wonder. I've talked about it before in several
places in this book, but I have to pull it all together and look at
the whole thing and its significance. It's hard to remember now
how much of what we take for granted in the West was missing
from people's lives in 1979. It was like going back in time about
a hundred years—but what took a hundred years to bring about
in the West was crammed into a heady ten years in China.

When I started living in China in the autumn of 1979, there
were more horses than motor vehicles in the streets. It was not
yet an automobile culture—the streets belonged to bicycle riders
and pedestrians, and what autos there were were forbidden to
keep their lights on at night, because they would blind the people

in the street. Car lights could be flicked on and off, but not kept on.

As for personal lives, people had very little choice of food. The only green vegetable we had all that winter was *bai cai*, or Chinese cabbage. Most foods were rationed, and what you could buy even with ration coupons was not much—about an egg a week per person, for example, almost no meat at all, very little fish. The diet was mostly rice, with pickled vegetables. People had almost no choice of what to wear. Not only was very little cloth available, and almost no ready-made clothes in the stores, but social pressures made it almost impossible for either women or men to wear anything but "Mao jackets" and loose pants. The only jewelry I saw was on baby girls. There were no cosmetics. For winter clothing, housewives and grandmothers spent a lot of their time all summer in knitting warm underwear and making plain cotton jackets and pants stuffed with cotton batting. In winter, the little kids looked spherical. There were no tape recorders, no privately owned cameras, no television sets except in special rooms in dormitories or hotels. There were no free markets. Everything was sold in State-run stores in which a lot of the shelves were empty. There were no washing machines, no refrigerators, no gas stoves or electric stoves (cooking was done on tiny coal stoves). No running hot water. No telephones in people's homes.

Only foreigners could go into the "Friendship Stores" where all kinds of things were for sale that were not available to Chinese people. We could buy bicycles without ration coupons, for instance. Once in 1979, I had the good fortune to spend a day with a couple of Beijing opera performers, and the woman asked me, as a present on her thirtieth birthday, to go to the Beijing Friendship store and buy a bicycle for her—with her money. She was admitted as my interpreter, and we picked out a bicycle, and carefully watched while the salespeople tightened all the nuts and bolts, and she went off riding it, in great delight.

On the other hand, I remember once in Tianjin joining a crowd on the street, watching the results of an accident. A young woman had just missed being run over by a truck by diving sideways off her bicycle. She was not seriously hurt, but her bike was demolished. A police officer was scolding her loudly. She was crying. The onlookers were arguing with the officer. Leave the poor girl alone! Doesn't she have enough trouble? Her bicycle is a wreck, and it may take her a year to get a ration coupon for a new one!

As for entertainment, there was very little to do in the evenings except study or go visiting. It was only on special occasions that people went to restaurants. There were movies, and operas, but as I've told you, during the Cultural Revolution only a few "politically correct" ones were shown, and people were bored with them.

Were the people unhappy? No, I don't think so. There's a psychological principle involved here. As long as everybody around you is living the same way you are, it's hard to feel deprived. It's when alternatives appear, and especially when you begin to see people who have much more than you have, that frustration and anger develop.

In 1982, washing machines began to appear in the stores. They were primitive—small cylinders, not hooked up to water pipes or drains, with no spin dryers or wringers. As was common at the beginning of Deng's decade, people thought about the social implications. One of my friends was a teacher of English at Nankai who spent the year 1982 at a university in Australia. When she came back, she told me that a socialist in Australia had been shocked to hear that the Chinese were buying such material goods as washing machines. "So there goes Chinese socialism!" he said. My friend boiled over. "Listen," she said, "my husband and I work long hours at our jobs six days a week. Sunday is our only day off, to do our major shopping, spend time with our children, see our friends, and catch up with our preparations for class. But I have to spend a full half of that day washing the family laundry in hand basins—and you have the nerve to tell me I'm a bad socialist for wanting a washing machine!" The same kind of argument was caused by the appearance of many of the material advances of the decade: Is this compatible with socialism? Until, that is, somewhere around 1989 ~~1996~~. By that time people simply shrugged and went for the goodies. Black cat, white cat, what does it matter?

Now, people have state-of-the-art washers and dryers. They have a wide variety of foods to eat, at home or in restaurants, and to see a ration book you must go to the museums. There's a wide variety of clothes and styles. The women wear cosmetics and jewelry—and so do most urban little girls. Cloth shoes are hard to find in the stores now. Everyone but eccentrics and old grandmothers wears leather shoes with heels. People have cameras, and colour film, and big colour TV sets, and tape recorders, and compact disks, and video-compact-disks, and telephones, and cellular phones, and pagers. People ride in taxis now. There were none in 1979, except at the big hotels where foreigners lived. Now people have matching furniture, and kitchen gadgets, and pictures on the walls. People are beginning to have their own autos—though this will take longer to catch on—and they are buying their own apartments.

All such things came in steadily over the decade. At first, new things were amazing, but gradually people got used to the idea of change, and began to take new material goods for granted. (When refrigerators first came in, some of my friends used them only to chill watermelons, before they realized that the new gadgets could change their shopping habits.)

Along with material changes came new freedoms, and the acceptance of new freedoms as part of the good new life. Look at how freedom of choice was affected: in 1979, no choice of what to eat, what to wear. No choice of what music to listen to—all they had was what their transistor radios picked up from the State-run broadcasters. Tape recorders and audio tapes and CDs let them choose what music they wanted to hear. TVs and VCRs let them choose what to watch. The freedom from ideology also let them decide what to do with their time. More and more, as the decade went on, people indulged in hobbies (stamp collecting, flowers, photography, fishing, keeping pets, and many others). Dancing had been taboo as late as December 1979 (when it was sternly forbidden at Nankai University by the Party). But it became very popular soon after that, and before long was even taught in the schools. Karaoke bars were introduced from Japan and quickly became popular. Many new restaurants opened their doors, a lot of them modeled on the Western ones that were appearing in the big cities.

From year to year, students in my classes were less and less restrained by ideological orthodoxy, more and more free to speak out their own opinions.

So, with all these good things happening, how to explain why the students, who in 1980 carried a banner saying "Hi there, Xiaoping", were calling for his resignation in 1989? I think Deng himself could never answer that. I imagine him saying, "Look at all the things I've given them! What do they want from me?" That's another way of saying that he seems never to have realized that when you give people economic freedoms and personal freedoms, sooner or later they are going to think about political freedoms, too. I think the reason he angrily repudiated the students of the spring and summer of 1989 is that he never made the connection. His model, apparently, was Singapore, which combined economic liberalism with political and social repression.

Well, to begin with, the economic prosperity through the decade was not all roses. Increasingly, as the decade developed, there were problems. One was that the increase in productivity resulting from doing away with the communes did not last. It was, indeed, suspect from the first, in spite of its acclamation by the government and its very good press. For one thing, the immediate increase in grain production was partly deceptive. The communes had stored grain to deal with possible future shortages. When the communes were disbanded, that stored grain came on the market and was counted as part of the increase in grain. For another thing, there was misleading accounting. It's true that independent farmers were making more money, but they were losing other things. In the communes children had free education. There was free medical care, free upkeep of infrastructure, and so on. Also, a lot of what they received in the communes was not cash, but grain. Altogether, to compare only their cash income before and after is very misleading. And it quickly developed that when farmers were free to choose what to grow, they opted for money crops like cotton rather than grain, so the total grain production failed to keep up with expectations.

Another problem was that during the decade a wide gap developed between the rich and the poor—something that was strictly controlled in the socialist period. One of Deng's most famous mottoes for the new life was "To get rich is glorious!" He called the new rich "pioneers, showing the rest of the country how to do it." But when we talk about people having VCRs and cellular phones, and saving up to buy automobiles, we must ask what people we're talking about. An increasingly rich middle class, yes. No question about that. But many more people could only look on and feel left out.

On the National Day weekend in October, 1996, I went up to Beijing to visit three friends. One, whom I had supervised for her MA program at Nankai, had a job with the China Travel Service. The second, whose PhD program at Nankai I had helped supervise, was working for the National Television Company. The third was an old friend, a Chinese-Canadian , who was now the Beijing correspondent for a business magazine published in Hong Kong. My two students were living in a world with very few of the new material advantages. The correspondent lived in the new prosperity. He and his wife (also an old friend) took me to dinner at a fancy new restaurant, one of a chain. They told me they'd been lucky to find it, because it was so good but so inexpensive. But later, when I asked my students if they'd ever gone to that restaurant, they laughed. There was no way they could possibly afford to go there. That was for the new rich. (I'm comparing incomes here, not personalities. I'm fond of all these friends.)

Another problem of the decade has been that as the government concentrates on helping business develop, it has cut back on other things, such as support for the arts and for education. At my Chinese university, Nankai, money became so tight that the Foreign Languages Department was ordered to raise 40 per cent of its own budget. Imagine a Western English Department trying to do that, and what an upheaval that would cause in its programming and its morale! Today, all my Chinese colleagues at Nankai are moonlighting, teaching private classes evenings or weekends—not to buy automobiles or cellular phones or be part of the new prosperity, but just to keep up with daily expenses. Today, also, students must pay tuition to go to university, so the system is more and more restricted to those whose families can afford it, just as in the West.

Another big problem has been in ideology. It's true that people welcomed Deng's slogan, "Black cat, white cat, what does it matter so long as it catches mice?" They were ready for an end to the ideology of the Cultural Revolution. But really, what does the slogan mean? It all depends, doesn't it, on what's meant by *mice*? If you said that *mice* meant socialist advancement, Chairman Mao would welcome the slogan. What, exactly, did it mean to Deng and to the Chinese of the 1980s? Actually, if you stop to think about it, Deng was not getting away from ideology at all—he was substituting the ideology of capitalism for the previous ideology of socialism, wasn't he?

But he was cautious not to do this too openly or too quickly. At the beginning of the decade, in fact, he said, "If China ever goes capitalist our grandchildren will never forgive us." And although he repudiated the Cultural Revolution decisively and promptly, he did away with some of the old basics more carefully, step by step. For example, one of the precepts of socialist China was that for one person to hire another person to work for him or her would open the door to exploitation, so only the State could hire people. At first, under Deng, it became permissible to hire one person, and soon young women were flocking from the countryside to become live-in maids in the cities. Then the rule was relaxed to hiring two people, then ten, and finally the restrictions were removed altogether. As the decade developed, there was more and more concentration of ownership and of wealth, with individuals owning several factories. Today, people tell me, there are a million millionaires in China, some of them members of the Chinese Communist Party. The Vice-President of China is a multi-millionaire, known popularly as "the Red Capitalist".

Perhaps the biggest change of the 1980s has been from socialist idealism to hedonism. "We used to say 'Look to the future!' Now we say, 'Look for the money!'" In the early years of the decade, this was widely resented and widely debated. You remember the case of the old man in the Shenzhen train station who asked a young man to help him with his heavy bags. In old tradition, the young man should have been pleased to help. But in the new spirit of the decade, he said, "I'll carry them to the front door only, for fifty cents a bag." The outraged old man wrote a letter to a newspaper. There followed hundreds of letters, split about evenly, the paper said, between those who supported the old man and wondered what the country was coming to, and those who supported the young man. We are in a money economy now, they said, and people deserve to be paid for their work.

As the decade developed, perhaps the feeling against the new materialism lessened. I think so, but I'm not sure. Certainly that feeling got less and less publicity. But many people I know are still expressing the old man's sense of outrage at the way everything these days seems to be based on money. They point out the connection between the attitude of getting as much as you can and the fact that crime has steadily increased during the decade. They point to the fact that gambling and prostitution are reported in the press as "rampant", and that cases of economic crime involving millions of dollars are increasingly frequent. They believe that materialism led to corruption and corruption led to popular support for the student demonstrations in 1989, in which students carried banners calling on Deng Xiaoping to resign.

12

Tiananmen

[I wrote about the Tiananmen "incident" in my journals in 1989 day by day as events occurred. In 1993, I pulled those entries together into one account of what happened. I started to re-write it again for this book, but on reading it over I thought, "Let it stand! It catches the spirit of those days." So here it is, just as I wrote it then. I'll follow it up with some notes on what happened later.]

The massacre in Beijing on June 4, 1989, stunned the Chinese. My students and colleagues and other friends were in a state of shock for days. We had all thought there might be violence, and the students were braced for it, but we were thinking of teargas and clubs, not tanks, armoured personnel carriers and assault rifles. No one could have imagined that the demonstrations would end in the slaughter of unarmed civilians by the Army. And yet, after coming out of my own shock and grief and anger enough to think about it, I could see that the brutalities of that day, and the following witch-hunt, jail sentences, and executions had precedents and ought perhaps to have been predicted.

It was not the first time a period of freedom of expression had been followed by a severe repression. In 1957, Mao Zedong said "Let a hundred flowers blossom and a hundred schools contend," but when people took him at his word and started criticizing the government and the Party, the response was the "Anti-rightist" clampdown. In 1978 came the "Early Spring".

Now that the Cultural Revolution was over, it was again time for re-appraisal. Chinese writers assumed a freedom to criticize. Unauthorized magazines sprang up. The *Democracy Wall* was covered with poems and declarations, and exposures of corrupt officials. In the clampdown that followed this brief period of openness many people were arrested and some sentenced to jail terms. A young man named Wei Jingsheng, who had edited an unauthorized magazine and who had declared that the Four Modernizations were meaningless without a fifth modernization, that is, democracy, was sentenced to fifteen years in prison.

There are many other examples in Chinese history of the suppression of intellectuals. Books had been burned and intellectuals beaten, imprisoned, or killed as early as the Qin emperor's crackdown about 215 B.C. and as recently as the Cultural Revolution.

But there was a special horror to the June 4 massacre because it was the sudden and brutal smashing of a wonderful, hopeful, joyous, non-violent mass movement.

The students who demonstrated in the spring of 1989 were a special generation. Those who were about twenty years old, as many were, would have been about seven years old in the year Mao Zedong died and the Cultural Revolution ended. They grew up in a period of peace and quiet, a period of a spectacular rise in the standard of living, a period of slowly but steadily increasing freedoms. Increasingly, the relaxation of controls, together with the expanding economy, made it possible for people to make their own decisions, in food, in clothes, in hairstyles, in lifestyles, in work, and in thinking.

The rural contract system that supplanted the communes made it possible for millions of peasants to decide individually for themselves what kind of work they would do, what hours they would keep, what they would do with their money, where they would go to sell their products or to look for work. In the cities more and more people set up their own small businesses. Along the streets there were barbers, fixers of bicycles or of broken pots and pans, people selling all kinds of things. Individuals could go into business, could hire others, could own factories, could make fortunes and spend their money as they liked.

All these freedoms made people, especially young people, impatient with the control of their personal lives. More and more they wanted freedom to concentrate on their own needs and desires, their personal enjoyment of life.

My student Xiao Guo said in class that she liked *The Great Gatsby* better than *The Grapes of Wrath* because Gatsby was handsome and adventurous and rich, so his life was full of possibilities, while *The Grapes of Wrath* was just one more story of peasants trapped in poverty. She also said to me once, "What did our grandfathers make a revolution for? Wasn't it so their children and grandchildren could have a better life? So why shouldn't we enjoy life?"

Tens of thousands of students went abroad to study, and compared their lives to the way the rest of the world was living. Many foreigners came to China, some to teach, some on business, some as tourists, all bringing ideas and assumptions new to the Chinese. My students said, "When we compared ourselves to Old China, we saw we had come a long way, so we put up with lack of housing and assigned jobs and control of our lives. But when we saw that people in other countries didn't have to put up with such stuff, we got angry."

It was a period of rising living standards, rising possibilities of personal choice, and—inevitably—rising expectations.

At the same time, though, it was also a period when many ordinary people, squeezed by inflation, were shut out of the new luxuries, while they saw officials living high and many people getting rich by bribery and corruption. They saw this, especially, in the families of the country's top leaders, as they learned about them by news items in the press and by China's efficient grapevine.

There had been economic reform, but no political reform, and the resulting patchwork system left lots of room for shenanigans. To take just one example, the State, to encourage the growing of grain, sold fertilizer to farmers at less than market prices. All well and good, except that the local officials who administered the program could with impunity sell the fertilizer in the market, at market prices, pay the lower cost to the government and pocket the difference, and then tell the farmers the subsidized fertilizer was all gone. The farmers, having no recourse—no power of the vote, no access to the courts in such matters—were helpless victims, whose anger sometimes broke out in mass raids on fertilizer storehouses.

After the boom period of the first half of the decade, the economy slowed down. At the same time, inflation was so severe that in some years the price of common foodstuff rose 40 per cent. People on fixed incomes, including pensioners, teachers, and government workers, were badly squeezed. (In China, that adds up to a lot of people.) By the end of the decade, most university teachers were moonlighting on second jobs, or tutoring, just to keep up with basic living expenses.

At the same time, they saw street vendors and the owners of the new businesses, and grafting bureaucrats, rolling in money. Bars and nightclubs opened, organized gambling and prostitution became, as the papers said, "rampant"—to give the flashy rich ones ways of spending their money. For forty years people had been taught to despise such things, calling them capitalist decadence and exploitation, but now the government seemed to be condoning and even encouraging them. And the gap between those who could enjoy the new prosperity and those who could not increased year by year.

Such contradictions, tensions, and frustrations were causes of popular unrest and eventually of those student demonstrations. It all came to a head with the death of Hu Yaobang in April, 1989. Hu had been the very popular national leader of the Party's Youth League, and later Secretary General of the Communist Party (one of the two top positions in China.) He had encouraged young people to open to new ideas and new freedoms. We saw him almost nightly on TV, in Western suit and tie, assuring foreign dignitaries that China was open to new ideas, new ways of doing things.

But after student demonstrations in 1986, Hu had been removed from his posts, the official reason being that he encouraged "bourgeois liberalization." (His firing, in spite of the fact that he was a protégé of Deng Xiaoping, was a sign of a power struggle going on at the top.) In spite of his firing, or perhaps even because of it, he continued to be a hero to the students.

He died on April 15. The next day there was a march on the Nankai campus by roughly 2,000 students. I heard them, at about eight o'clock in the evening, and ran out of my apartment building to see what was up. It was obviously spontaneous— there were no flags or placards, no shouted slogans, no singing— just a lot of people walking together out of the gate while others stood or sat atop the campus wall taking photos by flash, the lights popping all around us. The marchers went down the street three blocks to the gates of Teachers University. At first, those gates were locked and it seemed the crowd would break them down, but someone opened them and hundreds of Teachers University students poured out. They all listened to a few speeches and then gradually dispersed. The Tianjin police came hurriedly and late, but did not interfere, only stood on the sidelines,looking anxious. There was much excitement afterwards as people broke up into small groups and talked about it all.

One group formed around me and asked me if students in Canada had such demonstrations, and what I thought of this one. It was all very low key, but since nothing like it had happened in their lifetimes, they were excited.

I thought that would be the end of it, but of course it was just the beginning.

On April 22, the government held a memorial ceremony for Hu Yaobang in the Great Hall of the People, on the western edge of Tiananmen Square. The country's leaders praised him as a communist hero, but neglected to mention that they had fired him from office. Outside, in the square, 10,000 students were gathered. Their leaders knelt on the steps of the building with banners saying, "Please come and talk to us," and the students were shouting the same plea. But the doors remained shut.

My students, returning from Beijing and coming to talk to me about it, could hardly believe it. "What kind of government refuses to talk to the people?" (I could have mentioned several, but did not. Their amazement was a sign of how they had been taught to think of the government up to then.) If Premier Zhou Enlai were still alive, the students told me, he would have come out at once, and sat on the steps and listened to us. (In the following demonstrations, some students carried pictures of Zhou, just the pictures with no words necessary.)

The next day, as I was working at my desk in my apartment, I heard sounds of marching and singing, and running out I found hundreds of students marching along the main street of the campus and out of the gate—with flags, banners, and placards—marching in good order and singing the Communist Internationale and *"Qi Lai"*, ("Rise Up") the old revolutionary song. I walked alongside this demonstration for six hours through the streets of Tianjin, more and more impressed and caught up in the enthusiasm and in the certainty that I was watching history being made.

Students from Teachers University and Tianjin University joined the march, and as it went along others joined in from the Tianjin Foreign Languages Institute, and the Tianjin Medical University, and other universities and institutes—in all, according to TV reports the next day, over 20,000 students, marching ten abreast with the line extending out of sight in both directions. The outside line of students on each side held hands back and front making a chain to keep any trouble-makers from joining, letting in only people with student IDs.

The 1986 demonstrators had been confused in their demands, and most people thought of them as just trouble-makers. This time, the students zeroed in on three demands. They shouted them. Their banners and placards called for them: an end to corruption, especially at high levels of government, more democracy, and more personal freedom. These went to the heart of popular discontent, and people came running from all directions to cheer and clap. From the start, the demonstrations had the support of everyone except a few old people who looked frightened, perhaps remembering that the Cultural Revolution had started with student marches.

The Tianjin police did nothing to stop the march, but simply directed traffic around it. In Tianjin, as in China generally at that time, the police were unarmed, having neither guns nor clubs. As the marchers came to the Party headquarters building, we saw hundreds of these unarmed police massed on the steps in case there should be trouble. But the students were not there to make trouble. They marched past the building, holding up each other's hands and shouting in unison, "*Jingcha ai renmin!*" ("The people's police love the people!")—an old socialist slogan. Most of the policemen smiled, and some of them laughed, and I thought, "Where but in China?" Against this background the subsequent massacre was especially outrageous.

I say frankly that I loved these young people. What people had been calling "the Silent Generation", which supposedly cared for nothing but money and romance, marched for hours with heads high, joyously singing and chanting, so full of enthusiasm that they never tired, marching to change the country.

They were so orderly and self-confident you would have thought they were old-timers at this game. They shouted slogans all together, with great shouts. They sang with great spirit. They laughed, and waved to the crowds that were cheering them on.

I remember many demonstrations in Canada and in the United States, especially during the 1960s. There was a similar enthusiasm here, a similar joy in standing up together. But there was a crucial difference. In spite of the restraint of the Tianjin police, these young people were running very serious risks, and knew it. They remembered Wei Jingsheng's fifteen-year jail sentence. But the essence of their spirit, which the crowds around them shared, was not so much defiance as joy—joy that someone was at last speaking up, taking a stand, trying to do something about the common grievances. When you see thousands of young people stand up, at great risk, and joyfully give the world a push in the right direction, you know you'll never forget it.

Meanwhile, there were similar marches in other cities all across China. The centre of the movement developed in Beijing's Tiananmen Square, "the Gate of Heavenly Peace", where forty years earlier Mao Zedong had shouted "The Chinese people have stood up!" and announced the birth of socialist China. The government tried to convince people that it was all a local Beijing incident, but only foreigners believe that—it's called "The Tiananmen Incident", but as you can see by my report from Tianjin, it was far from that.

The government's first response came in an editorial in the Party newspaper *People's Daily* on April 26, edited and approved and perhaps written by Deng Xiaoping:

These people are not . . . advocating the advancement of socialist democracy or making more complaints of dissatisfaction. Under the banner of democracy they are trampling on both democracy and law. Their purpose is to poison people's minds, create national turmoil and sabotage the nation's political stability and unity. This is a planned conspiracy, a turmoil which, in essence, aims at fundamentally negating the leadership of the Communist Party of China and the socialist system.

Again, the students could hardly believe it. An attack on socialism? No student I talked to saw their movement as anything like that.

The American mass media was calling the demonstrations an attack on communism. A friend of mine in the United States, watching the news on TV, saw the demonstrations in Beijing and heard the American reporter say, "The students are demanding an end to communism!" The irony of this, as my friend pointed out, was that behind the reporter hundreds of students, as they marched, were singing the old Communist anthem, the *Internationale*.

As a matter of fact, one thing that struck me about these students is that they seemed to have shucked off labels like old clothes. They weren't using words like "socialism" or "communism" or "capitalism". They were only calling for reforms in their government and their society.

The students stayed in Tiananmen, and some of them went on a hunger strike, vowing to fast until the leaders spoke to them. As days went by and no leaders came, the numbers swelled until there were tens of thousands of students in the square, and 3,000 hunger strikers. Students came from many cities to take part. A thousand Nankai students pedaled the hundred and fifty kilometres to Beijing on bicycles, carrying banners and stopping to tell people what it was all about., and many more went up by train. Many Nankai students joined the hunger strikers. Young teachers went up to see if their students were all right and stayed to join the demonstrations.

The students became quite angry that the government wouldn't talk to them. But their anger didn't express itself in violence—right up to the day they were attacked by soldiers, their movement was non-violent. They spoke out their anger, and they wrote on their placards many satiric jingles, which in the original Chinese have catchy rhythms and rhymes and many witty puns which my translation can't match.

"Mao Zedong's officials had clean hands.
Deng Xiaoping's officials are millionaires."

"Xiaoping, go play bridge"
(Deng was an avid bridge player.)

"Premier Zhou we miss you
Your successor's not like you."

"Mother Deng, come quick,
Carry little Li Peng home."

"We want honest government,
not curtain government."

(The Empress Dowager, although her son was emperor, had ruled the country from "behind the curtain", as Deng had done since his nominal retirement.)

They also made up songs to sing as they marched, one of them to the tune we call "Frere Jacques", a tune with a long revolutionary history in China. Their words were a parody of an old revolutionary song that began "*Da dao tu hao!*" ("Down

with rich landlords!") suggesting a parallel between the oppressors
of those days and the people they saw at the top in their day.

Da dao quandao,
Da dao quandao,
Fan fubai! Fan fubai!
Women yao qiu minzhu! Women yao qiu minzhu!
Zheng ziyou! Zheng ziyou!

(Down with corrupt officials,
Down with corrupt officials,
Smash corruption! Smash corruption!
We want democracy! We want democracy!
Struggle for freedom! Struggle for freedom!)

As the days went by with no response from the government,
more and more people came out to support the students. In fact,
the support was so great that it was clearly no longer a student
movement, but a mass movement. On some days over a million
people were camped out in, or came to visit, Tiananmen Square.
People brought food. Teachers brought quilts for their students.
Doctors and nurses came after work to take care of the hunger
strikers. A group of nurses pooled their personal money to buy a
truckload of toilet paper. The Red Cross, when heavy rain hit the
area, quickly rounded up ninety buses for the hunger strikers to
shelter in. Workers came marching, with banners. Some farmers
brought trucks full of watermelons and put up signs saying "All
those with student badges help yourself free!" Groups of school
kids came to visit their "big brothers and sisters". Singers and
dancers came to entertain.

In Tianjin one day I rode the city bus to the railway station.
Most of the bus passengers were students with banners which
they hung out the windows. Twice, when we passed groups of
workers repairing the road, they stopped work to cheer and clap
as the bus passed.

I was going to the station to see a demonstration, and so, as it happened, were 50,000 other people. The large square in front of the station was jammed. A few hundred students were there, trying to raise enough money to buy tickets and go to Beijing and join the demonstrations. Just before train time, one of the ticket-checkers borrowed a bullhorn from the students and called out, "All those with student badges line up here. We're opening the gates. Get on the train! Go to Beijing! Never mind tickets!"

The next day, when I was in the Lhasa Street free market I noticed some old women shopping, anxiously as usual, because inflation had made it hard for them to buy enough food. A group of students came through with a flag, a drum, and a collection box, raising money to go to Beijing, and those old women pushed through the crowd to put money in the box. How could I help being deeply moved at times like this?

Nankai University was the rallying point of the big demonstrations in Tianjin. The rallies took place close to the apartment building where I lived, so I usually went out to see the students assemble before their marches.

At one such rally, the students were joined, first, by students marching in from Tianjin University and from Teachers University, singing and waving banners. A column of workers marched in from the Tianjin Watch Factory. There was a truckload of workers from the local television station. There was a whole high school, students and teachers. There was a group of street vendors, who made an amusing speech: "Yes, we are money-grubbers, but we love our country too. We've brought 500 yuan for your fund. And here's some good advice: you're smart, you university kids, but you're not good shoppers. You're easy to cheat. So look out! When you get to Beijing, don't let the leaders cheat you!"

And there was a group of Nankai University teachers. Many university teachers had signed a petition to the government saying the students must be listened to. Now some of them came out to march with the students, carrying a banner which said, "The students love their country and we love the students."

In Beijing, on May 16, a group of about two hundred young reporters from the *People's Daily* and students from the Graduate School of Journalism of the Academy of Social Science, marched to the square with banners calling for freedom of the press, and chanted as they marched, "The *People's Daily* belongs to the people!" The next day, about a hundred workers from the English-language *China Daily* marched in with banners saying "Support the democratic fighters and freedom of the press!" Over a thousand journalists in the Beijing area signed a petition demanding freedom to report the truth about the student movement. Then, to the delight of most people, they simply took that right, and for a week there was an amazing freedom of the press in Beijing. Both papers ran long sympathetic stories about the demonstrators and pictures of the encampment in the square.

Even after martial law had been declared and the newspapers became more cautious, the *China Daily* editors found a typical Chinese way to get the message out. The day after Li Peng declared martial law, his speech had to be the front page feature story, of course—but my Chinese students pointed out with glee that also on page one was a story from Hungary quoting Prime Minister Nemeth as saying that the Hungarian Army would never be used against the people. One reason Stalin was hated, he said, was that he had used the Army against the people.

On May 26, the Central Advisory Commission, the old men Deng had persuaded to retire by giving them this honorary and remunerative post, praised the government's position. Next to the story about that in *China Day* was a quotation from a member of the Soviet Union's newly elected Congress, calling the old Supreme Soviet "part of the mechanism of autocracy and dictatorial rule from on high in which the people were deprived of all power."

Finally, the government publicized a meeting between two Party hacks nobody had heard of before, and members of the old government-controlled union of students, but since the demonstrators had organized themselves as the Autonomous Union of University Students (as the workers who joined them organized the Autonomous Union of Beijing Workers) the government took refuge in the position that it could not talk to illegal organizations.

Government leaders were obviously angry that the students were occupying the square when President Gorbachev arrived for his historic meeting with Deng Xiaoping. There was to have been a welcoming ceremony in Tiananmen outside the Great Hall of the People. The students offered to move their encampment to the far side of the huge square, but the government moved the welcoming ceremony to the airport instead. When Gorbachev did come to the Great Hall for a meeting, the students put up banners welcoming him. Gorbachev the reformer was one of their heroes. But the government brought him in through the back door, so he and the demonstrators never saw each other. It's certain that Deng was furious at being robbed of the spotlight of world publicity in the great moment of his career—which may account for some of the ferocity of the government's response when it finally came.

The government's inaction was the result of an intense power struggle at the top. Behind closed doors two factions, reformers and hardliners, were fighting for control. Secretary Zhao Ziyang, who had succeeded Hu Yaobang as head of the Party, had for months been working to encourage openness in the mass media. On May 19, he finally came to the square and with tears on his face apologized to the students for not coming sooner. But he urged them to go home and trust the government, without any negotiations, and it was too late for that.

The next day, on television, I saw Premier Li Peng making a speech that showed that the hardliners had won the struggle. He described the situation in Beijing as out of control. He declared martial law and called out the army to restore order. As for Zhao, he disappeared from sight from that moment.

The situation changed abruptly. The first thing that happened showed dramatically that this was a mass movement, not just a student movement. As the 38th Army's tanks and truckloads of soldiers entered the city, many thousands of Beijing citizens poured out of their homes and filled the streets, blocking the way.

Again, I had to say "Only in China!" The Chinese people, right up to June 4 that year, did not hate the Army. During the wars of revolution, it really had won its official title "the People's Liberation Army". And in peace time (forty years without war inside their country, remember) the soldiers spent most of their time planting trees, repairing roads, helping the peasants get in the harvest, helping people in time of natural disasters. We saw them as friendly teenagers in baggy uniforms.

The commander of the 38th Army announced that they had not come to attack the people, but only to keep order. So when masses of people blocked their way, the trucks and tanks simply stopped, and after a while the tanks turned around and went away. The trucks full of soldiers remained blocked for two and a half days, during which time the people brought the soldiers food and tea and cigarettes and talked to them. Only in China!

But the mood had changed. It was obvious that there was real danger now and that the government had no intention of ever talking to the students. The hunger strike was called off.

But the students became more and more determined to press the issue, and the occupation of the square continued. The placard messages, though, were no longer humorous, but simple and extreme. "Li Peng, resign!" "Deng Xiaoping, resign!"

One of the ironies of the situation was that while Li Peng was deploring the "chaos" and "disruption of normal life" caused by the demonstrations, actually an amazing air of order and cheerfulness had developed in Beijing, and also in Tianjin. My students, going back and forth, described the Beijing atmosphere. When a student wanted to go somewhere, she or he held up a hand and was given a ride by the next car or truck. When people on bicycles bumped into each other, they did not shout at each other. When you went into a department store in Beijing, the clerks smiled at you. The Beijing salesclerks! That's revolution!

The *People's Daily*, *China Daily*, and the *Beijing Daily* all ran descriptions of this new atmosphere in Beijing. Food was coming in almost normally, they said, and farmers were refusing to raise prices to take advantage of the situation. (*China Daily* had photos of the markets full of vegetables and other food.) People on the street were smiling at each other and standing in clumps talking about it all. The *People's Daily* article, after citing examples of people being unusually friendly to strangers, said, "Beijingers are experiencing comradeship." The *China Daily* article ran under the headline, "The Soul of the City Has Been Awakened". And the *Beijing Daily* headline was "The Spirit of Communism Has Returned to Beijing". A startling report from the police said that the rate of crime in the city had dropped 30 per cent during the month of May.

Was there any hope, through all these weeks, that a peaceful, constructive solution was possible? I think there was, and I think that mistakes made on both sides tragically lost the chance of what might have been a great step forward for China.

The government, even aside from the June 4 massacre, has to have most of the blame. Why is it that governments, ruling in the name of the people, are scared to death of the people?

Why could they not have talked to the students after the memorial to Hu Yaobang? What did they stand to lose? A government responsive to the people would already have seen the need for reforms, and would have used the occasion to enlist the people in a campaign for reforms. But even a cynical politician could have seen that talking to the students would have taken the steam out of the movement. To tell the students that what they asked for was correct, was in fact government policy, and then to have announced even a minimal program for reform, or even a joint committee to decide what action to take, would have been politically smart. To do nothing while the situation escalated, was simply inept.

Later, as the crisis developed, the government took the position of stern parents offended by naughty kids. Although they said many times "The students are loyal citizens. We agree with their demands. There will never be any reprisals against these patriotic students," they also, inevitably, said, "Now go home, go back to your classes and let us decide how to run the country. Trust us." Which the students were not about to do.

The trouble was that the leaders were sharply divided in their ideas of *how* to handle the situation. Deng immediately called the movement counter-revolutionary and wanted it put down by force. Zhao, whose position as Secretary of the Party was a strong one, wanted to use the demonstrations as an opportunity to push for reform. It seems clear in retrospect that when the government acted inconsistently that was because two different lines were in conflict. The voice which said often that the students were right in their demands for reform, that the students were patriotic, that there would never be any reprisals against the students, was the voice of Zhao. The voice which spoke of chaos and counter-revolution and the disruption of normal life, and kept warning that patience was running out, was the voice of Deng speaking through Li Peng. The waffling of the government, which let the situation build up and get worse, grew out of this split in leadership.

The student leaders, although their share of the blame is far less, were not blameless. They saw themselves as having brought the government to a standstill. If they held on, with the support of the populace, they would surely win. But as time went on, they became increasingly demanding, even arrogant, which put the government in the position that to concede to the students would be a humiliating defeat.

Being inexperienced politicians, the students didn't realize that anybody they hoped to work with must be given a way to preserve his dignity, must be able to seem to be acting from reasonableness, not giving in to force. (Especially, in China, not giving in to force from a younger generation.) In the one meeting they had with Li Peng, which was, as they demanded, televised, one student shook his finger in the Premier's face and shouted, "Tell the truth! Stop evading the issues!" Well, loss of face is an especially serious matter in China, but what government leader anywhere in the world could respond to that with anything but anger and the determination to get even?

None of which, of course, excuses the ferocity of the action which the government finally took.

In the three days leading up to June 4, there were many rumours of impending violence. Some said the 38th Army had been withdrawn and a different army was being brought in. Some said the subway, which had been closed to traffic, was full of soldiers. Some said there were soldiers in secret tunnels under the square. Many people urged the students to call off the demonstrations and go home.

Some of the students did leave the square. There were only several thousand there by the evening of June 3. But the leaders vowed to keep the occupation going until the Standing Committee of the National People's Congress met on June 20, hoping to get concessions from them. Several thousand students stayed with them, although their numbers lessened day by day. And four non-students—two teachers, the head of a computer company, and a famous pop singer—joined the students and started their own hunger strike.

On the evening of June 3, a group of police suddenly issued from the government headquarters compound, near the square, and attacked the students there with clubs. The students fought back, and the police retreated. Later, a group of about a thousand soldiers came into the square and started attacking the students, but they were engulfed and pushed back, and finally retreated.

What happened next is a hotly disputed question. The government pronouncements about how many people were killed in the square have ranged from zero to 300 (of whom about half, they said, were soldiers.) That there are different accounts is not surprising, since everything happened in the dark and amid great confusion. Another reason for differing accounts is that some people talk about what happened only in Tiananmen Square while others include incidents in the streets outside the square.

But both foreign observers who had been watching the demonstrations closely, and students who rushed back to Nankai to tell me about it, agreed on the main points.

In the early morning of June 4, soldiers of the crack 27th Army, veterans of the war in Vietnam, sped very quickly along Changan Avenue in tanks and armoured personnel carriers. They smashed through barricades and ran over people who tried to stop them or were unable to get out of the way. (A photo of dead bicyclists who had been crushed has been widely reprinted.)

The soldiers suddenly rushed into the square from two directions, firing assault rifles as they came. A reporter for the BBC claimed to have seen tanks crush makeshift tents with students inside, and said that bullets killed three people near her. Other people say they saw a troop carrier chase a group of students and run them down, killing several. The television cameras of foreign news services caught rolls of film of wounded students being carried away by others.

As daylight came, a halt was called to enable the students to re-group and march out of the square. They left. But the shooting was not over.

Many people ran to the square to see what was happening, and shouted angrily at the troops, who responded by shooting into the crowds. Reporters saw forty bodies on Changan Avenue, between the square and the Beijing Hotel three blocks east. Through that day, and sporadically through the week that followed, troops went up and down the main streets in trucks or troop carriers, shooting at random. Once, people tried to escape by crowding into a clear area in front of the Beijing Hotel, off the street, but the soldiers fired into that crowd, too. Lines of tanks and troop carriers spread out into the city. From a line of trucks, soldiers sprayed the residential area of the foreign diplomatic corps with bullets, forcing one ambassador and his family to throw themselves to the floor while their windows smashed.

It was clear that the Army had declared war not only on the students but on the city of Beijing.

Reporters were told by doctors of one hospital that forty bodies and hundreds of wounded people had been brought there. I was told by a person who worked in another hospital that there were hundreds of dead and wounded there. Estimates of the total number killed vary widely. It has been charged (though who will ever know?) that the soldiers removed some bodies from the square and took them to crematoria, and heaped up other bodies in the pile of tents, blankets, and rubbish of the square which they then burned with flame-throwers. One radio reporter (who was quickly removed from his job) claimed that seven thousand people had been killed and many thousands wounded. Many later accounts repeated the phrase "hundreds, perhaps thousands". It is obviously impossible to arrive at a dependable figure.

The citizens of Beijing reacted with rage. Tanks were attacked with sticks. Two armoured personnel carriers were destroyed by home-made fire bombs and the soldiers inside one of these were killed when they tried to escape. Reporters saw in one place a row of twenty-nine military vehicles that had apparently been deserted by the soldiers and set on fire by the people. A few soldiers found themselves cut off from the others, alone among hostile crowds, and fired their assault rifles indiscriminately until they ran out of bullets, when the crowds jumped them and beat them to death. It was at least a week before the city was finally subdued and settled into a sullen silence.

Beijing airport was mobbed by foreigners desperate to get out. Several countries, including Canada, sent special planes to evacuate their citizens.

The anger of my Chinese acquaintances would be hard to exaggerate. "They're worse than the Japanese," one said, showing an ignorance of history but expressing his shock. "Nothing like this has ever happened in modern China, not even during the Cultural Revolution," said another. Students asked me if I thought there was some kind of chemical that might have been fed to the soldiers to make them berserk.

On the Nankai campus in the afternoon of June 4 there was a silent procession of students carrying hastily-made funeral wreaths. The student loudspeaker by the front gate played the *Internationale* slowly, all day long without stopping, so that it became a funeral dirge, and I'm sure I'll never hear it again without thinking of that day. As I went around the campus, eyewitnesses back from Beijing were giving their accounts of what happened, over student loudspeakers near the dormitories. Many students had stopped their bicycles to listen; the campus streets were dotted with motionless people, on their bicycles, heads down, silent, listening. It was a surreal sight.

In Beijing, in the days that followed, many universities had funeral wreaths at their front gates. An acquaintance at Beijing University told me that the mangled bodies of five students were displayed on mattresses, and that there was a memorial altar to a woman student who had stood facing the soldiers, shouting, "Brothers! Don't shoot the people!" and was shot.

For myself, I felt as if I were living an awful dream. Nothing seemed quite real. Whenever I saw a group of students, I thought, "This is the enemy that had to be attacked with tanks and assault rifles." When Deng Xiaoping publicly congratulated the Army on "a great victory", I could only think, in a stunned way, "The tanks and guns have won a great victory over kids camped out in the square." For a long time nothing else could occupy my mind. I am still haunted by it.

All this must sooner or later be put in a worldwide perspective. The crackdown in Beijing, if compared to the suppression of civilians in many other countries in this violent century of ours, was a minor event. Think of how many more people have been tortured, "disappeared", and otherwise violently oppressed in other countries, how many have been mowed down by government troops, how many men, women, and children have been the "incidental" victims of invasions, civil wars, and campaigns of terror.

Two things made Tiananmen shocking, even in this violent world. One was that by coincidence a great many reporters and television cameramen, from many countries, happened to be in Beijing just then. They had come to cover the historic meeting of Gorbachev and Deng, but they were on hand to give the world direct images of the violence, and direct witness to the outrage of the citizens. (Several of these reporters and cameramen later produced books about Tiananmen, of which I have thirteen. One of the best [meaning, I suppose, most gruesome], is *Beijing Spring*, with photographs by David and Peter Turnley and text by Melinda Liu.)

Another was that the "incident" was immediately condemned by the leaders of Western countries, who imposed economic and other sanctions on China. Why did they do that, when they have reacted so moderately to worse outrages in other countries? I have to suspect it was because China was a Communist country. Condemning China was condemning communism.

Inside China, the shock had deeper causes. To the Chinese people who knew what had happened, the crackdown was staggering out of all proportion to the number of people killed. It was an abrupt, explosive end to a period of civil peace, and to a whole generation's faith in the government. A popular mass movement calling for reforms had been labeled an evil conspiracy to overthrow socialism, and the beloved People's Liberation Army had been called out to kill Chinese civilians. It was, for sure, the end of an era. The leaders have paid the price of alienating a great many idealistic young people. When the leaders publicly denied that events which he had witnessed ever happened, one young Party member said to me, in tears, "They are lying! The *Party* is *lying*!"

Repercussions went on long after June 4. As soon as the city of Beijing was subdued, soldiers and security forces began a hunt for the student leaders. Soldiers went into university campuses and tore down posters while the police searched the dormitories for "subversive" materials and arrested students. When news of this got out, students started leaving the campuses quickly, for their homes all over China. For a few days, every time I looked out my window I saw lines of students with bundles heading for the bus station just outside the main gate. Soon, of the 400 or so students in my department, only 20 were left. Those who could not make immediate plans to return to other parts of China were taken into the homes of students who lived in Tianjin.

Nationally, within three weeks the police, according to the newspapers, rounded up over 1600 "leaders", and 27 were executed. News from various cities showed that the witch-hunt was going on everywhere. In Jilin Province alone, according to Chinese students in Canada who had heard from there, 28 people had been sentenced to death. Canadians returning from the city of Jinan, in Shandong Province, told me that 17 people had been executed there. It was a nationwide witch-hunt, in which many thousands of people were vulnerable, having signed petitions or made speeches or walked in demonstrations supporting the students.

With a rush the atmosphere was back in the worst days of the Cultural Revolution. Suddenly no one felt safe to speak his or her mind. Everyone was in danger of being turned in by their neighbours. The government officially praised a sister who had turned in her brother (who was later executed) and a mother who turned in her son.

An American TV reporter interviewed a man in the north-east, who made an intemperate remark about feeling counter-revolutionary. The Chinese took that sequence off the American satellite and replayed it on Chinese television and said that anyone knowing this man should phone such and such a number. Within four hours, he was in jail. The government published a list of the 21 most wanted student leaders, and displayed on national television their photographs, names, and descriptions, and asked people to turn them in. Those who did were publicly honoured and rewarded.

The government mounted a campaign against foreigners, charging that the Voice of America had made up the whole story of a massacre that never actually happened, and that foreign trouble-makers had masterminded the demonstrations from start to finish. I began to feel awkward about being the only foreigner in the apartment building where I lived, not knowing whether being friendly with my neighbours might get them into trouble. It was amazing how fast the joyous atmosphere of May turned into the sullen atmosphere of June.

Westerners have asked me how the government's campaign of disinformation could be effective in the face of known facts. In Beijing, of course, nobody believed the official version of what had happened. But most people across China get their information from the government's TV, radio, and newspapers. (Even in normal times, National Television had claimed that 500 million people watched the national TV network news at seven o'clock each evening.)

And the propaganda was thorough. The Chinese have learned (from whom, I've been wondering) how to use TV as a propaganda machine. Viewers all over China saw pictures of people attacking Army vehicles and were told that this happened *before* the Army moved in and was, in fact, the reason the Army had to be called in. The last TV news I saw before leaving China (that is, in the evening of June 10) showed such shots, then a group of people who looked like petty thieves being interrogated by police and identified for the viewers as counter-revolutionaries, then a ghastly shot of the body of a soldier who had been killed and his body incinerated. Then, for over an hour, many shots of soldiers as friends of the people—soldiers sweeping the streets, helping farmers load trucks, in primary schools letting little kids wear their hats, in hospital being visited by grateful citizens bringing them flowers and watermelons, one white-haired old woman with tears running down, thanking the soldiers for saving China.

One thing that made it hard for people to believe that such a massacre could have occurred was that it followed so many years of domestic peace. It's significant that the doctors in China's hospitals had not seen gunshot wounds, and didn't know how to treat them.

And it was hard to believe that the people's Army could ever do such things to unarmed Chinese people. It was even hard for us who saw the evidence to believe it, until that evidence became overwhelming. Those many shots on TV of the soldiers as the people's friends didn't have to be faked, just taken out of the archives. It's the idea of the army which most people had, and were reluctant to part with.

So yes, many Chinese people will believe the government version of what happened. That's not easy to prove, of course— if you were to ask people whether they believed the government, who would dare to give you a frank answer?

I have some evidence that people really did believe the government story. The waitresses at the Foreign Teachers' Guest House, on the Nankai campus, speak no English, and have no contact with the students; they come on campus, do their job, and go home. On June 9, they asked me why foreigners were leaving. I told them the foreigners were afraid the violence might spread, after so many people got killed. Oh, no, they said, very few people were killed, and those were only ruffians who attacked the army after the students had left the square.

And when a young teacher at Nankai went to visit a high school classmate who was now a factory worker, the minute he came in the door his friend's mother started shouting at him. "You see what your students have done? You see what all that marching and nonsense comes to? They opened the door for hooligans to come in and attack the soldiers!"

Before the end of June the editors of the *People's Daily* and *China Daily* had been replaced, and the same was expected for any publication that had taken the students' side. The journalists who had signed a demand for the right to tell the truth were required to stand up in meeting and admit their "errors" or lose their jobs. Factory workers were ordered to report in writing what they had been doing day by day at the end of May and the first week of June.

I went up to Beijing on the morning of June 10. As the train pulled into the city I looked out at the fine restored East Gate which is all that's left of the old city walls, as I always do. I was startled to see that atop its walls were rows of soldiers standing like statues, evenly spaced, in battle gear, with assault rifles at the ready. It didn't look very practical—who was about to attack the old East Gate? It was symbolic and ceremonial. Beijing was a conquered city.

As the train slowed and approached the station, there were equally ceremonial lines of soldiers on both sides of the train, facing us. I was close enough to see that their fingers were on the triggers of their guns. Behind them were large green tents outside of which off-duty soldiers were brushing their teeth.

I saw no other foreigners in the station. At the taxi stand I was mobbed by drivers of "black cabs"—that is, unregistered and unlicensed cabs which just recently had been busy hustling customers past the authorized taxi stands, and incidentally charging them outrageous prices. There must have been a dozen around me, since nobody else seemed to need their services.

I finally got a regular cab, and as we went along Changan Avenue I saw lines of statue-like soldiers on the overpasses, spit-and-polish professionals in steel helmets, their guns at the ready.

The Canadian Embassy had asked me to put up at the Kunlun Hotel for the night, to be ready for an early bus to the airport in the morning. I don't use big hotels, partly because working in China I don't have the income for such places. Besides, I don't like big expensive hotels anywhere, and think them grotesquely out of place in a poor country that calls itself socialist. And every time I do go into one of the monsters, I remember with nostalgia the "Welcome Guest Place" in Ningxia. Nevertheless, when I saw the Kunlun I couldn't suppress a twinge of sympathy for its present troubles.

The place was practically empty except for the staff. I wandered around the huge empty lobby, with a sign saying its wall-hung tapestry is the largest in the world, and along the wide, elaborate hallways, past the deserted coffee-shop terrace near the fountains, past the five or six luxurious restaurants, my footsteps echoing in the emptiness. At the door of the Japanese restaurant a pretty young woman in geisha costume bowed and smiled at me forlornly. Only the least pretentious place, serving Chinese food, had customers, and few of them were foreigners.

Poor Kunlun! I could almost hear the computers ticking off the lost income, moment by moment. It's no wonder the hotel managers of the city got together and urged that the city be "normalized" as soon as possible, and the soldiers put out of sight.

That was not to be. The government was clamping down in the most visible way possible. Not only must there be soldiers in the streets, but on TV pictures must be shown over and over again, of a loyal ruthless force smashing the enemies of China. There were many shots of burned-out vehicles destroyed by looters and smashers, and of marching troops, stern policemen, cowering prisoners. News of executions was broadcast daily. The Supreme People's Court publicly demanded that the lower courts deal with trouble-makers "without mercy".

An international revulsion suggested that the news of arrests and executions had better be downplayed. The point had already been made and the people knew that arrests and executions were still going on, and knew, too, that people picked up by the police had no protection in law, no right of *habeas corpus*, no lawyers, no due process, and were said to be beaten routinely.

A young reporter for *China Daily* who had been in the square on June 4, came to work on June 5 and 6, but then simply disappeared. Finally, the security guards at the newspaper went to the police and made enquiries and were told that she was in custody and some clean clothes should be sent for her. For many others, obviously, enquiries would not even get that much information.

The class distinctions which the Chinese deny exist were in evidence. According to newspaper reports, workers were being treated more severely than students, being crammed twenty at a time into cells meant for six, and having their hair shaved off. Those who had dared to join the Autonomous Workers Union were in trouble, and indeed in danger of execution just for that crime.

At the same time, a propaganda blitz was being waged. On June 9, Deng Xiaoping made a speech which has become almost a new *Little Red Book*. Everybody has been urged to study it in order to have a proper understanding of the issues. Soldiers study it. Workers study it in obligatory political sessions. University students were called back to campus early for indoctrination, featuring Deng's speech. Actually, the speech says nothing new or insightful. But it does set out the new orthodox line:

> What we faced was not just some ordinary people who were misguided, but also a large rebellious clique and a large number of the dregs of society. The key point is that they wanted to overthrow our State and the Party. . . . Their real aim was to overthrow the Communist Party and topple the socialist system.

The speech calls on the people to live a life of "hard struggle and plain living", though how the "plain living" is to be reconciled with "To get rich is glorious" and the high lifestyle of the new rich and of officials at all levels, is not discussed.

The seriousness of the political crisis was shown by the number of units and individuals who thought it expedient to express what amounted to loyalty oaths. The commanders of all the Army areas in the country telegraphed their loyal support of the government and its policies. The heads of all the provinces did the same, also the Central Advisory Commission, the Supreme People's Court, the chairman of the Chinese People's Political Consultative Conference, and many others.

It was painful to see how fast some writers and artists and intellectuals jumped into line. On July 7, the Propaganda Department of the Chinese Communist Party Central Committee called together the heads of the Writers' Union, the Artists' Union, and writers and artists of some degree of prominence, and asked them to support Deng and renounce "bourgeois liberalism", which they dutifully did.

Back in May, the leaders of four democratic parties (non-Communist organizations which exist at the price of cooperation with the Communist Party) had had the temerity to send a letter to Secretary Zhao Ziyang, the gist of which was reported in *China Daily* (May 18, 1989): "They hoped the students' requests will be met in a democratic and legal way because theirs was a patriotic movement and their reasonable requests are consistent with the views of the Party Central Committee and the State Council." But those same leaders one month later "unanimously voiced their support of Deng's speech and the crackdown on the recent counter-revolutionary rebellion in Beijing." (*China Daily* June 19, 1989) And so on and on, all swearing their orthodoxy—in order, one assumes, to be able to carry on their work.

The tone of life changed in China. June 4 was a watershed. For example, today many young writers and painters choose not to belong to the official unions. One such painter in south China who makes his living as a driver and paints in his free time, explained this to me. If he joined the union, he would get the best paints and paper and brushes at discount prices, would have places to exhibit his work, and might even be put on salary so he could give full time to his painting. But the price was to accept strict government supervision, and to accept that his job as an artist was first of all to support socialism—which in practice meant supporting the current policies of the current government. This painter's work was being exhibited in Germany, but he couldn't get an exit visa to go there and be present.

Government leaders make frequent speeches on television urging people to uphold the spirit of socialism. Ironically, I never hear any mention of socialism in China these days except in these speeches. The government is also trying hard to wrap itself in the historic mantle of socialism. They have funded the making of several blockbuster movies in praise of Mao Zedong, and dramatizing military victories in the wars of Liberation.

Today every school across China has been ordered to have a flagpole, and daily flag-raising ceremonies and pledges of allegiance, led if possible by one or more soldiers.

In an interview with Barbara Walters of ABC on May 2, 1990, Jiang Zemin, the new Secretary of the Chinese Communist Party, gave an interesting answer to her question of what lessons had been learned from Tiananmen:

> We have drawn very good experience from the Tiananmen experience of last year. We should learn to use the methods usually used by some Western countries; that is to say, we should build up an adequate riot police force and acquire enough non-lethal weapons for maintaining public security.

They have, indeed, been building up the police. The ordinary police in China, like those of Great Britain, are not armed except in rare emergencies. Now China has a force called "The Armed Police", made up largely of former soldiers. The regular police have also been greatly increased. And *China Daily* (December 3, 1991) reports that the streets of Chinese cities will be for the first time regularly patrolled by police. In this function, "regular police officers will be joined by traffic police, riot police, and reserve guards to cruise the streets of major cities as part of special patrol detachments, under a new policy dictated by the Ministry of Public Security."

I caught an interesting little five-word phrase in an article in *China Daily* for July 5, 1990 about the training of police dogs for "active service in the ranks of China's police and army." What are their duties? "China's special police dogs are widely used for investigative work, tracking down and arresting suspects, drug seizure, *riot control and public security.*" (my emphasis)

None of this would raise eyebrows in Western countries. Like the Tiananmen crackdown itself, what is striking is the contrast to China of just a while ago.

The government is also cracking down on published writing which differs from government policy—in fact, on past writing which differs from present policy. Anyone who wrote books or articles in the three years before Tiananmen, who was now judged to have been setting the stage for the student uprising, was in danger. Several of them hastily left the country, including the writer of the popular TV series "River Elegy".

One method of attacking dissent is to lump it in with pornography. As reported in an article in *China Daily* on October 26, 1990, the Deputy Secretary-General of the State Council defined anti-pornography as "the clearing of cultural and spiritual garbage". What that means is suggested in the rest of the news article: "12% of all newspapers, 13% of the periodicals devoted to social sciences and 7.6% of all publishing houses in China have been closed. . . . The country has banned more than 6.8 million illegal publications, 3,000 pornographic publications, *1,300 counter-revolutionary publications*, and over 4,000 pornographic video tapes". (my emphasis)

Across the country, new rules have been announced, including one banning all demonstrations which have not been approved by the police.

On the university campuses, life has changed. Now, all undergraduates must take military training, taught by soldiers. In some universities, including Nankai and Xiamen, this means that the freshman class gets one month of drill and lectures by army officers before starting regular classes. In special cases, such as Beijing University, for two years after Tiananmen incoming freshmen were required to spend a year in army barracks being trained and indoctrinated by the Army before they began their regular four-year undergraduate programs. In many universities there are now new codes of "proper dress" and "proper behaviour". No demonstrations of any kind are now permitted. No student clubs are permitted except with approval—this includes even discussion groups.

I spotted an interesting little note in a news article on the new uses of computers in university administration. (*China Daily* February 11, 1992) We are told "The system includes techniques of scientific decision making on the management of students . . .[and the] survey and appraisal of student ethics."

How have the students reacted to all this? For some, it's just more reasons for not going to university at all. It gets added to economic reasons: they know that if they become teachers, or doctors, or government workers, their incomes will be so small (and not indexed to inflation) that they could make more money selling things in the street. Why go through all those new hassles, too?

For others, it is all just more nuisances to put up with, like overcrowded buses. Some of them tell me, with smiles, that the grapevine tells them when dormitory inspectors are coming to see that curtains are not down in front of bunks, and no suspicious pictures or words are on the walls—so they roll up the curtains and clear the walls and look innocent. The Chinese have always had a great capacity for shrugging their shoulders and getting on with their lives.

For some, including the smartest, most idealistic, this is a traumatic period. A great many of them have lost the faith in socialism with which they grew up. One of them said to me bitterly, "If the government tells me it's raining I know I don't need an umbrella."

These groups have one thing in common: they turn their backs on politics. They refuse to discuss government, or socialism, or democracy, or capitalism. What does that leave them? Fulfilling their own personal goals and dreams. Some lose themselves in books and study. Some go all out for sports. Some frequent Lovers' Park. Some look for the money and the main chance, perhaps staying in university only to get the degree in hopes of getting a job with a foreign company and possibly— who knows?—even getting a chance to go abroad. Or, for women, making themselves attractive to men who are likely to succeed, socially and financially. Their tactics include pretending to be less intelligent than they really are, since successful men, by and large, shy away from brainy women.

However—as I find myself saying many times when talking about China—let's put all of this in perspective. What I've been describing is a trend, a direction. It does not mean that university life, or life in general, has gone to hell. Universities in China are in trouble, yes—in many ways. The administrators wrestle with inadequate budgets and government interference; teachers burn out moonlighting to make ends meet; students are disgruntled. All that is true, but it's still relative. What delighted me when I started teaching in China in 1979 has not all disappeared. In the graduate classes which I teach, I still get great students, academically of high caliber, socially aware, personally admirable, for all the mental turmoil they suffer these days. They are the largest part of what draws me back to China.

Another point I can't make too often. What the Chinese can't change, they deal with and get on with their lives. That does not mean they have changed their minds, have given up. The spirit of the student demonstrators is still there, though a newcomer to China might take a while to discover it. To paraphrase Hemingway, the spirit may be suppressed, but not defeated. Wait and see.

That's what I wrote in 1993. I can add only a few comments. The government has been trying hard since Tiananmen to restore people's faith in them. The way they do that is, first, to promote patriotism as hard as possible, and second, to restore the people's pride in the Army. We see on television almost daily shots of Jiang Zemin, the current leader of China (President, and General Secretary of the Chinese Communist Party) opening spanking-clean new factories full of high-tech equipment, or sitting in the home of poor peasants and holding the little daughter on his knee, or greeting foreign heads of state—looking for all the world like a rotund koala bear who never had any but peaceful thoughts. We see many, many shots of soldiers—during the awful floods in the summer of 1998, it was soldiers who were in the nightly news, hip-deep in water shoring up dikes, carrying old women through floods to safety. (I don't suggest at all that these shots were faked—the soldiers were indeed heroic—all I'm suggesting is that the country's leaders seem to have jumped on the opportunity to publicize the soldiers as the people's friends, so they got lots of special coverage, added to the publicity they get day to day.)

The government has also, since Tiananmen, publicized campaigns to clean up corruption and attack crime. Almost every day we see in the papers accounts of officials who are being sent to prison, convicted of accepting bribes and of using public funds to build themselves mansions, or giving elaborate banquets, or gambling on the new stock markets. This, too, I don't for a minute denigrate—but I notice that the war on corruption never seems to reach the top leaders and their families.

The new Premier, Zhu Rongji, is a technocrat who works very hard to solve economic problems. As a replacement for Li Peng, he's very much admired.

In short, the government learned from Tiananmen more than Jiang Zemin told ABC. They have replaced the hated top leaders. (Deng Xiaoping is safely dead; Li Peng has been moved to an inconspicuous post.) They have been working hard at appearing as a new team, interested only in peace and prosperity. And they have been trying very hard to make people forget that any kind of massacre or attack on peaceful civilians ever happened

Just before the tenth anniversary of the Tiananmen "incident", on May 30, 1999, a person described as "a leading official of the National People's Congress Foreign Affairs Committee" issued this statement at a Press conference:

> It is well known that some people with ulterior motives in and out of China created a political disturbance in Beijing in May and June 1989, in an attempt to overthrow China's legitimate government and subvert the socialist People's Republic of China.

The Chinese Government, of course, took immediate, correct and resolute measures and successfully stopped the disturbance, and thus maintained social stability and ensured the smooth development of the reform, opening-up and modernization drives.

The experience of the past 10 years fully proves that if the Chinese Government had not made these correct decisions at that time, there would be no political stability and none of today's remarkable economic and social progress and generally   recognized achievements in China.

Anti-China forces in the United States and some other Western countries played an inglorious role in that disturbance. They took an active part in it by making and spreading a host of horrifying rumours, by using their media to cheat and hoodwink the international community and by directly masterminding schemes and giving money and goods to support those making the disturbances.

After the abortion of the disturbance, the anti-China forces, disregarding international law and Chinese laws, provided shelter for the major criminals, and helped them flee China.

(China Daily May 31, 1999)

13
Women: Holding Up Half The Sky?

The women's movement has been one of the broadest and most important social revolutions during my long life. It's been different from other movements going on at the same time. For one thing, it's so widespread, with so many fronts and struggles, we tend to forget that it is one movement, that the attempts of Canadian girls to be allowed to play hockey on boys' teams in small towns where there are no girls' teams is really part of the same struggle as equal pay campaigns and abortion rights and getting bank loans for women running small businesses and freedom from harassment on the job and United Nations conferences on women. One struggle, with one overall goal: no less than changing the lot of half the human race and the attitudes of both halves.

The movement, although it includes victories won by hard political and social struggles, has for the most part been a deep, slow change in the way people (both women and men) think about women, so slow that many people have not noticed how sweeping the accumulated changes have become.

When I was young, my girl schoolmates could play basketball, but not by boys' rules: each girl had to stay in her zone; she couldn't run the length of the court because too much running would be harmful for girls' weaker constitutions. It was "common knowledge" that girls can't run, and can't throw balls—their bodies are just not built for such things. These days, when I pass schoolyards here in Regina and see primary school girls and boys playing baseball together, and the girls pitching, batting, running and catching on a par with the boys, I wonder if any of them ever think what a revolution they represent.

When my mother was young, she did not have the right to vote. Most professions were closed to her. As a child, she had been sent to a girl's school where she was told that the proudest, most glorious day in her life would be the day some man asked her to marry him. Over the years, my mother became an advanced thinker in many ways, but even so she would not let her own daughter climb trees, or go on bicycle trips with her brothers, or whistle. ("A whistling girl and a crowing hen will never come to a good end.")

When my grandmother was young, women could not own property, or rent a hall for a public meeting. The scientists of that day said that women's brains are weaker than men's, so it would be a big mistake to let girls go to university—the poor dears would get brain fever. Women's colleges started as a rebellion against this "science", and they met lots of opposition. In those days, the role of man was to run the world; the role of woman was to be "the angel in the house", modifying the natural aggressiveness of the man by her gentle moral influence.

Well, against the background of the changes that have occurred in the West, I was eager to find out all I could about the status of Chinese women, and how it had changed under socialism.

Under socialism, I discovered, the changes were immense. In few places have women had a heavier burden of patriarchal assumptions to deal with than Chinese women had. They've come a long way under socialism and modernization—which does not deny the fact that like women everywhere they still have a long way to go. At Nankai University once, when I was having tea with two Chinese colleagues, a woman and a man, somehow the subject came up, and I said I knew of no country in the world where women had achieved equality with men. He looked startled, and said, "What? Not even in China?" I said. "Ask her." He looked at the woman, who said nothing. She just grimly and slowly shook her head.

Old China had a heavy, ancient tradition of male supremacy. Among poor people (always the great majority in Old China) women were hardly even treated as human beings. Girl children were expendable in hard times. A girl could be advertised for sale by making her sit in the marketplace with a simple cross of sticks tied to her and extending above her head, or with a price written on a board hung around her neck. Or a girl child could be simply killed at birth.

When I was teaching at Xiamen University, a student once shocked her classmates with the story of how close her mother had come to being killed off as an infant. The baby who would become her mother was born into a desperately poor peasant family, and the baby's father couldn't face the prospect of feeding a girl. A son would have been different. It was the duty of sons to support their parents in old age. In fact, sons were the only resource poverty-stricken old people had, to keep them from starvation. But a girl, after years of being an expense to her parents, would marry into another family and help her husband support *his* parents. There was a saying in Old China: *Jia chuqu de nü, po chuqu de shui*, that is, girls, who leave the family, are like water that has been thrown out (and like that water they are gone—they can never come back to be useful.)

So the father carried the baby to throw her in the river. But he was stopped by a neighbour who offered to take the girl and raise her to be a wife to his little son. The neighbour thus got a life-long slavey for his own family, and an obedient daughter-in-law for his wife. (The story illustrates the sexism of Old China—which, by the way, has not exactly been eliminated altogether—but you have to understand that the ultimate background of this story is not heartlessness, but extreme poverty.)

So that baby girl lived, and grew up as the wife of a poor peasant—but *her* daughter grew up to be a university student, thanks to the socialist revolution.

In the more affluent classes of Old China, women were materially better off than the peasants, but were still very much subordinates in a man's world. The life of a middle-class girl was rigidly controlled, unless she had unusual parents. When she was a child, her feet would be broken back and tightly bound, so she walked on the inverted tops of her toes. Her adult foot was about four inches long. She would have no schooling except in such things as running a household, and in manners and perhaps poetry or music—things that would make her attractive to a prospective husband. She would have no say at all in the choice of a husband—the families would decide that. In fact, traditionally she and her bridegroom would never even see each other before the wedding ceremony.

Throughout life, she would be bound by the Confucian tradition that women must, in every way, be obedient, first to father, then to husband, and if she became a widow, to her sons. She would seldom be permitted to go outside the family home, and then only if accompanied.

One of my friends tells me that in her grandmother's generation married women didn't even keep any personal name. Her grandmother was never called anything but *Zhou Wang Shi*, which means "woman of the Wang family married into the Zhou family." (In socialist China, by contrast, women don't even take their husbands' names at marriage. They keep their own full names, as many of them have proudly pointed out to me.)

After Liberation in 1949, under Mao Zedong and his socialists, there was a big campaign to change the role of women in society. Mao popularized the slogan, "Women hold up half the sky." New laws forbade the buying and selling of people, the binding of feet, arranged marriages, child marriage, concubinage. One law said that anyone who had been married against her will could get a divorce. That law resulted in a rash of divorces. The Constitution of the People's Republic of China says in Article 48 (I quote the official English translation of the 1982 text): "Women in the People's Republic of China enjoy equal rights with men in all spheres of life, in political, economic, cultural, social and family life."

The Constitution is policy, not description of current conditions. To implement that policy in actual lives would take a long, hard struggle. But it *was* official policy: it set out the goals. And policy got a push from expediency. Women had played an important part in the revolution. During the Japanese invasion, and in the civil wars that followed, in the villages of the liberated areas, women's committees were often the leading force for change. The women pushed the men to "turn over" the village, "speak bitterness", overthrow the landlord, redistribute the land, support the Red Army. They were not about to go back to the old subservience after all that.

After Liberation, in the huge task of reconstructing their ruined country, the Chinese could not afford to let half the population simply stay at home. Women were as desperately needed in the reconstruction as they had been during the war. In 1976, everywhere I went I saw that Chinese women had come out of the kitchens and the farm fields and were working in every kind of job. I saw women interpreters and guides, women hotel desk clerks and post-office clerks and department store clerks, women conductors on the railways, women doctors, policewomen, women electricians installing power lines, women technicians, truck drivers, bus drivers, skilled factory machinists with tool belts around their waists, captains of ferryboats, army officers. In the huge parade in Luoyang, in May 1976, celebrating ten years of the "Glorious Proletarian Cultural Revolution", one of the military units I saw was an anti-aircraft battery staffed by women.

And you remember how impressed I was in 1976 by our guide, Fu Feiying. You remember the women factory workers I spoke to, and my friend Li who started as an ignorant barefoot girl in the mountains and became one of the directors of a big research institute, and my colleagues the women university teachers—and above all my great women students.

The new woman, who went out to work and had an income, became a different creature—one that many men had difficulty relating to. When I was teaching at Xiamen University in 1982, one of my men students wrote an essay describing the wife he wanted: one who would have a hot cup of tea ready for him when he came home from work, so he could relax while she cooked supper. He was expressing a conventional and time-honoured attitude, but the class jumped on him. What about the wife? She's been out working on a job all day, too. Isn't she just as tired as you are? Who brings *her* a cup of tea and says relax? It wasn't only the women students who were indignant—the men, too, told him he was selfish, unreasonable and intolerably old-fashioned.

Under socialism, as part of the campaign for equality, both government and the media publicized outstanding and influential women. In Tianjin, where I lived through most of the 1980s, a number of such women were honoured. A woman named Zhang Cizheng had been a clerk in a food store during the 1950s. Full of socialist idealism, she found more and more ways to make her work serve the people. She made home deliveries to handicapped or sick customers, and on her way to and from work she stopped to check up on them and be sure they were all right. She was named "Model Worker" ten years in a row, and eventually her hard work and know-how made her the manager of the huge Tianjin Vegetable Company.

Shu Xuezhen graduated from Beijing Medical College in 1949 and was assigned to work in the Tianjin Pharmaceutical Factory. When she was thirty-three, the Party asked her to change her career and become a researcher in the paper-making industry. She succeeded so well in this that she made important research discoveries, especially in the manufacture of photocopy paper. She became a member of the National Papermaking Research Association, the director of the Tianjin Paper Research Institute, and a member of the National People's Congress (China's legislature.)

In Tianmuchun County, outside Tianjin City, lived a fireball by the name of Bai Yuzhen, a member of the Hui ethnic minority. As director of the Women's Federation of her county, Bai started the county's first day-care centres. She organized women to do sideline work, so effectively that 95 per cent of the women in her county took up raising chickens, pigs, or cattle, or commercial weaving and knitting. Appointed vice-mayor of the county, she saw that agriculture (mostly growing vegetables for the city markets) needed updating in the development of new strains and in methods of irrigation. She soon became president of the Tianmuchun County Agricultural Technical College.

These examples from the Tianjin area, I was told, could be matched in communities all across the country.

At the national level, Chen Muhua was Minister of Foreign Trade and Economic Development when China was opening to the world economically. When the country's banking system got into trouble because it was not geared to the needs of the new economy, she became director of the Bank of China, in charge of all the banking institutions of the whole country. In the spring of 1988 she became vice-chairperson of the Standing Committee of the National People's Congress—the most powerful national government body. When she retired from government work, she became president of the All-China Women's Federation. In 1995, she was president of the Fourth UN Conference on Women, in Beijing.

Wan Shaofen, of Jiangxi Province, worked her way up from local work with the Women's Federation and the Party. In 1983 she was a member of the National People's Congress. In 1985 she became Secretary of the Communist Party of Jiangxi Province—one of the two most powerful positions in the province, and, practically speaking, the most powerful.

Gu Xiulan, daughter of peasant farmers, graduated from a technical school and became a lathe operator in a metal-working factory, then a technician. She worked her way up to become vice-minister of the State Planning Commission, a member of the Party Central Committee, and in 1983, the governor of Jiangsu Province—China's first woman governor. And remember that in the Chinese system the governor is in charge not only of everything we think of as government but also of everything we think of as business—this in the province with the highest industrial production of any in China.

Wu Wenying started as a mill-hand in a textile mill and worked her way up to be China's Minister of Textiles, in charge of modernizing the country's most important export industry. Qian Zhengying became Minister of Water Resources and Electrical Power. Xie Xida became president of the famous Fudan University. He Huanfen became vice-mayor of the key city of Wuhan. Women became deputy governors of Hubei, Jiangsu, and Liaoning Provinces. Many women became successful writers;

others became prize-winning movie directors. Zheng Xiaoying became a world-class conductor of symphony orchestras.

All these women owed their successes not only to their own competence but also to China's campaign to achieve equal opportunities for women. They were the pay-off of education for girls as well as boys, the policy of assigning women to all kinds of jobs, and the concept that women "hold up half the sky."

As in the West, some of the most obvious results of the new thinking about women were in athletics. It was under socialism that Chinese women began to shine in regional contests, World Cups, and the Olympics.

I like to think of two images that for me represent the lives of women in two periods. The first is the image of a young woman being married in Old China. I see her standing on tiny bound feet, swathed in heavy brocaded red cloth, her face completely covered by a heavy red veil, waiting with great anxiety to see what kind of man she's being married to, and trembling to think of the mother-in-law who will soon control her life. Whatever her wishes or her capabilities, she has nothing to say about her own fate.

The other figure I think about is a member of the great women's volleyball team of 1981. They burst on the world scene that year to win all the medals in sight. They were the darlings of China, and their games were the country's first big television events. Millions of people watched them win honours for China. Young, superbly fit, famous for never giving up, they stood in many people's minds as living examples of the new woman under socialism. The depth of the country's admiration for them was shown on the occasion when China's men's soccer team was defeated by the visiting Hong Kong team, and the Beijing fans rioted, tore up the pitch, and beat people up. The government asked the star of the women's volleyball team, Lang Ping (called by her fans "The Hammer") to talk to rioters whom the police had assembled in an auditorium. Lang told them "I am ashamed of you," and according to all reports the rioters left the auditorium in tears.

All this may be true, you'll be thinking, but can it be the whole truth? Are there no shadows in this bright picture? Well, yes, there are other sides to this story. For one thing, China didn't have to wait for socialism in order to have outstanding women. There were even empresses who, in effect, ruled the country. The best-known was Ci Xi of the late 19th century. And there was even one, in the late Tang Dynasty, who was the official ruler—Wu Zitian, a woman emperor. At less august levels: One of the policies of the Taiping rebellion in the mid-nineteenth century was the equality of the sexes. Taiping women generals led troops into battle. Many Chinese girls have treasured the exploits of the legendary or semi-legendary woman warriors Hua Mulan and Mu Guiying. Traditional Beijing operas, as I've observed from the audience, include a few, at least, about women who outfought all their male opponents. More practically, there were many women participants in the reforms of the May Fourth movement of 1919. At that time, schools for girls were established in Beijing and elsewhere, and the phenomenon of girls as students became commonplace.

On the other hand, even during the socialist period itself, there was opposition to the whole concept of women's equality. One respected Nankai University professor used to announce in a loud voice that at home he never lifted a finger to help his wife with her work. (He differed from many others only by his outspokenness.) She, by the way, was a very busy doctor who, like most working women, really had two jobs—one at the hospital and another at home, where she did all the cooking and cleaning and caring for the children. This was still the common practice while I was in China. Even men who did share the chores usually expected thanks for helping the wives with their work. I heard only one person ever say that a man doing household chores was doing his own work, or his share of their work, not just helping his wife with hers. It was still commonly assumed that man's work is more important than woman's, so if there was not enough time for both wife and husband to study to get ahead, the woman must of course tend to the children and so on while the man studied. (There was, after all, an age-old assumption that women find their natural role in service and sacrifice.)

In my area of the university—the humanities—I found a familiar pyramid: among undergraduates, there were many more women than men; in graduate classes, more women than men; in the department, about as many women teachers as men— but when you ask how many women were professors, or heads of departments, or administrators, the higher up that pyramid, the fewer the women. At the top there were rarely any women at all. The same pyramid was observable in government, in factories, practically everywhere.

You see what I mean when I say that the official policy, including those fine words in the Constitution, was an objective, not a description. Yes, of course, there were signs everywhere that socialism was changing the world for women—but it did not suddenly eradicate the customs and attitudes of centuries-old tradition. (One of my Nankai friends was not so sure that working at a job all day and then doing all the housework was much of a victory for women anyhow. She said, "Women have always held up at least half the sky. Why is it that after all these reforms we still get the dirty half?")

In short, although socialism brought very deep and important changes in the role of women in society, a hard struggle was still going on. The fine phrases of the Constitution still did not describe many people's lives.

During the 1980s, the struggle continued—but with a difference. Throughout most of that decade, the women's movement was actually losing ground. The pattern became clear to me in my classes. At the beginning of the decade, my women students were taking no guff from the men. They argued with them, contradicted them, and laughed at them, as often as they did to each other. They acted out, in short, the equality of women and men. The shift began about the middle of the decade. By the 1990s, the change was incredible. Most of the women were now holding back, waiting to see what the men would say, and never ever arguing with them. And they looked different. They had discovered cosmetics, and permanent waves, and pretty dresses, and leather shoes with heels. And they stopped arguing from theory, from ideology. They stopped even mentioning the equality of the sexes. I don't mean everybody, of course, but enough to make me despondent. Where had the militancy gone, and why?

It was parallel to a pattern I've mentioned before. At the beginning of the 1980s, when we began to hear about how "the market" would solve China's problems, there was a great deal of discussion. Remember the old man in the Shenzhen railway station who asked a young man to help him with his suitcases? When the young man said "Okay, but only to the main door and for fifty cents a bag," the old man was scandalized and wrote a letter to the newspaper asking what the world was coming to. He had expected the young man to say "Of course, sir. Glad to help." The newspaper reported over a hundred letters from readers, about half supporting the old man and half the young one. By the end of the decade, there would have been no support for the old man. Probably no one would have written letters about the issue at all. It had become a non-issue.

It was the same with attitudes about the new freedom of ordinary citizens to hire others to work for them. At first, there was lots of discussion about what should be done, what was right, what was socialist. But as the reforms went further, and all restrictions were gradually removed, discussion died out. It was the same with the changes in material goods. At first, was it right and socialist for some people to have lots of goods that lots of others couldn't afford? By the end of the decade, anybody raising such questions would have been stared at.

I noticed a difference in the way some men were speaking about women. It seemed to me that those who had never been happy about all the attempts to recognize women as equal to men had been keeping quiet, being "politically correct" but not changing their feelings. Now, as the ideological campaigns died down, they felt free to speak up. More than once, in the late 1980s, men students said to me, "Confucius was right: intelligence in a woman is not a virtue." At the same time, as the State gradually abandoned the custom of assigning graduates to jobs, the managers of businesses felt free to refuse to hire women. Remember the manager of the Tianjin Generator Factory? When I asked him why he was refusing to hire women, he was surprised, and exclaimed, "But this is a machine factory!"

When the government called on university undergraduates to find jobs over the summer as a way of broadening their experience of the modern world, many of Nankai's women students responded with enthusiasm—but came back to tell me that they met no enthusiasm among employers. The rejections were blunt. "No women." "We don't hire women." One student took her dossier, and the secretary handed it to the boss to read. He acted impressed as he skimmed through it, but then glanced up at her and said, "Oh, I didn't notice. You're a girl! We don't hire girls!"

Towards the end of the decade, the newspapers reported more and more evidences of this trend. *China Daily* July 20, 1987: "Employers tend to reject female university graduates . . . . [Even] the China Revolutionary Museum is determined not to accept women." *China Daily* February 26, 1988: "Many

Womens ^

enterprises are unwilling to employ women and an official of the All China ~~Workers~~ Federation recently called on society to pay attention to the problem." The Federation made a survey of 660 enterprises in many provinces, and found that "Only 5.3 per cent of the employers were willing to employ women for jobs that could be done by both sexes," [leaving me wondering whether we should be glad that some jobs are still considered "women's work."] On March 8, 1988, the Central Television Network found it appropriate to celebrate International Women's Day with a debate on whether China's working women should "go back to the kitchen" as one way to solve the problem of unemployment.

In a February 10 1988 article, *China Daily* reported that the problem engulfs university students and women in official positions, as well as job applicants: "Discrimination against women is prevalent in enrolling college students, assigning work to university and technical school graduates, recruiting workers and promoting cadres." This article adds:

> During recent discussions on the topic held by municipal and provincial women's federations throughout the country, some women cadres voiced their disappointment and confusion.

> "It's hard to accept the fact that there is no single member in the Party's Political Bureau to represent the 500 million Chinese women, after the country has promoted the equality of men and women for nearly 40 years," said Yang Yanyin, director of the Women's Federation in Shandong Province.

> . . . . The decrease in the number of women officials in China came as a shock to the All-China Women's Federation.

During the 1980s, women lost some important protections against exploitation. Prostitution, unthinkable at the beginning of the decade, soon became, as the papers said, "rampant". After the Tiananmen disaster, one of the "six social evils" that the government announced as targets for a campaign to show it really was fighting corruption, was the kidnapping of women for sale as wives in remote poverty-stricken villages. As the reforms in the countryside made many farm workers "redundant", small factories and other businesses sprang up. According to *China Daily* (March 7, 1988), many enterprising bosses hired child workers in these mostly unregulated new workplaces, and of the children 85 per cent were girls.

In many ways, it became obvious that once the government abandoned the campaign for equality, China's patriarchal traditions came out of hiding. One throwback that I saw constantly, on Chinese television, in newspaper pictures, and on the streets, was the custom of using pretty young women as ornaments. A line of attractive women with "sandwich boards" advertising a product or the opening of a restaurant or enterprise, walks down a busy city street. Young women wearing red sashes announcing a sale stand outside stores, calling out to people passing by. The example most commonly seen on television is at the opening of a new factory, tollroad, museum, or whatever, when a ribbon is ceremoniously cut. Those cutting the ribbon, sometimes three of them in a row, are, of course, men—usually government leaders. Beside each man stands a slim, pretty young woman in the old-fashioned *qipao* sheath dress, holding his official scissors on a velvet cushion.

What happened?

Well, as I pointed out in the previous chapter, the change from the Mao period to the Deng period was a change from class struggle to the GNP, and from ideology and a community focus to self-interest. ("Black cat, white cat, what does it matter as long as it catches mice?" "To get rich is glorious!") The result, on the one hand, was a steady increase, through the 1980s, of consumer goods, which raised a standard of living that desperately needed to be raised. On the other hand, as China opened to the world economically, what came in was not only Western technology and knowhow, but Western culture. The result was obvious: a joyous adopting of Western customs and values. Down came the posters about proper diet for children or the one-child family; up went billboards with commercial ads. Down came the signs on all the athletic fields, "Friendship First, Competition Second"; up went notices of price shifts in the new stock markets. Out went the ubiquitous Mao jackets and baggy pants; in came designer jeans, high heels, cosmetics. And, inevitably, in came Western commercialization of the image of women.

I remember very clearly the TV commercial in the mid-1980s that startled me into the realization that I was living in a different China. The scene, judging by the buildings in the background, is Beijing. The foreground is a park, with a wall covered with rambling roses in full bloom. In the centre, the only people visible (no crowds, just these two) are a young man and a young woman. They are taller than most Chinese, and their faces whiter than most Chinese faces. To judge by their clothes, they are very well off. As they stroll, the young woman is eating *tanghulu*, candied haw apples on a sliver of bamboo (much enjoyed by Beijing people—and by me). She is just finishing. She throws away the stick, sighs, and says, "I like them so much!" "Why not have another?" "Oh no. I must take care of my teeth." The young man pulls out of his jacket pocket a tube of toothpaste, and holds it so we can see the brand name. "Just use this toothpaste and you'll never have to worry about cavities." The next thing we know, as they stroll, she is holding a new *tanghulu* in each hand, and nibbling away with abandon.

Breathtaking! It's hard to know where to start, to list the implications. One, of course, is the message of American TV commercials: You don't have to have any self-discipline in this world. Do whatever you like and if something goes wrong, buy our product. Another is that women should be pretty and childlike, to attract such tall, handsome, well-off young men, and then follow their advice in everything. Her own agenda doesn't matter. He is like Daddy telling her what to do. It's about as far from the young woman on the 1950s poster, working on high-voltage power lines, as you could imagine.

Well, I could see what was happening. My question was *why* it was happening, and why so fast. It was Zhang Yuping, a teacher in the Tianjin Teachers University and a member of the Women's Centre there (about which, more later), who put it in focus for me:

> How can the public image of women change in such negative
> ways forty years after we thought we had achieved equality?
> One reason is that traditional patriarchal ideas had never really
> been questioned because official women's equality came with
> the victory of the Chinese revolution rather than as a
> result of a women's movement, conscious of its political power.
> In a sense, the government was still the father figure, granting
> women equal rights, making decisions regarding women's roles
> and determining our fate.

("Changing Images of Women, East and West" unpublished article, 1998)

Of course! Shades of the days when Blacks in the United States took over their own civil rights movement from the white leaders! Shades of the Nankai teachers who couldn't tell me how the One-Child program became law. ("We trust our leaders.") It's an old story, isn't it? One trouble with having a benevolent dictator has always been that it encourages people to think that Big Daddy will take care of everything, so the people have no experience of taking care of themselves. I remembered that Eugene Debs, when he was the head of the socialist-labour movement in the United States, used to tell his audiences, "If I could lead you into paradise, I wouldn't do it, because if I could lead you in, somebody else could turn you around and lead you out again."

Chinese women found themselves in a universal dilemma. During the revolution, and in the campaigns to build a socialist country, women subordinated their own needs to the greater good of the revolution, trusting that their concerns would be dealt with later. To insist on attention to women's own concerns would have been selfish and "splittist". But like others in that position, they discovered that "later" might be a long time coming. Also, like women in other countries, they realized that they had to deal not only with discrimination and neglect of their concerns by others, but with the fact that they had internalized the values of the patriarchal society and would have to change themselves at the same time.

The result has been the beginnings of a real woman's movement in China, starting about the middle of the 1980s and getting stronger.

Before I get into that, let me talk about the background— that is, the way the China in which a woman's movement is developing is different from Mao's China. In his China they had been content to have the rights which the government gave them. They settled for having their own jobs and incomes and the dignity those things bring, and were reluctant to raise the question of why they should, on top of those jobs, still have all the housework and child-care.

As I see it, the Army's smashing of the student movement of 1989 was a watershed in Chinese social history. If nothing else, it woke people up, and made them a lot less naive. No one today says, "We trust our leaders." No one says, "What kind of government won't talk to the people?" No one, I think, dreams of a mass appeal to the government which would result in consultations with government leaders and changes in government policy. Instead, there seem to be two worlds in China: the official world of the government and its supporters (most definitely including the mass media), and on the other hand, the people. One small example of this split is that in official speeches on Chinese radio and television I still frequently hear the word *shehuizhuyi*, ("socialism"), but I never hear that expression anywhere else.

The nature of this duality is, to put it succinctly, that you must not challenge the government or the Party unless you are ready to go to jail for your convictions—but in your own private life, or group life, you can do pretty much what you want and the government won't bother you. By and large, I mean, and within the law. You can certainly talk about things quite freely, as long as you don't go public. In November, 1998, I was amazed to see this statement in *China Daily* (November 11, 1998):

> Gays, lesbians, AIDS, trial marriage, DINK (double-income with no kids) families, extramarital love affairs—all these things people were unfamiliar with or felt ashamed to mention years ago are no longer taboo in social talk.

It amazed me to see this in print. Privately, I had been told in confidence by a woman student back in 1984 that most of her friends had pre-marital sex. Another had asked me if I could influence the university to get her an abortion that would not go on her record. Homosexuality, yes—that was new. AIDS, I remembered, had been brushed off by a government minister when the question first arose as to what China proposed to do about it. ("That is not a problem for China because we don't have that lifestyle here.") But to see this *China Daily* statement flat out in print as an almost casual aside was an eye-opener.

Besides social conversation, there was a new freedom to do whatever you wanted to, so long as it was not flaunted and did not challenge the government. A reporter for London's *Guardian Weekly* (December 27, 1998) told the paper's readers:

> [Chinese government] vigilance has so far not conflicted with a blossoming of intellectual activity. A theatrical renaissance, including plays dealing with controversial topics such as police brutality and corruption, is underway in Beijing. And a series of Chinese directors have been approved to make movies on sensitive topics, including the first film made inside a Chinese jail.

> Well-attended "salon" discussion sessions at bookstores continue in Beijing, probing issues such as the necessity for human rights, freedom and the right of assembly in China.

A reporter for the *New York Times* (September 2, 1997) even found a gay men's hangout in Shanghai, where he was told, "No one bothers us anymore. As long as we're not disturbing anyone else, we can enjoy ourselves and the police will leave us alone" and "The Government no longer has a problem with gays; it has a problem with organizations. As long as you don't organize or speak out, you can do what you want."

There has been a blossoming of non-governmental, volunteer organizations supporting various causes (which do not conflict with government policy): Groups for the cherishing of wild birds or the protection of the environment or encouraging people to stop smoking, and many others.

As for the women's movement, I see many references in the papers these days to what you might generally call women's self-help projects—women working together without counting on the government. In Qianxi county of Hebei Province, the local Women's Federation branch has an active "microcredit" program, lending small amounts of money to women to start their own businesses, from a fund provided by *Working Women Knowing All*, a periodical based in Beijing. *China Daily* (May 12, 1998) has a full-page article on how this program is helping women in poor areas help themselves and their families out of poverty.

Zhang Yuping made me change my mind about the Women's Federation of China. I had known that when the socialist nation was being set up in the early 1950s, the Women's Federation had been very active, sending teams throughout the countryside, using plays and other performances to educate the people about their new socialist state and the status of women in that new State, and setting up "Each One Teach One" literacy campaigns. But by the time I was teaching in China, what I heard from my students was that the Federation had degenerated into a cheerleader group to stir up support for any current policy of the government. One of my students at Nankai was having serious trouble with a man her parents said she must marry but whom she despised. He was writing poison-pen letters to the university and to prospective employers, and generally being a menace. When I asked her why she didn't go to the Women's Federation for help, she was scornful. "All they do is arrange the ceremonies for International Women's Day," she said.

In 1983, three women delegates from the Chengdu branch of the Federation came to Regina to investigate non-governmental Canadian women's organizations. My friend Zhou Xiaojing, who was living with my family while going to the University of Regina, became their interpreter and guide. She roped me in to be their chauffeur, and brought them home to have tea and talk. I told them frankly about my Nankai student's assessment of the Federation. They said that the student was right—that the Federation had degenerated into a captive support group for the government. But think about why they had come to Canada. They were part of a resurgence, a determination to find ways of really working to solve the problems of Chinese women.

Throughout the 1980s, I was depressed by reports in the newspapers of surveys that showed how women were being mistreated—from wife-beating to the exploitation of girls from the countryside who came to the city looking for work, exploitation including very long hours, low pay, beatings, and rape. When I learned of Zhang Yuping's admiration for the work of the Women's Federation, I went back to those accounts and found that all those surveys had been carried out by branches of the Federation. There were branches of the Federation in every province and in cities, towns, and counties, and at the top the umbrella group, the All-China Women's Federation. The All-China group conducted and publicized surveys, stepped into local struggles where needed, and lobbied the government for changes in laws and law enforcement. Its members included delegates to the People's Political Consultative Conference, an interesting body whose original business had been to set up the legislature of the new socialist State. Since then it meets annually to advise the government on problems and propose solutions. Such a body, obviously, could become ineffective—but the government seems to listen to it, and best of all the newspapers and television cover its meetings and its discussion groups in detail and report on its proposals.

For several years the Women's Federation lobbied the government for a law on the rights of women, and drew up a draft of such a law. When their proposal was accepted, and in 1992 the law was passed, the Federation decided to spend at least the next two years in a grassroots campaign to inform Chinese women about their rights and how to exercise them. (The law makes legally binding most of the provisions of the Constitution on the rights of women, though getting people to use and accept the law will still be a long struggle.)

China Daily for March 3, 1999 tells us that the All-China Women's Federation would propose several motions to the upcoming session of the National People's Congress. One would call for a ban on bar girls in night clubs. ("Many bar girls in

China become involved in the provision of sexual services.") The other motions the ACWF was proposing called for

> the establishment of an insurance system for women who are pregnant [to take away the common excuse of those who don't want to hire women, that pregnancy leaves are an unacceptable expense to the employer], guaranteeing equal rights to women farmers to contract land, and attatching greater emphasis to domestic violence and bigamy in the current revisions to the Marriage Law.

The All-China Women's Federation has also set up a research institute, the Institute of Women's Studies, which has published a good deal of statistical material, reports on the status of women, and a collection of brief biographies of influential women in China's history.

I think if I advised one of my Chinese students to go to the Women's Federation for help these days, she would probably go.

Another important development of the 1980s and 1990s has been the growth of women's studies programs and women's studies centres. I've told you about a conference on women's problems that I attended in April, 1989. One of the admirable women I met there was Min Dongchao, a teacher in the Department of History of the Tianjin Teachers University, who taught a class on women's movements. Her history of the development of women's movements in several countries was published in 1990. She and I met sometimes for lunch. We talked about her problems as a woman teacher in a male-dominated department, and about her students, and about the problems of being an unmarried woman in her forties in China. (You can't believe the social pressure on women who are unmarried after their twenties—I've known three who made hasty and unfortunate marriages because of that pressure.)

It seems to be easier to be concerned with women's problems at that university these days—that's where both Min Dongchao and Zhang Yuping are members of a very active Women's Studies Centre. Zhang's unpublished article "Education of Women in China" gives the details of one project—a study of the lives of women in Hebei Province in north China. The project combines academic study with consciousness-raising sessions, and the designing of programs to help the rural women raise themselves out of poverty. It sounds like a very exciting project to have been part of:

> Many women . . . said that for the first time in their lives they realized their own importance and acknowledged the inequalities in their lives. . . . Working together closely, friendships have deepened between our group members and the villagers. We eat together, live in their homes, and work together in the fields. We have taped interviews with many villagers, recording their life stories, and have interviewed successful women entrepreneurs of local enterprises. . . . The results of this research project will appear in two books. *The Influence of One Hundred Years of Cultural Changes on the Lives of Rural Women in Northern China* will be a compilation of papers written by Center members. Transcriptions of oral histories we have recorded will appear in *A Hundred Years of Changes*: the Oral Histories of One Hundred Rural Women in Northern China.

Altogether, in China as elsewhere, I have to think that in contrast to all the things going wrong in this world of ours, some things, like the women's movement, despite setbacks and a long road ahead, are going right.

14

Where To ?

I went to China in 1976 looking for socialism—remember? Here it is twenty-some years later as I sit here wondering what I can say to wrap up these memories. I feel much as I did that evening I sat on my porch in Xiamen, noting the solidity of the present moment and the present scene, but at the same time very conscious of the fact that everything is in flux, part of history, the present moment no less so than past moments. Twenty-some years! Well, I've learned some things—about China, about socialism, and about myself.

Socialism? People tell me now that it's dead and gone. In one sense they are surely right. The socialism I went looking for was an abstraction, an ideal which so far has never been on land or sea. The aspects of socialism that I found in China warmed my heart—but most of those aspects are gone. If one theme of this book has been how much I love old things in China, another has been how all things change. China in 2000 is very different indeed from China in 1976, which was already very different from 1950. The socialist China of the early 1950s ("We were brothers and sisters!" "We didn't have much, but we had each other!") is as lost in time as the Garden of Eden.

Not that it wasn't in itself a viable idea, I think, but that it now seems practically impossible in the interrelated world for one country to keep to its own ways, however idealistic, sealed off from the hostility of the rest of the world. And there were, you remember, fatal weaknesses in Chinese socialism from the start. Remember the time Nankai students first got a chance to see an American television program? How they crowded into the small TV room of the dormitory I was living in, and then how little attention they paid to the story? How they hungered for the life in which one ordinary family could have a whole house to live in, with carpets on the floor, and matching furniture, and could have its own automobile? I think I knew then, in my heart, that China's particular socialist dream was doomed—largely because socialism in China had already failed its own people. It was no longer teaching them what socialism was all about, only telling them what they must do and not do. Socialism to these students meant not a way of working together to build a good life, but a rigid system that would not let them have the good things other people had.

In March, 1999, the National People's Congress (to nobody's surprise) accepted the government's proposal to change China's Constitution. *China Daily* (March 10) showed the changes— the old passages in one column, the new ones in another. One of the changes seems to me indicative of the current attitude towards socialism. "China is at the preliminary stage of socialism" has been replaced by "China will be at the primary stage of socialism over a long period of time." When you consider that by current official theory China must first build up the means of production to the level of the advanced capitalist countries, and then move on to achieve socialism, this change puts off any consideration of socialism to some distant future. It ceases to have any relevance to the present.

So practically speaking, socialism is dead now? In one sense, yes. The socialist governments in big countries are gone—either overthrown, as in Russian and eastern Europe, or transmuted into something else, as in China—and modern armaments make it very unlikely indeed that there will again be an armed revolution bringing in a socialist society.

On the other hand, if we back off and take a broader view, socialism is not dead and never will be. If we consider the two polar impulses of human beings—self-interest and community—neither of these is going to die. There will only be different ratios or balances between them. Today the concept of capitalism, globalism on capitalist terms, profits as the be-all-and-end-all, seems to be solidly in command. But everything is in flux. There are already signs that the pendulum is beginning to swing the other way, and perhaps by the time you read this the global capitalist system will be seen to have cracks in it. As long as there are people who hold to that other concept—that we are all in this together, that in a real sense we really are all brothers and sisters and responsible for each other—there will be what I choose to call socialism.

As for China, it is at a strange point in its flux, a strange mixture of socialism and capitalism. On the one hand, Deng's motto "To get rich is glorious" does not sound very different from old John D. Rockefeller's "God wants every man to make as much money as he can." On the other hand, there is still a lot of humane feeling in China. Even in my own classes: I'm told that in the natural sciences departments, and the computer science and business administration departments, there is now as fierce cut-throat competition for grades and awards as anywhere in the West, but in my classes it's still different. (If it were not, I'd have stopped going back long ago. Why bother to go halfway around the world to find what you have left behind?) My students still take it for granted that they are there to help each other, and that their work should help society.

Chinese people are a mixed lot, as you'd expect when you consider that they are a quarter of the human race. There are money-grubbers, of course, and brutal corrupt people—far too many. There are silly people who are dazzled by possessions and by anything Western. (I hear there are now clinics in Beijing where Chinese young women can have their eyes "Westernized".) As for those who want a system closer to what I would call socialist ideals, they are for now stymied. As in the West, they can chip away at one or more aspects of the system, but as for changing the system, the times are far from ripe. We will not soon see another mass movement like that of the spring and early summer of 1989.

Well, what can one do, then, when there is no hope of changing the system? An old anarchist motto is "As much as possible live in the present world as if it were already the good world." There is still a lot of leeway, in China as elsewhere, to live your own life according to your ideals, and if enough people have humane ideals and live by them, the world will change direction. Besides that, the Chinese are very good at coping— at using current conditions to thrive and endure. One of the things I admire most about the Chinese is their ability to cope, to survive, to wait for the tide to change.

There are many bad things happening in China, yes, and a pessimist could predict from them that China is on the skids. The population problem is basic—China feeds roughly 20 per cent of the human race on 7 per cent of the world's arable land, and that formula gets worse every year as the arable land decreases and the population increases. (Contrary to what a lot of people think, China's population policy, while it has slowed down the rate of increase, has not stopped the population from increasing.) That puts enormous pressures on agriculture, on the environment, on government policy.

Another huge problem is unemployment, which if all the predictions were realized would mean that by the year 2001 over 100,000,000 people in China would be unable to find work. This in a country where workers have for half a century been told that jobs are for life. Unemployment is a problem of capitalist countries, they've been told over and over. A Chinese friend of mine went home in the summer of 1998, after eight years in Canada. She found that her family, the neighbours, their friends, all wanted to talk about almost nothing but the hardships of unemployment. "Every family has somebody unemployed," they said. "Why doesn't the government do something? All they do is say how many more people will be unemployed when the mines, or the textile mills, or whatever, get `rationalized' or `leaned down', and people are made `redundant'." It's a huge problem, and it's true that the government keeps announcing that one or another sector of the economy must be reformed to be made competitive—by firing a lot of the workers.

Other "evils of capitalism" which were supposed to be impossible under socialism include inflation and prostitution, which are now as the papers say "rampant" all over China. In 1995, when I asked Jan Wong, then the *Globe and Mail* Beijing correspondent, what she saw in her trips around China, she said, "I see corruption; I see poverty and nobody doing anything about it; I see privilege, I see the children of high officials getting away with sometimes literally murder; I see drugs in the south, and a reluctance to confront the problem; I see prostitution and the prostitutes treated like animals and no sense that we should try to educate the people about venereal disease. I try to look for positive stories, too, but it's very difficult."

Corruption is another huge problem. In every issue of *China Daily* you can see accounts of officials punished for bribery or extortion or misuse of public funds—in recent months many of these cases involve over a million yuan each—but everybody I talk to in China says the cases that get reported are a very small fraction of those that don't. Corruption became worse and worse during the decade of the '80s, and at its worst involves not only money, though as the old saying goes, it is the love of money that is the root. John Gittings, reporting from Beijing to the *Guardian Weekly* for January 24, 1999, says:

> China's biggest and most controversial dam project, the Three Gorges on the Yangzi river, has become the latest focus of a wave of allegations about corrupt officials taking bribes from unqualified contractors—allegations that are raising fears about the safety of the project.
>
> Nearly 100 cases of "corruption, bribery and embezzlement" related to the project were discovered last year, Beijing revealed this week. . . . Critics of the huge dam, which will raise the water level in the Three Gorges by 80m, [That's right—80 metres] have warned that any construction defect could have fatal consequences. . . . Renewed fears about the dam were sparked by collapse last month of a [recently constructed] bridge upstream from the Three Gorges . . . as a result of suspected faulty construction by a contractor who bribed local officials [to get the job.] . . . A local official has been arrested after allegedly taking a bribe of more than 100,000 renminbi ($11,500) from an unqualified contractor who built the bridge. [Other accounts tell us that 40 people died and over a hundred were seriously injured when that bridge suddenly collapsed.]

You've got the picture? A body of water 263 feet deep and miles long held back by this monster dam. And now many charges of corruption and incompetence in the building of the dam. And millions of Chinese people living alongside the river downstream.

Corruption is no longer a matter of individuals getting small kickbacks. Today, it's very big business. Smugglers, for example, now have high-speed motor boats, wear bulletproof vests, carry submachineguns, and bring in smuggled goods by the large boatload or in containers. Economic crime now involves not just a small scam but millions of dollars:

> Four people, including a tax official and three businessmen . . .have been sentenced to death in cases involving faked value added tax invoices. . . . 218 companies are involved in the case in which 65,000 invoices were faked, 89 criminal suspects were arrested and 6,234 billion yuan (US$751 million) was recovered.

> *(China Daily, November 5, 1998)*

That story was not even front page news, such crimes are so common these days.

Yet another huge problem is pollution. Beijing now has one of the highest levels of air pollution of any city in the world. You don't have to be an expert, or even read the newspapers, to see that the pollution of air, water, and ground are at horrific levels in China. To see clear water in rivers or lakes, you must go to the wilderness. In the mid-eighties, when I took a steamer to see Dianchi, the huge lake outside of Kunming, before we got to the lake itself the steamer went down a canal the water of which looked like dirty crankcase oil. Alongside the canal, local people were washing clothes in it, and washing vegetables before taking them to market, and carrying home bucketsful.

On the train from Kunming to Chengdu, almost a quarter of the way you are in tunnels. Every now and then you come out suddenly in a narrow mountain valley—many times in those valleys you see a dam, and an industrial town using the electricity, and a disgusting black cloud of pollution blanketing it. (Before they realize what that does to their health, the people refer to the black clouds as "Black dragons that are leading us to prosperity.")

I read in the papers that 71 per cent of the province of Guangdong is blighted by acid rain—mostly from the burning of high-sulfur soft coal.

Well, I could go on—for hours if necessary—detailing the internal problems of China, and the external ones growing out of China's having made itself dependent on the global economy, and about the threat of war over its claims to practically all the islands in the South China Sea, most of which are much closer to other countries than to China, and about charges that it has been selling nuclear capability to Pakistan and Iran. And so on.

But hold on here for a moment. Before we draw conclusions that China can't go on like this, let me remind you that it wouldn't be all that difficult to draw up a list of problems like this about any large country I've been to or heard of.

Canada has been called by the United Nations one of the best countries to live in, but in my home province of Saskatchewan, as I am writing this, nineteen of the former provincial government's ministers have been found guilty of the misuse of public money, and many of them are in prison. (If you think China is unique in such problems, let me urge you, if you live in Canada, to read Stevie Cameron's *On the Take: Crime, Corruption and Greed in the Mulroney Years*. If you live in the US, get your hands on Mike Royko's *Boss: A Political Biography of Richard J. Daley*.) The unemployment rate in many of the native Indian towns and villages in the north of my Canadian province is around 75 per cent, and their rate of teenage suicide is eight times the national average. As for pollution, think of this: Saskatchewan is three times the size of Hebei Province. Saskatchewan has one million people. Hebei has fifty-three million. So in Saskatchewan the weight of human activities on the land should be almost nothing, right? But the farmers themselves tell me that in Saskatchewan, because of the way we farm, the nutrition in the soil is only half what it was seventy-five years ago. And the runoff from the farm fields, loaded with pesticides and herbicides, has polluted the lakes and rivers so that you have to go to the "undeveloped" northern parts of the province to be able to eat the fish.

So don't think that China is unique in such heavy problems. I've tried throughout this book to give you a balanced picture—those things which I admire and love in China and those things which appall me. That's what I'd want to hear from anybody describing the culture of a country he or she has been involved with. I'm not going to wind up by telling you that China's problems are going to bring it down, nor that China's strengths are going to overcome all the difficulties and solve all the problems. I hope I've given you evidence, throughout the book, to encourage optimism that China's strengths will solve some of the problems, yes—that China will continue the struggle between idealism and materialism and idealism will score important victories in that struggle. What more can I say, and be realistic?

Well, actually, there is one more thing I want to say, or rather one more story I want to tell you—one more memory to share. Whether it has any bearing on the ideas I've just expressed, I leave you to decide.

One day in 1985 the bus I was riding in was delayed for twelve hours in a traffic snarl on a country road, waiting for our turn to board a little ferry and cross a river. It was raining lightly most of that time. It should have been a dreadful experience, but I hope to convince you that I remember it with pleasure. To make it harder for myself, I'll tell you that I was on a bus trip from Hai'an to Guangzhou which was supposed to take fourteen hours and ended up taking thirty-six, getting me to Guangzhou too late to make connections to go to Chengdu and spend Spring Festival day with Chinese friends.

The story starts in San Ya, on the south coast of Hainan Island, as far south as you can get in China, the only Chinese place I've found where it's nicely hot in winter. I had come in February to get some relief from the bitter winds and barely-heated buildings of Tianjin, with a guide and friend—a young man named Chen. He was a former Nankai student then working for the Tianjin City Foreign Affairs Office, and the office sent him with me on his first assignment as a guide. At first, Chen was nervous, afraid of making some dreadful mistake—which he never did. He turned out to have a real talent for getting information and for bargaining, and he was a good friend and guide. He had a knack of knowing what I wanted and helping me get it.

When we reached the hotel called Deer Looked Back (*Lu Hui Tou*), up the coast from San Ya, we were hot and tired from a long day on a third-class bus across Hainan Island. The desk clerks told us the only thing available was one of the modern units at 100 kuai a night for each of us. I started to argue, but Chen took me aside and suggested that I go look at the grounds while he talked to them. A few minutes later he came out grinning. We had one of the old bungalows right down by the beach under the palm trees, at 30 kuai a night for both of us.

The Deer Looked Back was really a lot of bungalows scattered through a large grove of palms. Ours was old, and was soon to be replaced. We had two large rooms and a bath. The doors sagged, the screens were rusted out, the water supply was erratic. In the bathroom, the handbasin drained right onto the floor. But we had a wide veranda with a railing just the right height for sitting with feet up listening to the surf on the beach and the breeze in the palms. We could smell the ocean, and the flowers that seemed to just spring up everywhere. The teenage girls who came once in a while to clean were lazy and talkative. I settled in fast, and my soul was at rest.

The name "Deer Looked Back", by the way, comes from a local legend. Once upon a time long ago there was a prince, the most famous of hunters. He saw a beautiful deer one day and chased it for hours through the forest. Finally the deer ran out onto a promontory—the same one we could see from our bungalow. Finding itself cut off from escape, the deer looked back, and saw the hunter coming fast. In desperation, the deer changed itself into a charming maiden, with whom the hunter quite sensibly fell in love. He took her home and made her his princess and they lived happily ever after. One of the locals told Chen that the proof the story is true is the fact that local girls have beautiful eyes.

The units they had wanted to give us were further inland and were hermetically sealed. They were the products of a joint venture with an American company, and when you were indoors you couldn't see any view or hear anything but the air conditioners or smell anything but the cheap new furniture. The manager was very proud of them.

We discovered a tiny restaurant just outside the hotel grounds, the one I've mentioned before, run by two brothers from Guangxi and their two young nieces. Chen preferred the hotel dining hall, where he got a discount, but I never did get around to trying the dining hall, I liked the little restaurant so much. There were about a dozen small tables, some of which were moved outdoors in the evening. It was the kind of place where I could stroll into the kitchen and inspect the tubs of live lobsters and crabs and fish, shrimp, and squid, and say, "I'll take that lobster and that fish and four of those big shrimps." The brother who cooked would grin and nod and say, "Okay. Go drink beer. We'll cook." And then cooked, wonderfully well. It was the kind of place where in the lazy afternoons I sometimes sat at a small table helping sixteen-year-old Jie Jie skin huge mounds of garlic and talked with her about her life.

Jie Jie had a healthy, pleasant country-girl face, a smile that made her suddenly pretty, and a handshake like a blacksmith's. She was always working but calm and good natured. They came from a poor village, she said, and the money they would take home at the end of the season would make a sensation. She was saving for her marriage. Without that money the family would, in effect, sell her to some farmer willing to pay for her. But now she could decide for herself whom to marry. She was going to take her time, and be choosy.

I spent many hours on the three incredible beaches of San Ya—the rocky one for looking at creatures in pools at low tide, the body-surfing one where the waves broke far out and came surging up the shore, the quiet and lazy scenic one for picnicking and sunbathing. There were very few people there, fewer than a dozen people to a kilometre of beach. "But just wait," the manager said. "If you come back in seven years there will be an international hotel and an airport, and lots of tourists." He was modest in his predictions—there are now three huge tourist hotels there, and an amusement park beside the beach, and an international airport that they say handles a million tourists a year. Well, okay, why be selfish? A lot of people ought to enjoy San Ya. But as for me, I keep thinking that in this case, as in others, I was very lucky in my timing.

The people who ate at my favourite little restaurant were mostly young foreigners who were staying in the cheap dormitory hotels in San Ya and came out to the beaches by bicycle or on little three-wheeled moped taxis the drivers of which had to help out their engines by pedaling on the hills. They were teachers of English or French, or foreign students of Chinese, come from many parts of China. And there was one burly American who worked for an oil company down the coast but was tired of seeing the same faces there every day. He had been a helicopter pilot in Viet Nam during the war, and had seen enough killing to last him the rest of his life. He had even given up hunting and fishing. Now he flew a 'copter out to the oil rigs in the ocean. He still needed physical challenge, he said, so he had taken up free-fall sky-diving, in which the object was to jump from a plane at high altitude and fall free for a long time before opening the parachute. There's no feeling like it, he said. I told him I'd take his word for that one but I had always wanted to learn to fly a glider. Now, of course, I was too old. He bristled. "What kind of talk is that? Man, you're not in a wheelchair. If you want it, go for it!"

We had to leave San Ya in a hurry, which is how our tribulations began. But I think I had reached such a calm and peaceful state by then that it carried me through the tribulations without the heebie-jeebies I might at other times have suffered.

Chen had been phoning daily to a bureaucrat in Guangzhou who had promised to get a plane ticket for me to Chengdu, to get me there for Spring Festival. One day the man said if we would come immediately he'd get me on a plane. Otherwise there were no tickets to be had. Unfortunately, to come immediately, though we really tried, did not turn out to be possible.

There was no airline serving San Ya then. We got bus tickets to Haikou, on the north side of the island, but to get even these at such short notice required Chen's ingenuity. He finally found the back door, which is to say he bought two tickets from a bus driver out behind the bus terminal, and we took off. There were no other foreigners on the bus—in fact, I was not to see another non-Chinese face anywhere until we reached Guangzhou at the end of our adventure.

The bus was built for about fifty people and held seventy-five or more. They crowded the seats. They stood in the doorwell.

They sat on masses of luggage in the aisles. On the roof was an ungainly heap of bundles, also a live pig and some chickens. It was an eight-hour trip across the island, during which I dozed a lot, barely hearing the voices around me speaking in a dialect I couldn't understand, with long drawn-out musical "a" sounds. At intervals on that eight-hour trip the driver declared a comfort stop, calling out "Men to the right, women to the left," and we piled out, like the circus act in which twenty people come out of a Volkswagon bug, and went off into the farm fields to relieve ourselves.

After a night in a Haikou hotel, a two-hour bus ride to the ferry, and a breezy refreshing two-hour ferry ride to Hai'an on the mainland, we found ourselves waiting in a compound for the deluxe express bus to Guangzhou.

The compound was large, with several buses sitting empty off to one side. Many people were standing around waiting, but no one seemed to know which bus we'd take or when it would start. Some said our bus was waiting for the cleaners to come to work. Others said our bus wasn't there yet but on the way. Meanwhile local buses came and went, with much hubbub.

A family of pigs explored the compound and grunted when they found anything edible. A number of skinny chickens scratched here and there, not finding much. Vendors wandered around—the most successful were those selling hard-boiled duck eggs, of which we bought half a dozen.

It had rained recently, and the ground was quite muddy. Some of us managed to find standingroom on a paved area, and a few others sat on the steps of the parked buses, but most people just stood in the mud.

I was struck by one young woman waiting near us for a local bus. She looked about eighteen years old. She was traveling alone except for the baby on her back, slung in a pretty embroidered cloth. Many packages were also slung in cloth bags from her shoulders. Her pants were rolled up clear of the mud, though her feet and sandals were very muddy. Her broad flat-cone straw hat was firmly attached to her head by straps and hatpins. She stood patiently, with an ancient peasant patience that I was to remember later.

The baby woke and cried, and the young mother reached a hand back and jiggled its bottom softly. Then, when that didn't work, she swung her body so that the baby's sling came around front and the bundles swung out of the way. Squatting on her heels, the mother opened her shirt and nursed her baby, looking calmly around. I was impressed by the competence of this young mother. In her familiar world she knew exactly what to do and how to do it. None of her bundles fell or touched the mud. The baby was comfortable and tenderly nursed. Although there was no dry place for the woman to sit or stand, she coped, and didn't seem to think anything was out of the ordinary. There was a strength there which I found more admirable the more I thought about it.

A bus terminal worker finally slouched over to one of the parked buses and unlocked the door and let us in. No one bothered to ask him why we couldn't have been waiting in the bus instead of standing around in the mud. I found out quickly why this bus was called deluxe: every passenger had a seat. After another long wait, a driver finally showed up and we set out, an hour and a half behind schedule, for the fourteen-hour run to Guangzhou. I couldn't have known, of course, that for us it would take thirty-six hours.

We passed through the south China countryside, with its terraced paddies and picturesque villages with houses huddled together to leave as much room as possible for the fields. Even now, in February, people were hoeing vegetable crops. The winter wheat, I estimated, would be ready to harvest in a couple of weeks.

The two-lane country road was full of traffic: two-wheel carts pulled by small horses, smaller carts pulled by forward-leaning men, many bicycles, some with bulky loads on the carriers. Many people carried heavy loads swung from bamboo carrying-poles, trotting with the curious rumba motion that keeps the loads from bouncing up and down. A lot of people just walking. It was no road for a driver to make time on, no matter how vigorously he kept sounding the horn.

Gradually, as the hours passed, I realized that it was not just normal traffic that was slowing us down. There were an extraordinary number of trucks and buses, many of them apparently brand new. When I asked about that, my fellow-travelers told me this two-lane road was the main traffic artery from the south coast all the way to Guangzhou, and that traffic on it was heavier year by year. There was no middle stripe marked on the pavement: the bus stayed right in the middle until something big came in the other direction, and then there was a chicken contest to decide which would pull over for the other. I had a good seat for watching the driver at work, but I had to stop watching and look out the side window instead.

As evening came on, we were already hours behind schedule, and all of us getting hungrier minute by minute. Finally, at about 9:30, we pulled into a walled compound and stopped. I never did find out what unit this was, but it had contracted to feed the bus passengers on this route. When we came staggering into the dining hall, we found all the chairs stacked on the tables and a team of barefoot young women, bossed by an older one, cleaning the concrete floor. First the older woman would flood the floor with a big hose. Then the others, all in a line, would push long-handled squeegees, pushing the water to drains on the far side of the room. Just when we thought they were finished and we could go in, they started all over again. But when that round was finished and the old woman shouted at them to start again, we rebelled. A fine noisy argument broke out, which was settled by all of us pushing into the room and taking the chairs off the tables and sitting on them.

We had to get up again, though, and go into the big steamy kitchen and help ourselves to food that had been kept warm for us. Finally, back at the tables with food and chopsticks, we set to. Rice. Duck. Vegetables. Either we were famished or the food was excellent. After that it was pile back into the bus, with a new driver now, and settle down as best we could for the night as the bus took off again.

In daylight next morning I woke, realizing we were not moving. And so began our twelve-hour wait for the ferry. We were caught in a traffic jam solid all the way to the river—a bypasser told us it was fifteen kilometres down the road. There we sat, while every time the ferry took a load the line moved up a tiny bit. I got out and climbed to the top of our bus and took pictures of the long line, and gradually the significance of what was happening—or not happening, rather—came to me.

Almost all this traffic was trucks and buses, and almost all of them were new. Most of the buses were imports from Japan. What was happening was that China's new affluence, the result of the New Economic Policy, was being expended on things like trucks and buses and there were now so many of them that the roads, bridges, and ferries simply couldn't handle them. Just now, when more people than ever before had the money to get home for the most important holiday in the Chinese calendar, the crowds swamped the system.

It struck me that this was a crisis like the one China had faced in the early 1950s, when the young socialist country had to build an infrastructure of roads and rails and aqueducts, and homes and schools and hospitals for 500,000,000 people, to make the new society possible. What was needed now was a massive new program to build thousands of new bridges, widen the highways, increase the railroads, improve river traffic. I had known all that intellectually, but it didn't really hit me until that day when I sat thinking about it for hours, caught in the traffic jam.

I thought, too, that now it was no longer possible to call on mass movements, with thousands of people each carrying a basketful of dirt. Today's society is not like that. Now, it would need massive amounts of money, for supplies, for heavy machinery, and for labour. And where was all that money to come from? Unless China reforms its tax system so that the people getting rich under the new system contribute a lot of their loot to the State for these purposes, I don't see any source for such amounts of money. In an odd way, it seems true that today, with the higher standard of living, the affluence, the advanced technology, it might prove harder to solve such problems than it was back in the days of low income and mass enthusiasm.

I had plenty of time to sit and think. And one of the things I thought about was the lines of people passing the bus in both directions. Since our traffic jam filled the paved road, all the usual traffic of bicycles and people had to pass along a strip of dirt about six feet wide, between our bus and a steep drop-off to the rice paddies about ten feet below. So there was a constant flow of people, going towards the ferry or away from it, passing just a foot or two from my face as I sat in the bus.

Sometimes some of us got out to explore the area. It turned out there were public toilets up ahead, and further along a quick-food booth that was a godsend. The farmers who had gone into business here beside the road were making a killing. The lines of people waiting to buy food were long and constant. What the farmers were selling was rice with stir-fried vegetables and a bit of meat, in styrofoam dishes and lids, accompanied by small throwaway chopsticks. In the old Chinese culture there was almost nothing that people would throw away which was not bio-degradable, so there was nothing in their traditions that would teach them not to litter. Here, at any rate, was litter enough to give me nightmares. People ate, and tossed the styrofoam boxes down—the area around the booth was ankle-deep in them and you could easily find the booth by following back the lines of litter from either direction.

Things like that fascinate me. Even that takeaway package itself combined old and new. The old was the good simple Chinese food, not modern junk food. The new was the container, a wonderful invention, cheap enough to be used once and discarded. And who could tell them that the styrofoam would desecrate the landscape until it finally evaporated and went up to cut holes in the ozone? Here was the meeting of two ages and two cultures, with a vengeance, and an example of the social problems that uncontrolled technology brings, which nobody seems to anticipate and nobody is in a hurry to solve.

I stood in the doorway of our bus by the hour, watching the local people go by in that narrow strip between us and the drop-off. People of all ages, going about their business. Sometimes one of them caught sight of me—the only foreigner in the whole traffic jam, probably—and was startled, but for the most part they paid little attention to us. For the last few hours we were there, a fine drizzling rain was falling, but most people seemed to ignore it.

I was struck by the fact that here, in the deep countryside, in what I'd been told was a poor area, the people all looked healthy. Their clothes were varied. Young women seemed to have picked up fashion ideas from the TV, and wore tight blue jeans and colourful shirts. Some of the young men had no shirts, but showed off their muscular chests. Older people wore the traditional Mao jackets and pants. One man wore a western business suit and carried a briefcase, though he also wore sandals, had his pants rolled up out of the mud, and carried by its gills a large fish he'd bought in the market. Many peasants passed wearing wide rice-straw hats to keep off sun and rain, and with their pants rolled up high on their muscular calves, but instead of traditional rice-straw capes they were wearing blue plastic raincoats—apparently some nearby factory specialized in them.. Perhaps that factory also made the blue plastic umbrellas some people carried.

It fascinated me to see with what calm and patience these two streams of people managed to go in two directions, in such a narrow space. They rubbed shoulders and passed. There were old women hobbling long. There were girls of about nine or ten with little brothers on their backs. There were men with carrying poles, with a bundle or basket swaying from each end— one man had a bundle hanging from one end of his pole, and from the other a basket holding two baby girls who sat still and watched the world. There were many people with bicycles, which were a problem, especially when in that crowd they met others with bikes going the other way. And once there was a real crisis when a man came pushing a motorcycle in one direction and met a man with a flatbed tricycle loaded with boxes.

I've often thought that the Chinese have a talent for making the best of things. Nobody seemed to be irritated. They were all in this together and it was nobody's fault, so they got along. When the motorcycle met the three-wheeler, there was a pause. Then, as if nobody needed to say anything, some young men got hold of the motorcycle and lifted it and carried it over the three-wheeler, and the two-way tangled procession started again.

There was a spirit here which reminded me of the young mother at the bus depot. There was none of the bad temper I had seen once in a Beijing subway, when the trains were late and the platform was crowded. More and more people kept arriving. There, I had no sense of a society, a community. It was a mob of angry, shoving individuals, and I was sure somebody was going to be pushed off the platform onto the tracks. I fought my way back up the stairs and got out of there.

There's a saying you'll hear over and over again in China: *"Mei ban fa!"* "There's no way—nothing can be done about it!" Sometimes that's a gesture of despair, but I've heard it more often in the sense of that other old saying, "The egg attacked the rock"—When you've ascertained that there is indeed nothing to do about it, relax. Swing with it. As those people passing by were doing, with a calm acceptance of the situation and a cooperative keeping going which was after all something to do about it. There's an important aspect of the Chinese character here which I must not forget

In our bus, when it was first apparent that we were going to be stuck in the traffic jam for a long time, there was much excited chatter and questioning. People got out and walked up ahead to see what the situation was and incidentally discovered the public toilets and the fast-food place and came back and told everybody about them. Gradually, as it became apparent that there really was nothing to do about it, they settled back calmly to wait. A group in the back of the bus clustered around two men playing *wei qi*, the ancient board game that the Japanese call "Go". Some, including Chen, were sleeping, some reading, some carrying on quiet conversations, some writing letters.

I fantasized that if the bus had been full of American tourists, they would be greatly upset, looking at their watches, talking loudly about the outrage, blaming the tour guide or the travel agency or the Chinese in general. They would waste a lot of energy attacking the rock. If it had been English tourists, I mused, they might have organized a sing-along. Others might perhaps have broken the windows.

Mei ban fa! Make the best of it. When there's something to be done, as when a motorcycle meets a three-wheeler, do it. When nothing can be done, cope.

The one exception to this attitude was a Hong Kong Chinese man who sat across the aisle from me. He looked at his watch frequently. At last he turned to me with an exasperated expression and said, in English, "How can you just sit there as if nothing was the matter?"

I started to tell him I thought this was an interesting opportunity to see how Chinese people dealt with such an emergency, but I got out only a few words before he shouted, "Interesting! You think this is *interesting!*" It was more than the poor man could stand. He jumped up, wrestled his large suitcase from the overhead rack, jumped off the bus and started striding through the rain towards the ferry—at that time about ten kilometres ahead.

He would slog through rain and mud and crowds with that big suitcase for ten kilometres, cross the ferry as a foot-passenger, and buy passage on one of the buses up ahead of us. Well, in his terms he was right. He would get to Guangzhou before us, and it would make him feel good to be doing something. It would have done me no good to go with him—it was already too late for me to get to Guangzhou in time to make my connection to Chengdu, even if the Guangzhou official had kept his word and bought me a ticket (which, I found out later, he had never done anyhow.) For me, it was *Mei ban fa.*

Can I explain why I felt at peace? I think it was an important experience. I learned something about China and about myself. Things go on.

We came to the river, finally, and ran the bus onto the ferry, amid trucks and tractors and a tight jam of foot-passengers and their bundles. There were three of these boats, one of which had come from another place to help. Two of the captains were women, I noticed. The ferrymen told me they had all been working for over twenty-four hours without a break, with others bringing them food to eat during the crossing.

We reached Guangzhou after dark, and checked into a small guesthouse run by the city. And I missed my connection, and spent Spring Festival Day alone in a strange city. (I sent Chen off to look up the friends with whom he had planned to spend Spring Festival while I went on to Chengdu. He asked me to come with him, but to bring an uninvited guest to Spring Festival was really not to be thought of.)

And it was all right.

I went to the wonderful Guangzhou "Flower City" where long lines of peasants were still arriving on bicycles, with enormous stacks of flowers tied to the bikes, bringing them to the market. The flowers were displayed for sale along three blocks, and hundreds of people were buying them to decorate their homes for the big occasion, or just wandering around carrying their flowers but looking at all the others, as if reluctant to leave. Little kids ran in and out showing each other the one flower each was carrying. It was pure enjoyment.

When I checked into my tiny room and looked out the window, I saw the tall sugar cube which was the new White Swan Hotel. There, I thought, is one of those international monsters. But there, come to think of it, there must be an American bar. And in an American bar there must be Scotch whiskey, which is exactly what one needs after a thirty-six-hour bus ride. So I went over, and met the barmaid I've described before, who asked proudly, "If I did not work on the holiday, how would the people be served?"

There are times, when things seem too frantic, or too frustrating, or too bloody awful, when I'm able to put myself back in that bus waiting for the ferry and simply coping. I think, sometimes, of that barmaid, and of Li Li, the guide in Beijing.

("You don't understand—I was needed in the factory.") I think of my stubborn Xiamen students studying English in the countryside and my colleagues and friends who lived through the Anti-Rightist Campaign, and the Great Leap Forward, and the Cultural Revolution, and never lost heart. I think of the many people I've met in China—teachers, merchants, street-sweepers, hotel clerks, administrators, factory workers, cab drivers—who in their individual ways were coping, making things work, doing what can be done with a spirit of patience and friendliness. They are the counterweight to some of the others I've described, aren't they? I think of my Nankai students, marching with joy to change the world, and the people who came out in their thousands to support them. I think of them with peace and with love and with hope for the future.

Index